HAPPY FEET

Keats Titles of Related Interest

The Practical
Health Guide for
Runners, Joggers, Race
Walkers and Just
Plain Strollers

HAPPY FEET

FRANK MURRAY

Keats Publishing, Inc. ☰ New Canaan, Connecticut

Happy Feet is not intended as medical advice. Its intent is solely informational and educational. Please consult a health professional should the need for one be indicated.

HAPPY FEET

Library of Congress Cataloging in Publication Data

Murray, Frank.
    Happy feet : for jogging, race walking, running, and walking /
Frank Murray : introduction by Robert R. Rinaldi.
        p.   cm.
    Includes bibliographical references and index.
    ISBN 0-87983-476-5 : $11.95
        1. Foot—Care and hygiene. 2. Leg—Care and hygiene. 3. Runners
(Sports)—Nutrition. 4. Runners (Sports)—Health and hygiene. 5. Walking
(Sports)—Health aspects.   I. Title
RD563.M87   1990
617.5'85—dc20   90-42376
                                                     CIP

Printed in the United States of America

Keats Publishing, Inc.
27 Pine Street (Box 876)
New Canaan, Connecticut 06840-0876

To
Julia Hodes, who also
loves to walk

Contents

Introduction

I was a youngster then, but I'll always remember the 1940s with newsreels at the movies, *Victory at Sea*, World War II and Lucky Strikes ("LS/MFT"). The fifties remain a memory for beer blasts, rock and roll music and pizza. Bra burners, draft dodgers and Vietnam leave the sixties with a tumultuous uneasiness of mind. It was the sixties, however, that paved the way for the seventies and eighties. I believe it started with football in the Rose Garden, Jack and Jackie Kennedy and the President's Council on Physical Fitness. Whatever it was, the seventies and eighties was a time in history when Americans became conscious of their bodies. The Physical Fitness Boom boomed and it has continued to boom for almost 20 years now. It is driven by athletic highs spirited by endorphins and an endless track of press articles, books, research and magazines.

The fitness boom started with plain ol' sweats and sneaks and soon the footgear manufacturers had a line of performance shoes specific for every sport imaginable. They upgraded their models each spring and fall. Sweats went high tech, too, with materials that were touted as actually assisting athletic performance.

Keeping up with the latest equipment and the current best diet and training techniques has become impossible. Along comes *Happy Feet*! It's more than another how-to book; it's a complete field guide to athletics. It works for the novice who is looking to get started. It works for the seasoned jogger and challenger runner because of its indexing of information on every aspect of performance in lateral motion sports. *Happy Feet* even works for the Armchair Historian Jock. Historical facts on the evolution of sports equipment from the Greek and Roman Empires are detailed.

Happy Feet has researched the research. It is, as a text, an enjoyable and informative book for anyone interest in the ability of human beings to excel in sporting activities using the feet and legs.

ROBERT R. RINALDI, D.P.M.
Stamford Podiatry Group, P.C.
Stamford, Connecticut

Chapter 1

These Feet Are Made for Walking

Although modern man, with and without shoes, has been on the move for about 92,000 years, our furry ancestors were walking upright 3.75 million years ago. In 1976, scientists discovered what are regarded as the world's oldest human footprints, which were made by a group of manlike creatures as they shuffled through damp volcanic ash near the Olduvai Gorge in Tanzania. The ash hardened, leaving behind the prints made over three million years ago. Judging by photographs of the prints, these nomadic creatures would not be able to fit into today's jogging shoes: they would require at least 18EEEEE clodhoppers.

Regardless of how long human beings have been on the planet, we have always been plagued with foot problems. The evolvement of shoes has helped but certainly has not completely solved the problems that we have with our lower extremities. And running and jogging, as well as other sports, each contribute their own forms of stress on our feet.

The human foot has been described as both an architectural nightmare or an anatomical wonder, says the American Podiatric Medical Association. Even so, this complex and delicate piece of our anatomy is still adapting to the job it is destined to do.

"Podiatrists say two factors account for many of today's foot problems," according to *Your Podiatrist and Shoeman,* a publication of the Association.[1] "One is the lag in the evolutionary development of the foot. For millions of years, man's ancestors walked in a crouched position, helping themselves along with their hands. When man finally straightened up, the feet had to do a lot of adapting and that process is not yet complete. The second factor is modern man's mania for paving every available surface. Human feet were made to walk on yielding, uneven surfaces—grass, sand, earth. Now feet must pound the pavements."

As it copes with the total weight of upright man and the hard even surfaces it has to walk on, the foot meets the challenge in high style. It does its work with the help of 26 bones, 107 ligaments and 19 muscles. With the interaction of these various components, two feet can balance a six-foot, 180-pound person, Refrigerator Perry or a sumo wrestler.

"The human foot absorbs a lot of punishment in a lifetime," notes the publication. "When one walks along at a comfortable 100-steps-a-minute pace, each heel strikes the cement with the equivalent of a 225-pound jolt 50 times a

1

minute—up to 600 pounds when running. In a lifetime, you will walk an average of 115,000 miles—tens of millions of jolts for each foot.''

A foot in action goes through these forward motions: 1) heel impact; 2) a transitional balance phase; and 3) the thrust of the toes to move smoothly into a repetition on the opposite foot—an action repeated millions of times. So, in essence, the foot is an engineering miracle that combines grace, durability and sensitivity.

As illustrated in Figure 1, each foot is a flexible aggregate of delicate bones and tough ligaments, muscles and tendons. As we walk or run, the weight of our body descends from the tibia or leg bone to the talus or ankle bone. As each foot is planted, the weight is divided between the tarsals and metatarsals in the front and the calcaneus or heel bone at the back.

The unusual strength of the foot can be compared to the ancient Roman ax handle—the fasces—which was made up of dozens of sticks. Although each of the sticks taken individually could easily bend or break, when bound together they possessed tremendous strength. In a similar way, the bones of the feet are quite fragile, but they are supported by tough, ropelike tendons and ligaments that provide considerable strength. The foot gets additional resilience and spring from the arches, which extend both crosswise and lengthwise across each foot.

Since the foot consists of so many complex structures, stresses of any kind, such as the weight of the body or the shocks of walking and jumping, can cause the feet to hurt. Much of this shock is counteracted by the arch of the foot, which is actually a series of arches. These arches curve in two directions—from ball to heel and from side to side—giving the foot the capacity of bearing a considerable load. And each arch is articulated, consisting of numerous small bones that can shift and adjust to the blows of movement. (For the three segments of the feet, see Figure 2).

"So long as this healthy structure is maintained, the footaches of sightseeing or hiking disappear with rest," explains *Building Sound Bones and Muscles,* by Oliver E. Allen and the editors of Time-Life Books.[2] "But chronic stress—caused by the extra weight of obesity or by continuous standing on the job—can eventually alter the healthy structure, so distorting it that the feet hurt chronically." The aching and burning of chronic foot strain develop because of excess stress and weight, which stretch the ligaments connecting the bones. The ligaments become so inflamed that they hurt.

"If the strain continues," adds the book, "the ligaments deteriorate, losing their ability to pull the bones back into the proper positions. The most common result is a permanent inward tilting of the ankle. Temporary tilting is necessary in walking, but ordinarily the ankle springs back up; when it does not, the foot flattens out, losing the strength and resilience of the arch."[2]

Most of the foot's movements evolve among the ankle bones or tarsals, which separate the leg bones from the five metatarsals. Thus, the muscles in the leg are mainly involved with ankle movements, flopping a somewhat rigid foot around at the end of the inflexible leg skeleton.

A book called *Human Structure* describes the arrangement of foot bones this way:[3] "There are seven tarsal bones, but the tibia and fibula only touch one

Figure 1

HOW DOES THE FOOT WORK?

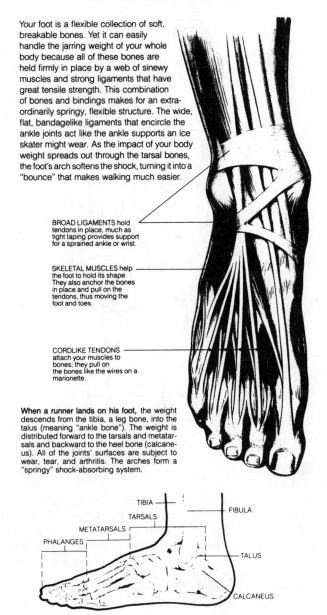

Your foot is a flexible collection of soft, breakable bones. Yet it can easily handle the jarring weight of your whole body because all of these bones are held firmly in place by a web of sinewy muscles and strong ligaments that have great tensile strength. This combination of bones and bindings makes for an extraordinarily springy, flexible structure. The wide, flat, bandagelike ligaments that encircle the ankle joints act like the ankle supports an ice skater might wear. As the impact of your body weight spreads out through the tarsal bones, the foot's arch softens the shock, turning it into a "bounce" that makes walking much easier.

BROAD LIGAMENTS hold tendons in place, much as tight taping provides support for a sprained ankle or wrist.

SKELETAL MUSCLES help the foot to hold its shape. They also anchor the bones in place and pull on the tendons, thus moving the foot and toes.

CORDLIKE TENDONS attach your muscles to bones; they pull on the bones like the wires on a marionette.

When a runner lands on his foot, the weight descends from the tibia, a leg bone, into the talus (meaning "ankle bone"). The weight is distributed forward to the tarsals and metatarsals and backward to the heel bone (calcaneus). All of the joints' surfaces are subject to wear, tear, and arthritis. The arches form a "springy" shock-absorbing system.

TIBIA

FIBULA

TARSALS

METATARSALS

PHALANGES

TALUS

CALCANEUS

Source: *ABC's of the Human Body*, The Reader's Digest Association, Inc., Pleasantville, New York, 1987. Reprinted by permission.

Figure 2

THE THREE FUNCTIONAL SEGMENTS OF THE FOOT

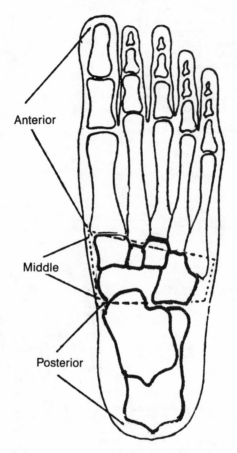

Anterior

Middle

Posterior

Reprinted by permission from *Foot and Ankle Pain*, by Rene Cailliet, M.D., F. A. Davis Company, Philadelphia.

of them. This is the talus, which sits atop the arch of the foot like a keystone. It articulates with four other bones, two above and two below. Its upper articular surface, shaped something like the curved surface of a spool, fits into a reciprocal socket formed by the two leg bones. The tibia and fibula press against the flat medial and lateral ends of the spool. Because the upper surface of the spool rests wholly against the tibia, body weight is carried downward to the talus through the tibia alone; the fibula bears no weight. (At its upper end, it does not even touch the femur.)''

The calcaneus, which is located below the talus, absorbs most of the weight, transmitting it downward to the heel in back and the two lateral metatarsals in the front. Weight is transferred to the metatarsals by the intervening cuboid bone. Additional body weight is carried from the talus to the bowl-shaped navicular bone, from where it is passed on to the three medial metatarsals. This transmission is made through three cuneiforms, one for each metatarsal.

"Most of the foot's movements occur at the joints between the talus and the neighboring bones above and below it," the authors continue. "The upper joint—between the talus and the leg bones—is a simple hinge, capable only of flexion and extension. Like other hinge joints, it has collateral ligaments on each side that help restrict its movements to a single axis of rotation. These ligaments are attached to conspicuous bony bumps, the malleoli, at the bottom ends of the two leg bones. You can feel these malleoli on either side of your ankle. The collateral ligaments run from the malleoli down to the calcaneus. The one from the fibular malleolus is a round cord; the one on the tibial side has a more broadly spread-out attachment, including bundles running to the talus and navicular. Its radiating fibers fanning out from the tibial malleolus give it a triangular delta shape, so it is called the deltoid ligament."[3]

As the foot swings from side to side around a single fore-and-aft axis, the sole of the foot is either turned toward the other foot or outward and away from it. When the sole is turned inward, this is inversion; the opposite is eversion. If people walked only on hard, flat floors with their feet close together, extension and flexion would be the only movements required. But when you stand with feet apart, you have to invert them to keep the soles planted on the ground. As you walk on uneven surfaces, your feet are alternatingly everting and inverting as they adjust to the changes in terrain. But if you make the wrong adjustment, your ankle buckles under the weight of your body and you experience a sprain, which is essentially the wrenching or tearing of the ligaments in the joint.

The major differences between the foot and the hand result basically from the medial shift of the calcaneus. With that shift, the heel is parked squarely in the middle of the limb. As the extrinsic flexor tendons approach this obstacle, they have to "duck around it" and enter the sole on the medial side of the calcaneus, instead of running through a midline carpal tunnel like that in the wrist. This arrangement means that the flexor digitorum longus tendons have to run obliquely across the sole to reach the four lateral toes and are not lined up with their digits. But their obliquity may be compensated for by a small muscle that is called flexor accessorius, which has no equivalent in the hand. A Y-shaped muscle, the flexor accessorius arises by two heads from the calcaneus. It extends forward to insert directly into the radiating fan of flexor digitorum longus tendons.

Since the metatarsals and toes are not as mobile as the metacarpals and fingers, the "thenar" and "hypothenar" clusters in the feet are somewhat simplified. Neither of these clusters incorporate an opponens muscle, and only the abductor and flexor brevis remain. The abductors—abductor hallucis and abductor digiti minimi—are not considered important as abductors; they are analogous to their equivalents in the hands. Apparently their only function is to assist the plantar aponeurosis in maintaining the foot's longitudinal arch while being stressed by such actions as running or standing on tiptoe.

The short flexors of the two marginal digits—flexor hallucis brevis and flexor digiti minimi brevis—arise more distally and deeply in the sole, deep to the extrinsic flexor tendons and flexor accessorius. Nobody really knows what function they serve. Flexor hallucis brevis forks into two tendons of insertion, which attach to the phalanx via two little sesamoid bones lying under the first metatarsal head. The sesamoids of the halux probably serve to keep the body's weight from squashing the big toe's long flexor tendon under the first metatarsal head. The sesamoids transmit the weight from the metatarsal down to the underlying skin (the 'ball' of the foot) and form a little bony arch underneath which the tendon can slide back and forth freely. (As in the hand, the tendon is surrounded by a lubricating synovial fluid). The flexor hallucis brevis may act as a sort of active ligament for adjusting the position of these two sesamoids.

The final cluster of foot muscles has no similar counterpart in the hand. This group of muscles is a fan of relatively short intrinsic toe extensors—extensor hallucis brevis and extensor digitorum brevis, which are located deep to the extrinsic extensor tendons on the back of the foot. These brief extensors originate laterally from the calcaneus and extend small tendons downward to feed into the extrinsic extensor tendons. Apparently the little toe does not generally receive a short extensor tendon, and the one to the big toe—the extensor hallucis brevis—joins directly to the proximal phalanx.[4]

If this is more than you ever wanted to know about the bones, ligaments and tendons of the foot, it is reviewed to illustrate the complexities of the human foot, which we obviously take for granted. When people abuse their feet, through the stress of running or jogging or by wearing improper shoes, it remains for the podiatrist or other health professional to get them walking again. As you can see, many things can be involved in making a proper diagnosis of a foot problem. It is also obvious that the more you understand about the complex nature of your feet, the more likely you are to be able to prevent serious injuries.

Plantar Fasciitis

Perhaps the most common athletic injury to the fascia is called plantar fasciitis. This involves the plantar fascia or arch ligament, which is the longest ligament in the foot. Fasciae are the numerous strong, thick, white fibrous strips that surround, protect and support all tissues in the body, including joints, nerves, blood vessels, muscles, and tendons.

"Fascia looks and feels to some degree like ligaments and tendons and contains the same four components: two types of fibers, fluid and connective tissue cells," explain Gabe Mirkin, M.D., and Marshall Hoffman in *The Sportsmedicine Book*.[4] "In athletes, fasciae absorb some of the pressure on tendons, muscles and joints, and help to protect them from injury."

Athletes with plantar fasciitis experience pain just under the heel bone, as well as anywhere along the bottom of the foot. Pain may begin with a sudden tear during exercise, or it may not develop until several days after the injury.

"The plantar fascia extends from the bottom part of the heel bone to each of the five toes," the authors say. "It serves as a guide wire to support the bottom of the foot, especially the arch. If sufficient pressure is exerted on the bottom of your foot—enough to spread out the toes or to flatten the arch—the fascia tears."[4]

Mirkin and Hoffman list four main causes of this problem:

1. A sudden turn that puts excessive pressure on the tissues on the bottom of the foot.
2. Shoes that do not provide adequate support for the arch of the foot.
3. Shoes with very stiff soles.
4. Feet that pronate or roll inward when you walk or run.

Dr. Mirkin discusses a leading middle-distance runner who got plantar fasciitis by running fast intervals. Since he was preparing for an upcoming Olympics, the athlete didn't have time to rest; instead he was given steroid injections (cortisone) to decrease the pain. But these shots do not actually heal the foot, and the injury did not heal in time for the athlete to participate in the Olympics.

"I do not believe that steroid injections should be used to treat plantar fasciitis," Dr. Mirkin states. "Not only can they weaken the fascia, but also they can stop the pain—nature's warning signal that you should be taking it easy—and by continuing to exercise, you can cause further damage."[4]

Allen Jacobs, D.P.M., chairman of the national scientific committee of the American Podiatric Medical Association, told the *Medical Tribune* that, with more people involved in athletics, plantar fasciitis has become a major problem.[5]

"It's much more common than stress fracture," he said. "In fact, it is probably the most common sports-related injury that we are seeing in our offices."

Dr. Jacobs, who is director of resident training in podiatric medicine and surgery at the Central Medical Center, St. Louis, Missouri, adds that plantar fasciitis is especially common among middle-aged athletes who have suddenly increased their level of activity following a sedentary lifestyle.

The medical newspaper quotes a study from the St. Anthony Orthopaedic Clinic, St. Paul, Minnesota, suggesting that 76 percent of sports-related subcalcaneal injuries involve running and jogging. Racquet sports account for another 9 percent of these injuries.

In addition to mechanical overuse, such as while running or jogging, the other common factors, according to Dr. Jacobs, are ill-fitting shoes and recent weight gain.

"The most important preventive measure is determining whether a person has a foot type that will predispose him to plantar fasciitis," Dr. Jacobs is quoted as saying. "Unfortunately, many physicians never take their patients' shoes and socks off to look at their feet."[5]

For those who are predisposed to plantar fasciitis, Dr. Jacobs prescribes suitable orthotics. As an example, if the foot is too flat, a suitable supporting arch is probably warranted. If the arch is too high, a device can be made to distribute weight evenly over the whole surface of the foot, thereby taking some of the load off the plantar fascia, he said. If overpronation is the problem, Dr. Jacobs advises the patient to select shoes with superior motion-control properties and firm midsoles. Another recommendation is to stretch the calf muscle and Achilles tendon during warmup and cooldown exercises.

"It [plantar fasciitis] can be an extremely difficult problem to treat," adds Dr. Jacobs. "Exacerbations are quite common, and in bad cases immobilization, non-weight-bearing, and even casting are not infrequently required."[5] He goes on to say that, even after a period of rest, the plantar fascia can begin to tear again when weight-bearing is resumed.

Haglund's Deformity

After placing fourth in the 1977 Fukuoka Marathon in Japan with a time of 2:14:24, Tom Fleming's elation turned to pain on his way home, when his right heel became so sore, hot and inflamed that he could barely walk, according to Dr. Richard Schuster in an article in *The Runner*.[6] An orthopedic surgeon diagnosed the problem as Haglund's deformity, which was caused by Fleming's running shoe constantly rubbing against a congenital ridge on his heel.

Because of the pain, Fleming had to reduce his training time from 140 to 50 miles per week. Surprisingly, he endured the pain and swelling for seven years, Dr. Schuster adds. The irritation had caused the bursa sac between the bone and the Achilles tendon to swell, and, in time, the sac calcified into a hard lump. Finally, a surgeon chipped away the bump until the heel was normal, and seven months later Fleming was back running marathons.

Although Haglund's is not a runner's injury, it can be triggered by running, says Dr. Schuster. It is an inherited condition and it usually strikes people who have been born with unusually shaped heel bones.

"Haglund's can also be blamed on the general shape of the back of the heel," Dr. Schuster continues. "The backs of most heels are relatively round; you can feel the shape with your hand. In cases such as Fleming's, however, the upper shelf of the backward extending heel bone protrudes farther back, sometimes like an overhanging cliff. Shoes, including running shoes, are not shaped for these out-of-the-ordinary protuberances, which usually occur in both feet, with one worse than the other. Before the running boom, in fact, Haglund's deformity most often plagued women who wore dress shoes with hard, unyielding counters. Consequently, the problem is sometimes referred to as 'pump bumps'."[6]

Pinched Nerves

Pinched nerves in the foot rank about eighth on the list of overuse injuries, according to Dr. Richard Schuster.[7] This happens when a nerve becomes squeezed between bones or in "tunnels" of bone, tendon, ligaments and other tissues. He goes on to say that runners have a higher rate of nerve irritation than the general public.

"Nerve entrapments strike runners for a couple of reasons," he explains. "Pressures on the foot of a runner equal many times more than his or her body weight. Unlike average individuals, runners use their feet for long periods without restful interruptions. This nonstop pressure not only causes pain, but also can result in a fibrous thickening of the nerve trunk which in turn increases pain. This thickening is known as a neuroma. Doctors suspect the problem if pain is aggravated by tapping or squeezing the inflicted area.''[7]

Nerve pressure in the forefoot is called Morton's neuralgia, Morton's neuroma or Morton's foot. This is not the same as another problem, also called Morton's foot, which refers to a short first toe. In Morton's neuralgia, Dr. Schuster says, pain occurs when the head of one metatarsal bone presses against the next metatarsal, squeezing the nerve between them. The pain can radiate to the toes, and, if the nerve is thickened into a neuroma, the pain can be even more intense.

"Morton's neuralgia generally involves the nerve between the third and fourth metatarsals, although experts have reported cases in which all four nerves are involved," Dr. Schuster continues. "During an examination, a doctor may sometimes detect a click when squeezing the forefoot as the thickened nerve slips out from between the bones. An entrapment of this sort may result from an unusually-shaped metatarsal bone or a malalignment of bones due to supination or pronation. In most cases, however, nerve pains in runners can be blamed on shear or back-and-forth sliding forces.''[7]

Dr. Schuster points out that the foot slides forward in the shoe during running, which forces the forefoot into the shoe's narrow toe box. The metatarsals are, therefore, squeezed together, pinching the nerves that are between the toes. Running shoes often flare inward at the ball, even though most running feet flare outward. This causes pressure on the outer metatarsal bones and the inter-metatarsal nerves, he says.

He adds that when a patient is diagnosed as having Morton's neuralgia, the doctor first determines if the shoes match the functional shape of the patient's feet. Unlacing the bottom two or four eyelets can help to clear up the problem by reducing the pressure from the sides of the shoe. Also, a pad can be inserted between the toes that are sensitive. Or the doctor may choose to elevate and separate the metatarsal bones with a pad underneath the area where the nerve is pinched.

"If pronation is causing a malalignment of the bones, a podiatrist or sports physician may prescribe an orthotic device with a modified metatarsal correction," Dr. Schuster states. "The success of this remedy ranges from partial to complete. If these solutions fail, surgery or relatively new laser treatment to remove a section of the nerve may be the answer.''[7]

Other Common Foot Problems

One of the most vulnerable sections of the foot is the Achilles heel or tendon, which connects the lower leg muscle to the heel. It is named after the Greek warrior Achilles, who, when he was an infant, was dipped into the River Styx by his mother, who hoped to make him immortal. To keep him from drowning or floating away, she had to hold him by a heel. Since that heel was not completely immersed, it remained his only vulnerable spot. And, of course, as a young man in battle, he was killed when an adversary shot an arrow into his heel.

The Achilles tendon not only puts the spring in our step, but also allows us to stand on tiptoe. But, unlike other tendons in the body, the Achilles has no protective covering, making it easily vulnerable to inflammation and injury. According to *ABC's of the Human Body*, "If ill-fitting shoes inflame or tear the tendon, you will feel excruciating pain in your heel and ankle. If violent exertion causes the tendon to snap, you may have to spend six to eight weeks in a cast. In some cases, the snapped tendon cannot simply be 'set' and allowed to heal, but must be surgically repaired."[8]

Another annoyance for runners and other athletes are heel spurs, which are small pieces of heel bone that protrude in the area of the plantar fascia's attachment. These spurs are another cause of some cases of plantar fasciitis. Since some people have heel spurs but do not experience any pain, some orthopedists leave the spurs alone; other physicians may decide to remove them.

Hammertoes are aptly named because of their shape; they might be seen to resemble the little hammers or mallets that strike piano strings. This foot deformity is caused by an inherited muscle imbalance or an abnormal bone thickness or length. "The condition develops when the joints closest to the web bend, raising those toes above the others and curling the top joints under," writes Marc A. Brenner, D.P.M., in *Prevention* magazine.[9] "The ligaments and tendons contract sharply and pull the front of the toe downward."

Dr. Brenner, a foot specialist in Glendale, New York, adds that surgery is the usual procedure for correcting the problem, and that 80 percent of the patients can have it done in a doctor's office. Most people can walk within 48 hours; they should be able to play tennis or go dancing in three to four weeks, he says.

Other common foot problems, which affect athletes and non-athletes alike, are discussed in *Your Podiatrist Talks About Foot Health,* which is published by the American Podiatric Medical Association.[10] These include:

Corns and calluses.

They result from friction and pressure on the feet. Since they do not have "roots," they may be caused by a bone deformity. When friction or pressure is exerted on a part of the foot for an extended period (such as by badly fitted shoes), a corn or callus forms a protective shield. Since there is a specific reason why they form, corns and calluses cannot be eliminated until the source of the pressure is found.

Warts.

Often mistaken for calluses, a wart is a skin growth that has a blood and nerve supply all its own. Warts are very painful, and they can spread if left untreated.

Bunions.

These are misaligned big toe joints that may become swollen and tender. Although generally caused by a weakness in the structure of the foot, bunions can also result from hereditary imperfections and ill-fitting shoes.

Athlete's foot.

As explained elsewhere in this book, this is a skin disorder caused by a fungus.

Ingrown nails.

An improper trimming of the nails can cause this problem. But these painful nails are also caused by poor foot structure, heredity, injury and fungus infections.

Caring for Foot Injuries

In *Your Podiatrist Talks About Foot and Ankle Injuries,* another publication from the American Podiatric Medical Association, a number of accepted myths are dispelled:[11]

"It can't be broken because I can move it." With certain fractures you can walk, such as breaks of the thinner of the two leg bones, small "chip" fractures of either foot or ankle bones, or fracture of a toe. But these need medical attention just as much as compound fractures do.

"If you break a toe, immediate care isn't necessary." If an X-ray shows a simple, undisplaced fracture, your podiatrist can usually bring rapid recovery. If the break is displaced or angulated, a prompt "setting" by your podiatrist will be important to help speed healing. A post-fracture deformity of a toe can result in a very painful corn.

"If you have a foot or ankle injury, soak it in hot water immediately." In truth, hot water makes the blood vessels dilate or open wide. This allows the blood to rush to the injured area and increases the swelling. More swelling means greater pressure on the nerves and more pain. Instead, an ice bag wrapped in a towel contracts the blood vessels. This produces a numbing effect and prevents further swelling and pain. In perhaps 48 to 72 hours, warm compresses or soaks may help.

"Applying an elastic bandage to a severely sprained ankle is adequate treatment." This type of injury usually causes torn or severely overstretched ligaments. Therefore, it requires immediate care by a professional, including an X-ray to determine the extent of the damage, the immobilization by professional strapping to reduce motion that pulls on the injured ligaments. Casting and physiotherapy may also be required to speed recovery. In some cases, surgery may be necessary so medical attention should not be delayed.

"The terms 'fracture' and 'break' are different." No, they both signify a broken bone.

The Association recommends that, when you have a foot injury, you follow these procedures until you can see a podiatrist:[11]

1. Reduce your activity. If pain continues, get off your feet entirely.
2. To reduce swelling and pain, elevate the injured foot higher than your waist.
3. Apply cold compresses or an ice bag wrapped in a towel in a 20-minutes on/40-minutes off cycle.
4. Wear a soft shoe or slipper, since your regular shoes may not fit after the podiatrist has applied bulky dressings.
5. If you have bleeding lacerations, cleanse and apply pressure with gauze or a towel and cover with a clean dressing.

6. If blisters are not painful or swollen, do not open them; let the podiatrist look at them first.
7. Slivers, splinters or sand in the skin can be removed with a sterile instrument. If broken glass, a needle, or the like has deeply penetrated the skin, this should be removed professionally.
8. An abrasion is similar to a burn, in that raw skin is exposed to the air and can become infected. Cleanse the wound to remove foreign particles and apply a first-aid ointment and sterile bandages.

Proper Running Technique

Correct running technique can help you avoid injury and "getting off on the wrong foot." This familiar expression, incidentally, originated with the ancient Romans, who believed that it was bad luck to enter a house with your left foot first. To insure that this did not happen, it was customary to have a footman stationed at the door to make certain that this rule was not violated.

Dr. Joseph D'Amico, who is head of the Orthopedics Department at the New York College of Podiatric Medicine, says that a survey he conducted showed that 81 percent of the runners he questioned had pain either during or after running.[12] He attributes much of this to the fact that the runner takes over 1,000 steps a mile and that much of this stress falls on the heel, which is actually smaller than a golf ball.

According to Dr. Kim Sloan, Director of Sports Medicine at the New Jersey College of Medicine and Dentistry, injuries can often be prevented by training first. He adds that many runners do not know how to run correctly. "You can't be a 30-year-old in a desk job today and a runner tomorrow," he says. "You're trying to be an athlete and all athletes need to train."[12]

Unlike sprinters, in which running on the toes extends the length of the stride, distance runners and walkers should hit the ground with their heel first, according to Gary Yanker in *Gary Yanker's Sportswalking*.[13] Exceptions are steep inclines and stairways with short steps.

As explained by Yanker, good foot action is necessary for good leg action, and the more smoothly your ankles flex during walking, the faster and more energy-efficient your stride will be. Those who land on their forefoot will automatically have a shorter leg extension and stride. They also shorten the rolling surface of their feet, thereby curtailing the smoothness and fluidity of the walking action, he says.

"Like posture," continues Yanker, "foot placement should be adjusted to terrain and changes in walking speed. The advanced walker learns to change the distance between his or her feet, depending on the speed and the terrain. On a smooth surface, a fast walker can 'walk the line' by placing one foot in front of the other. On more rugged and inclined surfaces, a sportwalker can vary foot placement distance to provide maximum stability."[13]

In addition, he continues, the foot of the forward-moving leg should hit the ground at the back edge of the heel. When putting the heels down, your toes should be pointed straight and upward at a 45-degree angle with the ground. Such an angle permits your feet to roll forward correctly. Check to see that your feet are not turned inward or outward, otherwise they can't roll to the left or right. And the closer you can swing your feet to the ground, the more energy you can save and the faster your leg can move forward, he says.

When you are walking properly, your foot unrolls smoothly on the ground, on the outer edge instead of the flat part, and up to the forefront and then the toes. You use the outer edge of your feet, Yanker explains, because it is the smoothest rolling surface and acts like a rocker. This keeps your knees from turning inward as you walk. The rear of the foot should not leave the surface until you have completely rolled it up to the toes, not just the forefoot, he continues. This can add an average of three inches to your stride.

As you walk faster, he goes on, your feet will be just about vertical before you leave the ground. The extra inches allow additional time to swing your forward foot farther out in front, and insure that your rear driving foot is pointed in the direction you are headed. Some sportwalkers tend to point their feet outward, so it pays to monitor your foot's position from time to time, he says.

For exercise walking, Yanker suggests that arm pumping and swinging are important for working the upper body and helping it propel forward with the legs. For sportwalking, he says, the arms pump closer to the body, and the shoulders, assisted by the torso muscles involved, begin and absorb the forward propelling forces of the upper body. He adds that longer strides and clean foot placement require a tighter arm swing. So bend your arm at a 90-degree angle or less and swing it across the chest at midchest. To keep your arms from tiring, he recommends that you shift some of the counter-rotation work to your shoulders, bringing your arms even closer to your body. You can do the cross-chest arm swing but rotate the shoulders a bit inward. The arm-shoulder movement permits your oblique abdominal muscles to propel your hips forward, your arms relax and you can then concentrate on the body action of your hips, abdominals and shoulders, he continues.

As you swing your arms, he adds, practice synchronized breathing. So breathe normally and rhythmically as you walk, using the most comfortable lung-diaphragm breathing combination for optimum oxygen consumption. Yanker points out that some sportwalkers often hold their breath too long while climbing.

Kenneth Forsythe, M.D., writing in *Athletics for Life,*[14] says that the same foot-strike pattern just described also applies to distance running, in which the heel hits the ground slightly before the rest of the foot. This procedure not only results in a smoother run, he says, but also it minimizes the chances of getting shin splints, plantar fasciitis, Achilles tendinitis, knee pain and even back pain.

He goes on to say that an alternative, forefoot-strike pattern, in which the ball of the foot hits the ground first, is ideal for sprinters, since it extends the length of the stride by running on the toes. To illustrate this point for yourself, extend your leg and point your toes downward. This will reveal how this lengthens the lower leg.

"Moving your ankle into this position and increasing your stride length is effective if speed is the only consideration," Dr. Forsythe continues. "This explains why 100- and 200-meter sprinters are never heel-to-toe runners, and why 10,000-meter and marathon runners are almost never forefoot runners. In longer races or distances, where endurance is the primary concern, the forefoot-like pattern leads to much more rapid lower leg fatigue."[14]

For the runners who manage to sustain a forefoot foot-strike pattern during long-distance races, Dr. Forsythe says that they pay the price for running on their toes with an increase in injuries. He mentions one runner, Jill, who ran a rather respectable 2 hour and 52-second marathon several years ago. However, she hasn't increased her time in two years, mainly because she has had two stress fractures, recurrent Achilles tendinitis and plantar fasciitis. "Jill illustrates the attachment most of us develop to our routines, even when they are clearly harming us," he says. "I told her that I was convinced her gait was a major factor in her injuries. But like many athletes who have achieved a certain degree of success, she was reluctant to change her style of running. Instead, she continues to attribute her rash of injuries and inability to improve to bad luck."[14]

Since the foot-strike pattern is so critical, Dr. Forsythe recommends that you have a friend who is familiar with running observe you as you run back and forth on a makeshift 10-meter track. Your friend should especially observe the foot nearest him or her as it hits the ground. Having someone observe how the foot hits will reveal rather accurately your own particular foot-strike pattern, he says. Also, look at the sole of your shoe. If the area outside the ball of the foot is worn down more than the heel, this probably means that you are a forefoot striker. For a definitive analysis, go to a clinic and have them professionally analyze the biochemical components of your gait with a high-speed videotape.

Dr. Forsythe goes on to say that arm motion can win or lose a race, and he illustrates this with an example from the 1983 New York Marathon. In this race, Geoff Smith, running his first marathon, was 200 meters ahead of veteran Red Dixon. To make up the time, Dixon began swinging his arms in pendulum fashion from the shoulders in order to get a greater stride frequency. This textbook-perfect use of his upper body made his running faster, Dr. Forsythe explains, and it gave him the slight edge he needed to pass Smith and win the race.[14]

Researchers at the Center for Locomotion Studies at Penn State University, using a computer, have confirmed that the heel of the foot bears the most weight (60 percent). This is followed by the forefoot (28 percent); the mid-foot (8 percent); and the toes (4 percent). This is an added incentive for buying walking shoes with a solid heel and forefoot padding, says Thomas McCall, M.D.[15] He adds that this same weight-bearing percentage applies to the daintiest of women as well as heavy men.

In the December/January 1988 issue of *The Walking Magazine*,[16] a 51-year-old woman wrote in to say that she walked barefoot five or six miles daily along a beach and wondered if this would harm her feet. The editors replied that most podiatrists actually recommend walking barefoot on the beach, unless you have a history of foot problems.

Running in Winter

As might be expected, the most common cause of winter running injuries is slipping or falling on ice. However, runners who change their running style to protect themselves from a fall can suffer muscle strains or other overuse problems, according to the American Podiatric Medical Association.[17] As an example, to increase traction, runners often land with their whole foot on slippery surfaces, rather than the usual heel or toe strike. Changing your running style can cause an injury. And when the foot lands on an icy area that slopes to the outside of the body and the foot slips in this direction, a pulled groin muscle can result.

"However, there are several ways runners can reduce injury potential in the winter," says the Association. "First, stretch your muscles gently before and after you run. In the winter it is important to run slowly for the first 10 to 15 minutes. Also, you may want to shorten your stride on slippery areas to help maintain your stability, but be sure you still run heel to toe. If the area you plan to run on has occasional patches of ice, you may want to invest in spikes that can be slipped over ordinary running shoes. These spikes can minimize slipping and improve traction on icy roads. And lastly," cautions the Association, "if the weather looks too bad or the conditions are really rough, don't run. It is far better to miss one day of running than to spend a couple of months recovering from a fall."[17]

The Association provides these additional cold-weather tips for maintaining healthy feet:[17]

1. Keep feet warm and dry, especially in extremely cold or damp climates. If feet do become wet, shoes and hose should be changed at the earliest opportunity.
2. In snowy areas, shoeboots are easier on the feet than shoes with boots or galoshes.
3. Hose comfort is as important as the fit of shoes, and if socks are too small they will bunch the toes together. The resulting friction can cause a painful blister or corn to develop.
4. Those who perspire freely must take extra care with foot hygiene, including regular bathing of the feet and applying a good foot powder. This not only promotes comfort, but also assists in combatting various fungus infections.
5. Injuries caused by frostbite, slips and trips are common in winter months. Such problems should receive immediate professional attention before infections or other aggravations set in, to avoid a period of long, drawn-out recuperation.
6. The cold weather and dryness of winter months can often lead to deep cracks in the skin of the heel. These fissures, common to those very active in winter sports, can be controlled by regular application of a moisturizing lotion to keep skin soft.

References

1. *Your Podiatrist and Shoeman* (Bethesda, MD: American Podiatric Medical Association, undated).

2. Oliver E. Allen and the Editors of Time-Life Books, *Building Sound Bones and Muscles* (Alexandria, Va: Time-Life Books, 1981), p. 69.

3. Matt Cartmill, William L. Hylander and James Shafland, *Human Structure* (Cambridge, Harvard University Press, 1987), pp. 298–321.

4. Gabe Mirkin, M.D., and Marshall Hoffman, *The Sportsmedicine Book* (Boston, Little, Brown and Company, 1978), pp. 117–134.

5. Rick McGuire, "Inspect Feet to Help Stamp Out Agony of Plantar Fasciitis," *Medical Tribune*, November 24, 1988), pp. 3, 14.

6. Dr. Richard Schuster, "Down at the Heels," (*The Runner*, May 1986), p. 24.

7. Dr. Richard Schuster, "What Nerve," (*The Runner*, October 1986), p. 14.

8. *ABC's of the Human Body* (Pleasantville, N.Y.: The Reader's Digest Association, Inc., 1987), pp. 178–181.

9. "What Are Hammertoes?" (*Prevention*, March 1986), p. 16.

10. *Your Podiatrist Talks About Foot Health* (Bethesda, Md: American Podiatric Medical Association, 1987).

11. *Your Podiatrist Talks About Foot and Ankle Injuries* (Bethesda, Md.: American Podiatric Medical Association, 1987).

12. Janice Hopkins Tanne, "Everything You Ever Wanted to Know About Your Feet," *New York* (August 24, 1981), pp. 52–57.

13. Gary Yanker, *Gary Yanker's Sportwalking* (Chicago: Contemporary Books, Inc., 1987), pp. 124–127.

14. Kenneth Forsythe, M.D. and Neil Feineman, *Athletics for Life* (New York: Simon and Schuster, Inc., 1985), pp. 52–55.

15. Thomas McCall, M.D., "Soft Steps," (*American Health*, March 1988), p. 38.

16. "Barefoot's Best," (*The Walking Magazine*, December/January 1988), p. 11.

17. *Winter Sports and Healthy Feet* (Bethesda, Md: American Podiatric Medical Association, 1985).

Chapter 2

Choosing the Right Shoe

Because they are so vulnerable to thorns, sharp rocks, animal bites, snow and ice, hot sand and other dangers, protecting the feet has been one of man's major concerns since prehistoric times. Footwear has evolved for both practical and ornamental purposes, and as a symbol of social status. As soon as *Homo erectus* began chasing animals and birds for his food, he discovered that tender feet were not only slowing him down, but were also causing considerable discomfort. That's when he began to strap leaves to his feet in what is considered the forerunner of today's shoes. Later, he discovered that tree bark and animal hides were even more comfortable and durable.

"Sandals of yucca leaf with corn husk linings, which were tied to the feet with twine, have been found in Arizona," according to *The Complete Handbook of Athletic Footwear*.[1] "Some artifacts from these early eras—such as stone tools and bones for scraping leather, and needles and awls for stitching the leather—have survived to the present. No doubt some of these leather-working tools were used for shoe making. The earliest known footwear dates back some 10,000 years. Sandals of this age were found in 1932 by archaeologist Luther Cressman as he explored a cave in Oregon."[1]

Until shoes could be mass-produced, the average person walked about barefoot. However, ancient Egyptian wall paintings detail the sandals worn by kings and priests, which were often made of plaited reeds. Paintings of Tutankhamen show him wearing shoes of finely tooled leather. In colder climates, people began wearing shoes early on, as indicated by Egyptian wall paintings at Beni Hassan of about 2,000 B.C. and at Thebes (1,450 B.C.), which show Syrians and Minoans from Crete wearing a variety of sandals and boots. On the reliefs from Calah (modern Nimrud) and Nineveh, around 800 B.C., can be seen the sophisticated sandal designs of the Assyrians.[2]

The first professional tanners worked some 5,000 years ago among the Hittites, who lived in present-day Turkey, say Irene M. Franck and David M. Brownstone in *Clothiers*.[3] These tanners perfected a mixture of alum and tannin to produce the best leather of the time. At the same time, the Egyptians piled layers of hides that were four feet deep. Crushed tannin pods were placed between the layers and the skins were held in place with a pile of stones. This tanning operation was left alone for several years, allowing the damp skins to absorb and become permeated with the tannin. The resulting soft leather was

17

colored with black, red, yellow or blue vegetable dyes and used for cloaks and armbands.

It is not clear whether the Egyptians made sandals from papyrus or leather, continue Franck and Brownstone, although papyrus sandals have been found on mummies that have been buried 2,000 to 3,000 years. It was Herodotus, the Greek historian, who maintained that the Eygptian priests wore paper sandals that were made like sheets of writing paper. To do this, papyrus reeds were flaked, dampened, molded together and left in the sun to dry. The paper sandals were then worn with twisted leather thongs.

"Greek sandals were developed from those of earlier Middle Eastern peoples, with many individual designs of straps over the instep and intricate lacing up the leg," says *The Encyclopedia Americana*. "To prevent the laces from slipping down, the heel piece was often extended for several inches up the back of the leg and was provided with eyelets through which the laces were passed after being twisted around the leg. Robert Graves writes in *The Greek Myths* that Greek warriors wore only one sandal—on the left foot, their shield side—because that foot was advanced during a hand-to-hand struggle and could be used for kicking an enemy in the groin. Thus the left was the hostile foot and was never set first on the threshold of a friend's home. The custom survives among modern soldiers, who begin marching with the left foot foremost."[2]

Roman sandals were more ornate than those designed by the Greeks, and they generally covered all of the foot, leaving the toes exposed. The Romans also wore the calceus, which covered most of the foot to the ankle, as well as buskins that extended halfway up the calf. Roman senators wore black buskins that featured a crescent-shaped clasp of silver or ivory at the instep. These shoes were often open up the front, with laces, and they were lined with the skins of small animals, with the heads hanging down over the tops for ornamentation. Roman soldiers were called *caligati*, a name derived from their sturdy boots, *caliga,* which were often studded with nails.

Shoemaking has always been regarded as an art, rather than a trade, explains Thomas Wright in *The Romance of the Shoe*.[4] Consequently Apollo, god of the arts, was the tutelary deity of the shoemakers of Greece and Rome. "Recognizing the link between god and craft, the Emperor Augustus placed at the entrance of *Sandaliarium vicus* (sandal street), where the shoemakers congregated, a statue of 'the god with loosely-floating hair'—held back, no doubt, by a brainband—Apollo Sandaliarius," says Wright. "In its hand was probably a lyre, and at its sandalled feet a reticulated omphalos (a stone in the temple of Apollo at Delphi, which supposedly marked the center of the earth) and a crow—the bird which the jealous god sent to spy upon his mistress Coronis. Anciently almost every shoemaker indulged in a crow which he taught to talk, and there is a hoary jest of one who kept his bird in a cage in order to see whether it would live 300 years."[4]

Shoemakers were also to be found among the early Christian saints, according to Franck and Brownstone.[3] As an example, St. Anianus of Alexandria was converted to Christianity by St. Mark in the first century A.D. As he repaired one of St. Mark's sandals, Anianus pricked a finger with an awl, resulting in a bit of profanity. After giving him a sermon about using God's name in vain, St. Mark, in a miracle, commanded that the wound go away. St. Anianus later became a leader of the church, from 70 A.D. until his death at the age of 86.

In some of the countries of northern Europe, people wore hose fitted with feet, similar to a baby's leggings, for protection against the weather. Over these socks, the wearer often used oblong pieces of leather bound to the feet with leather thongs. During the late 14th century and early 15th century, according to *Encyclopedia Americana,* as headdresses and hats rose into points on the head, the toes of the shoes were also extended to balance the design.[2] As an example, princes wore shoes that had toes 24 inches long, stuffed with fiber or straw to keep their shape. The shoes were called *poulaines* or *crakows,* indicating that the designs may have originated in Poland. Since the long toes were difficult to walk with, they were often tied to the knees with chains. But the frequency of the accidents caused Edward IV of England to restrict the length of shoe toes to two inches.

"During the 14th and 15th centuries shoes were often made of such delicate materials that cloglike overshoes, called *patterns,* were introduced for outdoor wear. They were made of iron, wood or even cork (for kings), and their toes and heels were thickened or fitted with pegs to lift the sole above wetness and dirt," says the encyclopedia. "The patterns, held on the foot by straps over the instep, could be easily slipped off by the wearer before he entered the house. Similar to patterns were *chopines,* high platforms, to which shoes or mules were permanently attached. In the 16th century, chopines became very high, like stilts. Hamlet, addressing one of the Players, says: 'Your ladyship is nearer to heaven than when I saw you last, by the altitude of a chopine.' "[2]

Heels were apparently introduced in the 1590s by Queen Elizabeth I of England to make her look taller. The idea quickly became fashionable, and it is said that the people of medieval and Elizabethan England were the best shod in Europe because the enormous amount of meat that they ate made leather cheaper and more readily available.

"The city of Lynn, in Massachusetts, became a shoemakers' center because the first tannery of the North American Colonies was built there, in 1630," state the authors of *Clothiers.*[2] "This came before the first guild of American shoemakers, chartered in Boston in 1648. With the leather left over from individual commissions, shoemakers began making shoes for display in their shop windows hoping to attract more customers. The American shoemakers gradually gathered into larger and larger establishments. No longer were they occupied primarily in work that had been ordered by clients. Instead, teams of workers turned out shoes by routine, and customers bought what pleased them. By 1767, John Dagyr's manufactory in Lynn, the biggest shoe workshop in the Colonies, was making 80,000 pairs of shoes a year."

Until the mid-1800s, shoes were made by rather simple hand tools. Most people either wore homemade shoes or purchased them from a nearby shoe-maker or door-to-door salesman. About this time, machines were developed to stitch shoe parts, rather than having the leather nailed together or stitched by hand. In 1882, Jan Ernst Matzeliger, who worked in a Massachusetts shoe factory, invented the shoe-lasting machine, and this and other devices resulted in the mass production of shoes by 1900. This, of course, greatly reduced the price of shoes.[5]

Incidentally, our current method of shoe sizing was adopted in 1324. At that time, King Edward II of England decreed that, in measuring shoe sizes, a standard inch would be equal to three average-size barleycorns, according to Walter E. Cohn in *Modern Footwear Materials and Processes*.[6] And even today the length of one of those barleycorns—one-third of an inch—represents the difference between whole sizes for shoes, even though the length of barleycorns has changed during the past 664 years.

"However romantically archaic an origin this is—and it is not even uniform through the English-speaking world—those poor barleycorns have been blamed for more deficiencies in shoe sizing and last grading than they really deserve," says Cohn. "After all, a standard is a standard, no matter how arbitrarily it may originally have been set. Napoleon based the metric system on a terrestrial measurement in 1790, which could be rechecked from time to time; barleycorns wilt."[6]

History of Athletic Shoes

The origin of sports shoes goes back many centuries, when man finally began to meet his needs for water, food, shelter and warmth and had the time for friendly competition, says *The Complete Handbook of Athletic Footwear*.[7] Archery was a popular hunting skill in mesolithic times, some 8,000 years before Christ, and those early games probably centered around the fastest and most skillful hunter. The authors quote the *Guinness Book of Sports Records* as saying that the earliest sports records go back to 2,450 B.C. for the sport of fowling, which was a javelin-type sport in which sticks were thrown for distance.

In early Greek footraces, notes *The Complete Handbook*, which date back to religious festivals and were held by the first tribes of the Peloponnesus in Olympia, kings and commoners competed in the same races, usually running in their birthday suits.

In tracing the evolution of sports footwear, as of sports itself, continue the authors, the Olympic Games are the best chronological guide. At the first Olympics in Greece in 776 B.C., the winner of the Dolichos (5,000 meters), Goroebus of Ellis, ran in his bare feet. But by the end of the first Olympic era, the Greek athletes favored a type of sandal shoe called *ligula* or *krepis*. The Romans later called them *crepida* or *soccus* (sock). By 480 B.C., a Vatican vase painting shows the introduction of sandals on female runners. Today, "it seems symbolic that Nike, the Greek goddess of victory, was chosen the brand name of what has become one of the world's largest athletic shoe companies."[7]

One of the first American companies to specialize in running shoes, these authors state, was the A. B. Spalding Company. Both rubber soles and the usual leather soles were tried, and the company even sent some of its experts to the 1908 Olympic Games in London to get some suggestions for improving their running shoes.

The "pedestrian" or marathon era, which grabbed headlines during the mid-1860s, influenced the development of flat-soled sport shoes, and, by the end of the century, pedestrianism was in vogue on both sides of the Atlantic, the authors continue. These grueling contests, which often lasted for six days, required highcut leather boots to support the athlete during these grueling run-walks. The maximum distance covered during these six-day races, which consisted of 144 hours of running, walking or resting, was 623¾ miles, completed by George Littlewood in 1888 on a small indoor track.

If there is a historic low point in the development of athletic shoes, add the authors, it was obviously the pedestrian era. At a time when human endurance was being pushed to the limit, the shoe industry was literally dragging its feet by contributing little aid or knowledge about how shoes could help. There are many horror accounts of blisters, taped toes, blood-stained shoes and the pickling of feet, which was done to tighten the skin.

The authors say that those who entered the 1927 Redwood Highway All-Indian Marathon, which covered 482 miles of Northern California, apparently wore double-soled highcut leather boxing shoes.

The first notable athletic shoemakers began making shoes around 1900, say Melvyn P. Cheskin and co-authors. These popular brands were manufactured by George E. Tackaberry of C.C.M. in Canada, Joseph W. Foster (Reebox) in England, the Dassler family in Germany and Marquis Converse in the United States. Adidas, originally owned by the Dassler family, provided shoes for Uli Jonath, who won the Bronze medal (100m) in the Los Angeles Olympics in 1932, and Jesse Owens, the winner of four Gold Medals in the Berlin Olympics in 1936.

In 1948, the authors say, Rudi and Adi Dassler split the company during a family argument. Adi continued with Adidas, said to be the world's largest athletic shoe company, and Rudi founded Puma, which is reportedly number three in rank.

In 1924, Harold Abrahams and Eric Liddell, an Englishman and a Scotsman, made history, as recounted in the movie, *Chariots of Fire,* as they won the 100m and 400m races at the Paris Olympics. They were wearing Foster's running shoes.

"Joseph W. Foster's Reebox Company . . . attracted such early track stars as Alf Shrubb, Arthur Postle and Lord Burghley in the 1928 Olympics," the authors continue. "J. E. Lovelock wore Fosters to his 1,500-meter Gold Medal win in 1936. During the 1950s members of the famous Moscow Dynamo soccer team made sure they had Foster boots with them upon returning from their first ever trip to the West. . . . In 1958, Joseph and Jeffrey Foster left Foster Bros. to form Reebok in the U.K. Reebox has remained Britain's largest indigenous brand and is now number four in worldwide sales volume."[7]

By the 1930s, the major brands were already internationally known, the authors report. These included such personalities as J. E. Sullivan and G. L. Pearce of the Spalding Company; the Dassler brothers; Richings of the Riley Company (now New Balance); Chuck Taylor of Converse; and J. Law of England, who designed Roger Bannister's four-minute-mile shoes.

By the mid-1930s, the authors report, the very young sport shoe industry in the United States couldn't decide whether to use leather or vulcanized rubber/

canvas for making shoes. Such brands as Hyde, Riddell and Brooks favored leather, while Converse, Pro Keds, Red Ball and P. F. Flyers were known for their rubber/canvas models. As might be expected, many of the rubber shoe makers were owned by the tire companies, such as Uniroyal, Dunlop and Goodrich.

The 1940s, the authors add, with the world at war, saw the development of the sneaker in the United States, with Converse and Keds leading the way. During this period, sport shoe manufacturers also introduced the side-laced running shoe, which had an elasticized gore top for a snug fit, as well as sponge rubber innersoles and outersoles.

In the 1950s, the stage was set for what was essentially a small industry to become a major segment of the footwear business, the authors continue. Adidas, Puma and Tiger in Japan increased their share of the market with innovative designs, centralized shoe marketing and testimonial advertising.

After they conquered soccer, the Japanese turned to track and field; they then used their expertise to make new inroads into most of the world's major sports markets, the authors say. Spot Bilt, the U.S. brand, had the biggest share of the track shoe market at this time. Tiger, formed in 1949, concentrated mostly on their chosen area: long-distance running and track and field. Their efforts in introducing new materials, such as nylon uppers and blown rubber wedges and midsoles, easily gave Tiger an historical place in the 1960s. The same efforts also laid the foundation for an off-shoot company, Nike, which has played a major role since the 1970s.

About this time, Nike was joined by Pony, Brooks, Hyde, Converse and others in the highly competitive sports shoe industry. While working for Tiger in Japan, Bill Bowerman developed new running shoes, and, in 1965, in collaboration with Jeff Johnson, another Oregon runner, they introduced nylon uppers and full-length cushioned midsoles. In 1971, when those two runners and Phil Knight formed Nike, they developed the waffle sole, air cushioning and variable width lacing system, the authors report. Beginning in 1975, Nike was joined by Etonic, Brooks and Saucony in making shoes which featured ethylene vinyl acetate (EVA) material, rearfoot motion control devices and molded insoles that could be removed.

In 1961, these companies were joined by New Balance, a company that was founded in 1906 and known for its orthopedic inserts and shoes. Especially interested in shoes for long-distance runners, New Balance experimented with ripple soles for traditional traction, as well as heel wedges for more shock absorption. It was also apparently the first company to introduce width fittings to athletic shoes, the authors continue.

The 1980s has seen the athletic shoe industry reach full maturity, although sport shoes have become less traditionally crafted with natural materials, and more emphasis is being placed on protection, foot support and a reduction in injuries. Interest has increased in expanded rubbers and plastics as cushioning materials, and biomechanical, electronic and computer testing are still being perfected.

What to Look for in a Running Shoe

Because of the stress placed on the heel or lateral edge of the foot during running, manufacturers continue to improve on running shoes to protect athletes. In fact, those portions of the feet pound the surface with a force two to three times that of the athlete's total body weight, according to William T. Bates, a sports physical therapist in Brighton, Massachusetts, writing in *The Physician and Sportsmedicine*.[8] This impact occurs to both feet over 1,000 times per mile. Bates suggests that, when purchasing a pair of running shoes, you carefully check the construction of the shoe, the materials used in making the shoe and your own physical characteristics (such as high instep, or wide foot). With the improvement in running shoes has come a variety of new terms such as wedge, throat, heel counter, toe box wing, (see Figure 3), which need to be learned before choosing the right running shoe.

"The shoe should not have a built-in varum or valgum wedge," Bates cautions. "Make sure a vertical line through the back of the shoe is at right angles to a flat surface. Check balance at the middle of the shoe by pressing a pencil straight down on the heel sock liner. The front of the shoe should lift up with no side-to-side motion. Also, press down on the inside of the shoe at its widest point, the metatarsal arch. The heel should remain on the surface."[8]

Bates also recommends that you inspect the outsole, looking especially for things like ragged edges. And the shoe should flex or bend easily at the metatarsal arch. If the midsole and the wedge are separate pieces, examine the bonding between the two pieces as well as the bonding of the outsole to the midsole. The insole should feel comfortable and the sock liner should feel soft and strong with no seams that could lead to irritation while running, he says.

Also critical in the selection of a running shoe are a firm heel counter and a comfortable heel fit, Bates continues. He suggests that you see that the heel counter is at least four inches forward from the rear part of the heel and that it is sturdy and not easily misshapen. Heel fit is a difficult matter in shoes with only one width for each length. As an example, he adds, a 5 foot 7 inch, 140-pound person and a 6 foot 2 inch, 200-pound person, each with size 9 feet, might be given the same width shoe, with resulting foot problems.

"Check the upper for workmanship in the toe box wing, the eye stay, the saddle and the foxing," he continues. "Look for a smooth stretch of the vamp (the front part of the upper of a shoe) at the featherline. Make sure that both shoes are sewn symmetrically. Check for double stitching, especially at the toe and heel counter."[8]

Bates points out that inadequate cushioning in the heel and sole is a frequent complaint, even in expensive shoes. It is his recommendation that the height of the heel lift should equal the thickness of the midsole (normally ⅜ inch), the wedge (½ inch) and the outsole. The proper heel lift is useful in reducing pressure on the Achilles tendon and in scattering shock as you run or jog. He also suggests that you see that the heel flare is not wider than 3 inches on a size 9 shoe, because this can throw the runner's foot into an unnatural position and contribute to overpronation.

He goes on to say that a well designed outsole, using a combination of

HAPPY FEET

Figure 3.

RUNNING SHOE CONSTRUCTION

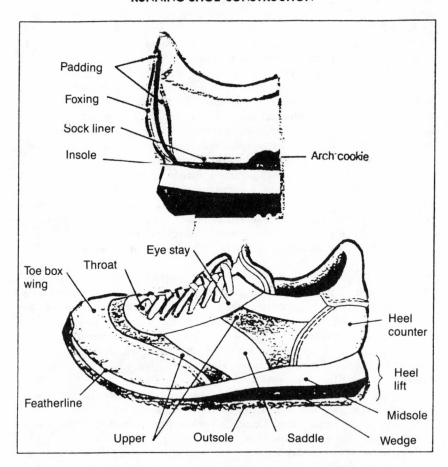

Source: *The Physician and Sportsmedicine*, March 1982. Reprinted by permission.

natural rubber and EVA, will last for quite some time. Manufacturers have found that EVA dissipates shock better than rubber. The upper part of the shoe should be made with nylon oxford or nylon mesh, Bates says. The mesh is especially useful in warmer climates. To test, place your hand inside the shoe and blow from the outside. If the fabric "breathes" sufficiently, you should feel the incoming air.

Some running shoes have a rubber liner that eventually molds to the foot, while other manufacturers insert a flat insole with a supportive arch "cookie," Bates explains. This area is critical, he says, because runners generally have either a high- or low-arched foot. A sock liner made of nylon tricot without seams will prevent irritation.

"Valuable clues can be obtained from your old shoes," Bates adds. "If the wear is on the inside of the heel and the rear of the shoe cants (tilts) inward, you probably pronate too much. In this case you need a firm heel counter and a firm or semi-firm shoe overall. If the upper rolls over either way (though it usually happens toward the outer part of the shoe), mention this to the salesperson. In this instance a strong upper and proper width sizing will help."[8]

He goes on to say that the main difference between training and competition shoes is that the latter have been made 30 to 35 percent lighter by decreasing the soles so that little shock dissipation remains. For that reason, he adds, elite runners usually train in heavier training shoes and use the lighter weight competition shoes for racing or speed work.

More salient tips for buying running shoes are provided by Damien Howell for the Indiana University Runners Clinic and publicized by the Road Runners Club of America.[9] Howell is a physical therapist in Richmond, Virginia. He recommends:

1. Buy a good-quality running shoe designed for running. Expect to pay between $30 and $100. Keep in mind that the most expensive shoe may not necessarily be the best shoe for you.
2. Find the right store. Choose a specialty sports store, one that is owned and operated by a runner. The second choice is a general sports store that sells a variety of sports equipment. The least appropriate place for buying a running shoe is a regular shoe store or department store.
3. Find the right salesperson. Ask for a knowledgeable salesperson who has running experience. Avoid salespeople who try to hurry you or who are inexperienced.
4. Ask the salesperson for a training shoe, not a racing shoe.
5. When trying on shoes, wear socks of the thickness that you will wear when running. If you forget to bring your running socks, ask the salesperson for a "loaner."
6. If you have any special problems, describe them to the salesperson and ask for special help. Some of the problems that the proper shoe can help control are: unusual widths; flat feet; rigid, high-arch feet; excessive body weight; and toe shape. Avoid shoes with a wedge unless you have an identified need for a wedge.
7. It is wise to look at more than one pair of shoes.
8. Choose shoes that fit both feet while you are standing. Ask if you can try running in the shoes on a non-carpeted surface. Some stores will allow a short test run.
9. Inspect the shoes closely and carefully for quality control. It is not unusual for at least one shoe in a pair to be poorly constructed and to be put on the market without proper inspection. Things to look for include:

    a. Place the shoe on a flat surface and examine the heel from behind to see if the heel cup is perpendicular to the sole of the shoe, as it should be.

    b. Pull on the upper part of the shoe and see if it separates from the sole. It should not.

    c. Feel the seams inside the shoe to make sure they are uniform, smooth and well stitched.

    d. Loose threads or extra glue spots are usually signs of a poorly-constructed shoe.

    e. If you compare one shoe to another, or one pair to another pair, you can usually find defects.

    f. If you find a defect, ask for another pair if available. If you cannot find what you want, you can still go to another store.

10. The running shoe industry is changing very rapidly. New technology in shoes is described in fairly objective evaluations in the running magazines. Other runners' advice regarding shoe selection can be helpful. But be careful not to be misled. Body type and running stride may differ.

In another booklet, *Buying a Fitness/Walking Shoe,* Damien Howell provides this check list for diagnosing your own foot problems and selecting the proper shoe:[10]

Your foot type is:

_____Flexible

_____Rigid

You need a shoe which is especially good at:

_____Controlling excessive motion

_____Absorbing shock

_____Both controlling excessive motion and absorbing shock

_____Arch support

_____Heel control

_____Curved last

_____Allowing an orthotic in the shoe. That is a shoe with a removable sock liner, extra eyelet for laces, no anatomical last, deep heel cup. The shoe should be no larger than your typical shoe size.

Here are some additional tips from Dean M. Wakefield of the American Podiatric Medical Association:[11]

1. Buy shoes in the afternoon, when your feet are generally at their true size, having naturally swollen a bit during the day. Wear socks you'd ordinarily wear while using the shoes and pay most attention to getting a comfortable width.

2. If you're accustomed to wearing insoles or orthotic devices with regular shoes, probably you ought to consider them for athletic shoes as well. A serious athlete will want to consult a podiatrist for a foot examination and advice on this matter.

3. If you are a professional walker, then professional walking shoes are in order. If you are not, then the answer is the same as the answer to the question, "Do I need a Jaguar or a Chevrolet to drive to work?"

4. For strenuous exercise (jogging, running, tennis, aerobics, etc.), podiatrists are generally recommending socks with a blend of acrylic and a natural fiber. As an example, orlon tends to "wick" off moisture, especially when the shoe has a leather or mesh upper, thus your sock and foot don't get as

sodden. When the feet sweat profusely, wool and cotton socks tend to hold the moisture longer. For exercise walking, when the feet sweat less, the absorbency of wool and cotton are probably appropriate.

Tips From Shoe Experts

In selecting shoes for aerobic sports, they should fit closely enough to fit snugly and provide support, but should not be so tight that they don't give the foot room to expand, according to Will Albers of Brooks Shoe Inc., in Rockford, Michigan.[12] An experienced athletic footwear salesperson can be helpful in measuring the feet and verifying a good fit.

In addition, Albers continues, the shoe should provide those performance features that best satisfy your personal running style, including durable outsoles, shock-absorbing midsoles, strong heel counters and anti-pronation features. Expect to pay about $60 for a good running shoe; prices for functional running footwear range from $40 to $120.

"Feet are a combination of straight or curved and high-arched or flat and any combination in between," explains Albers. "Many models of shoes are made on lasts (foot molds) that are better suited for people with curved or straight feet. This characteristic is usually advertised as a feature of the shoe. Arch supports in shoes can accommodate most people's arch height through over-the-counter orthotics that are available for special needs. It's simply a matter of trying on several different shoes and selecting the one that feels best. A podiatrist can identify foot morphology (shape) and recommend brands of shoes and/or arch supports."[12]

Outsole wear is a good barometer in determining whether or not you need a new pair of shoes, Albers says, although quite often the midsole loses most of its shock-absorbing qualities after several hundred miles. Although some athletes can get 1,000-plus miles out of their shoes, a good rule of thumb is to replace shoes after 300 to 600 miles, he says. He does not recommend resoling old shoes for running.

"Outsoles are usually made of carbon rubber for durability and cushioning," Albers adds. "Midsoles are made of EVA or polyurethane. These materials provide cushioning. Sometimes units of pressurized gas or silicon are used to add extra cushioning. Different densities of EVA or polyurethane provide stability features and resistance to compaction. The upper is usually made from a combination of leather and nylon mesh. The mesh provides breathability, while leather reinforces the stress points. Heel counters are made of PVC plastic or laminated fibers to provide support and strength."[12]

The serious athlete should avoid cheap and non-branded athletic shoes, Albers continues. These shoes are suitable for casual wear, but they do not provide the comfort and protection that is necessary for functional use, he says. He adds that machine washing and drying can damage athletic shoes. Therefore, these shoes should be washed by hand and air dried. Most shoes have replaceable sockliners.

"People living in a warm climate might prefer shoes with nylon mesh for breathability, but I don't see that this makes much difference, since the shoes are designed for all climates,'' Albers concludes. "Of greater concern is the terrain on which you run. Running on pavement requires cushioning; running on grass or trails requires more traction.''[12]

Researchers have been looking at people's feet for a long time, says Ernest Shiwanov, American Sporting Goods Corporation (Turntec), Irvine, California.[13] As an example, the U.S. Army was among the first organizations to analyze the problems involved in keeping their foot-soldiers on the move. The Army did some of the first large population studies on foot types. However, during the past 20 years, other researchers also have looked into feet, especially with sports performance in mind. As a result, says Shiwanov, three distinct foot types have been identified: the high-arched foot; the normal or average-arched foot; and the low-arched foot. The three foot types have different shapes, and, although their function is the same, there are marked differences among them. We can discuss generalities, he says, but none of the discussions are etched in stone.

"The high-arched foot tends to be rigid, which during the foot-strike, generates higher pressure-per-unit area (pronation) along the lateral border of the foot," explains Shiwanov. "In contrast, the flat foot is quite flexible. Its pronation path generally follows the medial aspect of the foot. Since we have little in the way of structure in that part of the foot, the arch has compressive forces that work against the muscles, tendons and ligaments in that portion of the foot and ankle. That leaves the average-arched foot somewhere in the middle."

He goes on to say that the consequences of these foot types are the following: The high-arched foot's greater pressure on a smaller area of the foot transmits more impact force to the foot, ankles, knees, hips and so on. Therefore, most injuries related to the high-arched foot are shock-related. Conversely, foot types that are subjected to over-pronation have stress-related problems. That is, the flexibility of the foot's associated structures stresses the bones of the foot (usually metatarsals two and three), the plantar fascia (the connective tissue of the bottom surface of the foot), the Achilles tendon and the medial part of the knee, to name a few. Shiwanov quotes Dr. L. D. Lutter's study,[14] which found that 65 percent of runners' injuries belonged to the low arch type, 25 percent to the high arch type, and 10 percent to the average arch type.

"It is clear why manufacturers have targeted the most-likely-to-injure category in their design efforts," Shiwanov says. "Therefore, if you know something about your feet, you can avoid the pitfalls associated with purchasing the wrong shoe, regardless of the activity it is being used for. The Shoe Selection Chart (Table 1) should help to sort out these features."[13]

In addition to the considerations in Table 1, proper fit is critical, Shiwanov continues. Although most salespeople in specialty athletic shoe stores know how to fit shoes properly, a couple of points should be emphasized, he says. For example, in the case where the individual has a very flexible foot, care should be taken to allow more than the usual space allotted for elongation after foot strike. In a running shoe, he says, the rule-of-thumb of one-half inch space between the *longest* toe and the end of the shoe may not be enough for this foot

Table 1

SHOE SELECTION CHART

FOOT TYPE	RECOMMENDED SHOE FEATURES
RIGID HIGH ARCH	1. Impact protection should be the most forgiving (softest) material allowable. 2. Curve lasted 3. Low or moderate rearfoot stability 4. Slip lasted or flexible shoe
FLEXIBLE HIGH ARCH	1. All of the above features apply, with the addition of greater arch support 2. Orthotic compatible (Compensated interior space for the room an orthotic device requires inside a shoe)
NORMAL ARCH	1. Impact protection should be less forgiving by using a higher density midsole material 2. Standard or natural last 3. Moderate rearfoot stability either in the midsole and/or external stabilizing device 4. Slip, combination or board lasted shoes are all workable possibilities 5. Orthotic compatible
RIGID LOW ARCH	1. Impact protection should be the most forgiving (least dense) material allowable. 2. Curve lasted 3. Low or moderate rearfoot stability 4. Combination or board lasting or a shoe with minimal midsole flex 5. Uppers with substantial medial and lateral support 6. Orthotic compatible
FLEXIBLE LOW ARCH	1. Impact protection should be the least forgiving (highest density) midsole material allowable 2. A straight last 3. High degree of rearfoot stability 4. Combination or board lasting or a shoe with minimal midsole flex 5. Uppers with substantial medial and lateral support 6. Orthotic compatible

type. He recommends that you go a half size larger, especially if the person complains of a history of good store fit, but gets black toenails during jogging later. In any case, the longest toe should be the guide in making the adjustment. He goes on to say that about 25 percent of the population has a longer second toe, so this fitting exception should be kept in mind. For other athletic shoes, ultimate length is often a matter of personal preference, keeping in mind the flexible foot's idiosyncrasies. In addition, he cautions, for those who wear orthotics, allow enough space in the rear of the shoe to accommodate them.

"You would be surprised how an obviously good-looking, well-wearing athletic shoe is actually worn out," Shiwanov says. "In the case of athletic shoes with midsoles, it is time to retire them when there is a measurable difference between the midsole height of the lateral verses and the medial side of the shoe. This difference could be between two to four millimeters, but this is contingent on the type of midsole configuration (i.e., multi-density midsoles). Another measure of a shoe's life," he continues, "is the integrity of the heel counter(s) after prolonged use. A once-rigid heel counter that can now be easily deformed by hand pressure should be retired. Another common test is the table-top examination. Place your athletic shoes on a table top and examine the rear-foot area straight on, at table-top level, for relative true to perpendicular. A shoe that lists five degrees out-of-true in any direction should be discarded."[13]

The types of fabrics and supports used in athletic shoes are influenced by the type of sport as well as cost and production considerations, Shiwanov points out. Pigskin is used because it resists shrinkage and retains its shape. Suede is selected because of its relatively low cost. Synthetic suede is often the choice because it is lightweight, it does not absorb water, it does not stretch, it is low in cost, it is uniform in thickness and it does not bleed dyes. As for mesh, either nylon or polyester, it is cooler than nylon fabric or leather. Manufacturers decide on their own whether to make heel counters out of PVC, TPR, or the various other thermoplastics.

Shiwanov adds that temperature and humidity can affect the shock-absorbing properties of most midsoles. Low temperature can reduce the flexibility and resilience of midsoles, whereas high temperatures increase flexibility and resilience. Humidity can exacerbate these problems.

He concludes by saying that sweating is the body's normal way of regulating temperature, and that those who do not sweat have serious problems. Sweating is an individual problem; therefore, you should not be concerned if you sweat more or less than your jogging or running partner. As for foot odor, that also varies from athlete to athlete. For an excessive foot problem, see your podiatrist, he suggests.

Heel wear is often a sign that you need a new pair of shoes, says J. Kolb of Adidas, Warren, New Jersey.[15] Therefore, each athlete needs to pay attention to how his or her shoes are wearing out. As an example, Kolb says, a serve-and-volley-style tennis shoe will tend to wear the toes of the shoes down very quickly. Another clue to excessive wear are minor aches and pains. These physical signs are often indicators the shoes have lost the cushioning and support properties the athlete needs, he says.

Kolb adds that a shoe designed for one sport is probably not appropriate for a different sport. Thus, the proper equipment, including shoes, can help to prevent injuries. In sports such as running injuries are so common that properly-fitted running shoes are good investments, because they can minimize the chance of an injury, he stresses.

Runners should begin with a training shoe and then move on to racing flats, according to Harvey B. Simon, M.D., and Steven R. Levisohn, M.D., in *The Athlete Within*.[16] Select a shoe that is comfortable and feels supportive without being snug or constricting, they continue. The tongue and the Achilles pad should be well padded to prevent irritation and tendinitis. Uppers should be light and flexible.

"The shoe lining should be comfortable and moisture-absorbent," they continue. "Most insoles are made of a firm foam rubber. Some insoles provide built-in arch supports, which can be helpful but are not truly necessary for runners. In fact," they continue, "if you have structural or biomechanical abnormalities of your foot, you should consider a specially-molded-to-measure insole called an orthotic to provide support and gait correction."[16]

They add that the heel counter should be firm, to provide hind-foot stability, and the heel itself should be raised on a heel wedge so that the height of the sole and wedge in the back of the shoe is two to three times greater than the sole beneath the ball of the foot. Since runners land on the heel, this gives greater shock absorption as well as taking pressure off the Achilles tendon.

"The midsole of the shoe should be flexible," they continue, "and the toe box should be rounded and at least one and a half inches high. Flexibility is important so that you can push off properly, and a large toe box is important to avoid injuring your toes and nails by excessive pressure during push-off. Many sole materials and designs are available. Try to find one that is rated high for durability. Look for reinforcement in the heel, particularly along the outer side. This is where most runners strike first, and hence is the area that will wear down first. A studded sole is particularly useful for running on slippery or wet surfaces."[16]

Breaking in a new pair of walking or jogging shoes should take one to two weeks, according to Gene R. Hagerman, et al., in *Efficiency Walking and Jogging*.[17] The shoes can be worn for longer and longer sessions each day, and they should be alternated with older shoes to prevent blisters, tendinitis or other injuries.

Biomechanical Analysis

In recent years, considerable advances have been made in the design of walking shoes, especially with the aid of biomechanical analysis, say Anne Kashiwa and James M. Rippe, M.D., in *Rockport's Fitness Walking for Women*.[18] With this procedure, the motions of any activity can be broken down into small segments using high-speed filming techniques and computer technology. The forces involved are also monitored with the use of a force plate.

"When biomechanics have been applied to fitness walking, it has been discovered that the walking stride is unique and very different from the running stride," according to Kashiwa and Rippe. "In the running motion, the individual typically lands with significant weight on the heel, then rapidly transfers this weight to the ball of the foot as he or she springs off the ground. In walking, the heel hits at a greater angle than in running, and the weight is slowly rolled forward on to the ball of the foot.''[18]

The forces involved in the walking stride are also considerably less than those of the running stride, they add. In running, you land with several times your body weight each time your foot hits the ground. In walking, since one foot is always in contact with the ground, the forces are only 1 to 1.25 times your body weight on each stride.

In research during the past three years in association with the Biomechanics Laboratory at the University of Massachusetts in Amherst, Kashiwa and Rippe have found that a properly designed walking shoe is better able to cushion impact on the heel during fitness walking than a comparably priced athletic shoe. They also report that well-designed walking shoes were better able to control excessive pronation, in which the heel rotates from outside to inside, during fitness walking than comparably priced athletic shoes. And they found that women land with more pressure on their heels than do men during fitness walking, when the forces are normalized for weight. Consequently, they add, a woman should buy an especially well-designed walking shoe and ideally one that is specifically made for women.

"Several years ago," they add, "many people doubted that there was a need for shoes specifically designed for walking. However, research in our laboratory and at other laboratories makes it clear that each activity has its own unique biomechanical needs and hence deserves its own piece of specifically designed equipment. This is completely consistent with the history of other activities where advanced technology has led to improved performance, safety and pleasure.''[18]

Because of the force of the body weight during running, runners who have shoes with heels that are too low experience excessive pull on the calf muscles and the Achilles tendon, according to Rob Roy McGregor, D.P.M., one of the founders of Sports Medicine Resource, Inc.[19] Consequently, chronic limpers can usually be helped by raising the heel height, either with heel lifts or a new pair of shoes.

A heel cushion that is too rigid causes the heel to be bruised, Dr. McGregor continues. He refers to this as "jogger's heel," or the first socially acceptable foot problem. On the other hand, if the heel is overly cushioned, you sink into your shoes and miss some of the rebound energy that goes with each footstrike. The soft heel cushion also increases fatigue, he adds.

The heel counter, situated at the back of the shoe, encircles and holds the heel in place. To properly control heel motion, the heel counter should be rather stiff. The ideal is to prevent excessive rolling in or out, he adds. The feet also need to have support against the rolling out of the arch as you run, and the best support is achieved, he says, by adding a wedge from the heel to the ball of the shoe.

Since biomechanics have determined that the greatest amount of vertical force absorbed by the feet is just behind the ball of the foot, proper cushioning should be built into the sole of the shoe, Dr. McGregor suggests. He explains that the reason why some people who run in tennis sneakers experience a burning sensation is because the ball of the foot doesn't have sufficient cushioning.

Dr. McGregor goes on to say that if the shoes do not bend where the foot normally bends—at the ball—these stiff shoes can result in shin splints, Achilles tendinitis or lower leg pain. That is because the stiff sole causes the foot and leg muscles to work unnecessarily.

If there is not sufficient room in the shoes for you to wiggle your toes up and down, continues Dr. McGregor, there is added pressure on your toes, resulting in blisters, calluses, corns or runner's toe, in which a blood blister forms under the nail.

Shopping for Shoes

When buying shoes for sportwalking, Gary Yanker recommends that you go away from fashion to function, considering as well socks, orthotics and other foot aids. Custom biomechanical orthotic devices can stop excessive motion of the foot and leg, and are perhaps advisable for people with leg problems. But leg problems should be analyzed by a trained sports medicine podiatrist, he recommends in *Gary Yanker's Sportwalking.*[20]

He recommends at least two kinds of walking shoes for sportwalking: a sturdy pair and a lightweight pair. And he suggests multiple sets of each type for training and testing. The sturdy pair needs to be thicker, firmer and stiffer and probably should be made of leather or a leather-synthetic fabric combination. This is the pair you will wear the most, especially when it's wet. The lighter pair can be a jogging-style shoe with thick cushioning, and can be quite flexible, he continues. You switch to the lighter shoes to give your feet a change and a rest. So, it's a good idea to carry the lighter shoes in your day pack in case you decide to switch.

In buying walking shoes and boots, Yanker suggests that they should be cut below the ankle bone to allow for maximum foot flexing. He admits that hikers often prefer shoes which cover and protect the ankle, but he says most mountain walking, excluding technical climbing, is done on trails, where a stiff heel counter provides ample support. Some hiking boots, of course, have padding along the tops to prevent dirt and pebbles from getting into the shoe.

Since walkers spend a great deal of time walking over a variety of terrain in all kinds of weather, including rain and snow, waterproof shoes are essential, he says. If your feet become wet, your skin softens and this is the ideal way to start a blister.

"Leather (treated with waterproofing wax) is still the best proofing," he adds. "Unfortunately, synthetic materials resist only moisture and light rain at best. As soon as it rains moderately to heavily, puddles form, so you need more than water resistance. This is when you switch back to your sturdy shoes."[20]

For running, too many people gravitate toward lightweight shoes, perhaps because this type seems glamorous and more likely to improve speed, according to Kenneth Forsythe, M.D. and Neil Feineman in *Athletics for Life.*[21] But if you are just beginning a running program, don't even try them, Dr. Forsythe warns.

He says that these lightweight models are designed for elite marathoners and long-distance runners who rarely weigh over 150 pounds, and these shoes simply do not provide adequate protection for heavier athletes. Unless speed is the main object in a running program, even runners with slight builds would benefit more from a heavier, more cushioned shoe, he contends.

For those just beginning a running program, who are maintaining their weight or performance, or who are training for a 10K run, Dr. Forsythe recommends a casual running shoe that is suitable for seven to 30 miles per week. For those training for a marathon and running over 30 miles a week, he recommends a more advanced training shoe. In any case, he cautions, don't consider price when buying shoes. Even the most expensive shoe is less expensive than several visits to the doctor's office, he points out.

To get some help in selecting shoes, Dr. Forsythe recommends that you read such things as the *Runner's World* annual survey of running shoes, which rates and comments on the leading brands. A local high school or college track coach can tell you where his students buy shoes, he adds.

One of the newest developments in soles is the air sole. Dr. Forsythe cautions that these soles feel fabulous when you first try on the shoe, but that they are not without problems.

"Nike developed the air sole in response to a study suggesting that a rare anemia might be caused by the fracturing of red blood cells in the heel during running," Dr. Forsythe reports. "The air sole is particularly shock absorbent and may prevent this fracturing. The vast majority of runners never experience this problem, so you should consider the air sole for its shock absorption, rather than its protection from anemia. Before you buy a pair of these shoes, however, you should know that they lose their absorptive properties approximately twice as quickly as shoes made with other materials. Even so, many runners who use the shoes feel that the comfort and protection, while short-term, are worth the expense of replacing them more frequently."[21]

Dr. Forsythe adds that sorbothane heel lifts are available in many stores to decrease the stress of the foot striking the ground. Sorbothane, he says, has the longest life and the highest ability to absorb shock of any synthetic material. It's too heavy for an entire sole but is ideal as a heel lift, he says.

"While no substitute for correct running form, these heel lifts have helped some of my patients who suffer various foot and ankle problems, such as Achilles tendinitis," he adds. "Thus, while the heel lifts should not be put in running shoes as a matter of course, they may be useful if you have problems."[21]

One of the advantages that walkers have over other athletes is that virtually all of the attire they need, with the possible exception of shoes, is already in their closet, according to John Pleas, Ph.D., assistant professor of psychology at Middle Tennessee State University, Murfreesboro. In general, he says in *Walking*,[22] any pair of shoes that is comfortable and feels good can be suitable for walking. The bottom line, since you will probably be walking hundreds of miles in the months ahead, he adds, is that you have shoes that add pleasure, maximize comfort and minimize the possibility of injury.

"Most walking and jogging shoes have a double or triple layered heel to absorb the impact of each step and waffled or treaded sole and heel to assure adequate traction for your heel when it strikes the walking surface—and for pushing off with your toes," he explains. "High heels tend to throw the body out of line and exert pressure on your toes and instep, and smooth soles without heels (including tennis shoes) tend to exert pressure on the Achilles tendon. Neither type of shoe is usually suitable for sustained walking."[22]

Dr. Pleas says that most walking shoes are constructed with a soft absorbent padding that conforms to the arch of the foot. But this is not an arch support, he adds, so if you have a history of fallen arches or if you are prone to injuries in this area of your foot, a worthwhile investment would be to see a podiatrist and have a special arch support constructed for your foot that can be transferred from shoe to shoe.

Dr. Pleas goes on to say that, since salespeople are often more interested in style and making a sale, you should remind them that comfort and safety are your main interests. You might mention that you plan to walk from three to seven miles per day and you need a walking shoe for that purpose. He adds that a jogging shoe or a leather walking shoe are both recommended for sustained walking. When purchasing your second pair of shoes, assuming that your first pair has been suitable, you can save money, he says, by looking for sales that sporting goods stores and other outlets often have several times a year. If possible, leave your name and telephone number with a clerk so that they can call you the next time the store has a sale. Never purchase walking shoes through the mail or have someone else buy them for you, Dr. Pleas cautions. You really need to try on the shoes before purchasing them and it may take two to three weeks to get a refund if the shoes do not fit.

When in the shoe store, Dr. Pleas adds, have the salesperson measure both your right and left foot, since one foot may be larger than the other. Try on a shoe for the larger foot first. During the process of elimination and selection, you may have to visit several shoe stores in order to get the right fit, he continues. After standing, wiggling your toes and checking the fit of the heel and the pliability, walk around the store. Check further by walking back and forth past a mirror.

But, he adds, shoes that feel comfortable while you are walking on carpet in the store may have a different feel on concrete or other hard surface. So ask if you can walk around the block. This may be met with skepticism in a department store, he adds, but is a routine request at a sporting goods store that caters to walkers and joggers.

Upon reentering the store, he continues, check the shoe out in the mirror once again. Are the shoes the ones you want? Is the color right? If not, do they have a color you want? Do the shoes make you look and feel like a walker? Finally, he says, ask about the care and maintenance of the shoes. What special precautions should be taken?

When buying athletic shoes, it is imperative that you take along a pair of socks that you will be wearing with the shoes, explain James G. Garrick, M.D., and Peter Radetsky in *Peak Condition*.[23] It's certainly counterproductive to try on running or aerobic shoes in your regular dress socks or pantyhose.

"Leave one of your old shoes on one foot, put one of the new ones on the other foot, and walk around for a while—that gives you a valid basis for comparison," they report. "Then reverse the process. Then put both new shoes on and see how they feel. . . . Above all, test for comfort. Generally, shoes will not stretch in length at all, although they may spread a bit in width. But for the most part, shoes are never going to feel much better than they did in the shop."[23]

Dr. Garrick says that the best way to cushion a shoe is to put the resilient material outside the shoe, between the soft innersole and the hard outersole. In that way, he maintains, the whole shoe sinks instead of you sinking inside it. Until you flatten out the foam in the heel, you will be sliding up and down each time you take a step. Therefore, he says, buy shoes that cushion below the heel rather than inside it.

Another problem, he continues, is that manufacturers often contour heels for the so-called "normal" foot. Shoes cup forward in the heel, so that, in profile, they resemble a shallow "C." Unfortunately, he adds, all feet aren't so symmetrical; some heels are cuplike, but others are almost straight from the Achilles tendon to the bottom of the heel. For this shape of foot, especially in tennis shoes, the counter of the shoe will cut into the heel, he says. So crush the back of the shoe with the foot.

"Yikes! sixty dollars down the drain!" Dr. Garrick says. "But, no, it won't hurt the shoe, and it could make life lovely for your Achilles tendon."[23]

When buying outdoor athletic shoes, he adds, look for the ones with cleats molded into the sole, because they are safer than the longer, conical, screw-on cleat. They bring fewer knee and ankle injuries, he says.

Athletic shoes for youngsters are generally deficient in arches, so Dr. Garrick recommends the Spence or Dr. Scholl's arch supports. Since kids grow so quickly, they can actually outgrow their muscles, and this puts a strain on the tendons that are attached to those muscles and bones. If the tendons are tight, he adds, there is a possibility of injuries. And if the arch remains unsupported so that the heel drops, there is also a chance of injury.

At the end of 1984, when Dr. Garrick was researching his book, there were over 28 different kinds of aerobic dance shoes on the market. They were generally all the same—a bastardized running shoe—he says.

"In a survey we did of the popular brands of aerobic dance shoes, there was no difference in the injury rates at all," Dr. Garrick continues. "None! The most popular shoe was the best-looking, but in every one of the other seven categories in which we compared them—including durability—it was below average or tied for last. . . . Unfortunately, it seems that the most important feature of aerobic dance shoes, so far as the customers are concerned, are looks."[23]

He adds that, "Bottom line: the main thing you should look for in a shoe, no matter what athletic demands you're going to place on it, is comfort. All the business about traction, shock absorption, durability, etc., won't make a bit of difference to you if your feet hurt. So buy a shoe for comfort. Consider anything else frosting on the cake."[23]

Serious exercisers must do their homework when buying shoes to insure that the shoes not only look good, but also are the best ones for their athletic needs, according to Lisa Gundling of the American Running and Fitness Association, Bethesda, Maryland. She quotes Paul Taylor, D.P.M. (team podiatrist for the Washington Bullets and past-president of the American Running and Fitness Association) as saying that these shoes can be "fashionable" or "functional." The so-called fashionable athletic shoes are now lighter, softer and more color-coordinated, but their use for exercising can lead to injuries, Dr. Taylor said.[24]

"Functional shoes, which have greater stability and shock absorption, are imperative to athletes because the body becomes more susceptible to stress when it is fatigued," Gundling said. "This fatigue, coupled with poor shoes, can lead to shin splints, knee problems and stress fractures. Wearing proper athletic shoes will help you to stick to your exercise program by decreasing your chance of being injured."[24]

Pat Devaney, promotional manager of Reebok, is quoted as saying that the bulk of their business is from people who buy running shoes to wear to the grocery store or the subway. He estimates that only 10 to 15 percent of running shoe customers use their shoes for actual running.

With all of the variables in selecting and buying properly fitted shoes, it is obvious that most of us need to take more time when buying shoes. By taking that extra time, trying on a number of different pairs, and even visiting several shoe stores if that is what it takes, we can not only prevent a lot of pain and foot problems, but also enjoy our jogging, running and walking even more.

References

1. Melvyn P. Cheskin, Kel J. Sherkin, D.P.M., and Barry T. Bates, Ph.D., *The Complete Handbook of Athletic Footwear* (New York: Fairchild Publications, 1987), p. 1.

2. Margaret Stavridi, *Encyclopedia Americana* (Danbury, Conn.: Grolier, Inc., 1987), pp. 745–749.

3. Irene M. Franck and David M. Brownstone, *Clothiers* (New York: Facts on File Publications, 1987).

4. Thomas Wright, *The Romance of the Shoe* (London: C. J. Farncombe & Sons, Ltd., 1922), pp. 1–19.

5. *The World Book Encyclopedia* (Chicago: World Book, Inc., 1987), pp. 350–352.

6. Walter E. Cohn, *Modern Footwear Materials and Processes* (New York: Fairchild Publications, Inc., 1969), pp. 3–21.

7. Melvyn P. Cheskin, et al., op. cit.

8. William T. Bates, MS, ATC, RPT, "Selecting a Running Shoe," *The Physician and Sportsmedicine* (Vol. 10, No. 3, March 1982), pp. 154–155.

9. Damien Howell, "How to Buy a Pair of Running Shoes," (Alexandria, Va.: Road Runners Club of America, undated).

10. Damien Howell, "Buying a Fitness/Walking Shoe" (undated).

11. Dean M. Wakefield, American Podiatric Medical Association, Inc., Bethesda, Md., personal letter (February 12, 1988).

12. Will Albers, Brooks Shoe, Inc., Rockford, Mich., personal letter (January 6, 1988).

13. Ernest Shiwanov, American Sporting Goods Corporation (Turntec), Irvine, Cal., personal letter (February 9, 1988).

14. L. D. Lutter, "Pronation Biomechanics in Runners," *Contemp. Orthop.* (2 (8): 1980), p. 579.

15. J. Kolb, Adidas, Warren, N.J., personal letter (January 4, 1988).

16. Harvey B. Simon, M.D., and Steven R. Levisohn, M.D., *The Athlete Within* (Boston: Little, Brown and Company, 1987), pp. 190–191.

17. Gene R. Hagerman, John W. Atkins, John G. McMurtry and J. Richard Steadman, M.D., *Efficiency Walking and Jogging* (New York: Bantam Books, 1987), pp. 12–14.

18. Anne Kashiwa and James M. Rippe, M.D., *Rockport's Fitness Walking for Women* (New York: Perigee/Putnam, 1987), pp. 47–52.

19. William Southmayd, M.D., and Marshall Hoffman, *Sports Health* (New York: Quick Fox Publishing Co., 1981), pp. 374–376.

20. Gary Yanker, *Gary Yanker's Sportwalking* (Chicago: Contemporary Books, Inc., 1987), pp. 216–224.

21. Kenneth Forsythe, M. D., and Neil Feineman, *Athletics for Life* (New York: Simon and Schuster, Inc., 1985), pp. 58–62.

22. John Pleas, Ph.D., *Walking* (New York: W. W. Norton & Co., 1981), pp. 60–66.

23. James G. Garrick, M.D., and Peter Radetsky, *Peak Condition* (New York: Crown Publishers, 1986), pp. 65–69.

24. Lisa Gundling, *Choosing the Right Shoe Keeps You Exercising* (Bethesda, Md.: American Running and Fitness Association, October 24, 1988).

Chapter 3

Jogging

If you are not convinced that jogging is one of the most stressful forms of exercise, simply observe a group of joggers—many of whom are overweight—as they huff and puff along city streets or in parks, their faces contorted in hideous, Goyaesque configurations. Jogging should be fun! And it is for the thousands of regular joggers who set realistic goals, have a suitable checkup before they begin and wear appropriate clothing, especially shoes. As with other forms of exercise, warmups and cooldowns are imperative. For those who lope along at a moderate speed, jogging can be an energizing outing. It can be enjoyed by people of all ages, and you really don't need a lot of gear.

Although some people use the terms "jogging" and "running" synonymously, it should be pointed out that running is generally less stressful than jogging, because the runner is usually not hitting the pavement with such force. Some joggers pound the street or track as though they were driving posts into the ground. That style of running is bound to result in injuries and perhaps damage to various parts of the body. If jogging has become too stressful for you, have a professional check out your style or gear. As a compromise, alternately walk and run, both at a moderate speed.

How to Jog

There is actually no correct way to jog, according to the President's Council on Physical Fitness and Sports, Washington, D.C. Therefore, jogging techniques will vary as much as the way people walk. To make jogging more enjoyable and to minimize muscle and joint soreness, the President's Council offers the following advice:[1]

1. Stand up straight, keep your back as straight as is naturally comfortable; keep the head up and don't look at your feet while jogging.
2. Arms should be held slightly away from the body and bent at the elbows so that the elbow and hand are about the same distance from the ground. Arms should be moved rhythmically with alternate legs. While running, occasionally shake and relax arms and shoulders. This helps to offset tightness that can develop while jogging or running. To relax, periodically take several deep breaths and exhale gently.

3. There are several recommended ways for the foot to hit the ground. One is to first land on the heel of the foot slightly before the bottom of the foot touches, then rock forward and take off from the ball of the foot on the next step. If you find this unnatural or uncomfortable, land on the entire bottom of the foot, with most of the weight on the ball of the foot. Avoid landing only on the ball of the foot, since this can contribute to unnecessary soreness in the foot and leg.

4. In any case, keep steps short by allowing the foot to hit the ground beneath the knee, instead of reaching it out in front. The slower you are running, the shorter the stride should be.

5. Do not hold your breath, but do expel the air naturally and rhythmically. If it doesn't feel too much like rubbing your head and patting your stomach at the same time, you can develop a breathing rhythm by exhaling on two steps and inhaling on two; or exhaling on three steps and inhaling on three.

6. If you become excessively tired or uncomfortable while jogging, slow down, walk . . . or stop!

For a beginning jogging program, the President's Council recommends that you jog every other day or at least three times a week. A daily program often leads to foot and leg problems.

"After the bones, ligaments and muscles of the legs get used to supporting body weight while jogging, then a daily program can be developed," continues the President's Council. "On the days a person doesn't jog, they should try to perform some stretching exercises or calisthenics and go for a brisk walk or swim. If this program is too difficult, replace some of the jogging with walking or reduce the total distance covered each day. Be sure to always start each workout with a warm-up (a walk and some stretching exercises for 10 to 15 minutes), and end it by tapering off with a walk for at least several minutes. These procedures will help reduce any muscle soreness or cardiovascular complications that might occur."[1]

After the beginning jogger has completed a 16-week program, he or she can design a personal exercise program to fit individual needs, schedule, facilities and interests, the President's Council advises. However, it is important to exercise regularly—every day or every other day.

Where to jog? Soft jogging tracks, dirt paths, and smooth, grassy areas are preferable, since they cushion some of the jolt as you move along. Hard surfaces, such as concrete or asphalt roads, should be avoided if possible. Golf courses, parks or rights-of-way along highways can be useful, especially since they provide a change of scenery. However, because of pollution, try to avoid areas with heavy automobile traffic. During inclement weather, you can jog in your basement, at a local Y, school or church gym and other protected areas. The President's Council suggests that you give the right-of-way to automobiles, bicycle riders, dogs and policemen, "who may think you look suspicious." It was not mentioned, but if you jog too close to a bluejay's or other bird's nest, especially when there are young birds present, you are likely to be dive-bombed by both parents.

Almost any time is acceptable for jogging, says the President's Council, except for immediately after a meal (wait an hour or so), in the middle of a hot and humid day, or when air pollution is especially bad. Most joggers like to set aside a specific time for jogging, such as early morning just before breakfast. This time schedule also generally insures that the jogger will stick to a regular routine. Jogging with family members, friends or co-workers will also insure that the training program will not be interrupted.

"Any minor illness, injury or infection that might be influenced by jogging should be taken care of immediately," continues the President's Council. "Care should be taken to prevent blisters, sore muscles and aching joints. Use of proper shoes and socks and taking it easy at the beginning will help avoid many foot and leg problems that might occur. Any persistent illness or injury should be brought immediately to the attention of a professional. Overweight individuals need to be extra cautious at the beginning of a jogging program to avoid foot, ankle and knee problems."[1]

To avoid undue stress, a jog should be a moderately-paced run in which you should be able to carry on a normal conversation comfortably, says John La Place, Ph.D.[2] If you have been inactive and are just now beginning a jogging program, he suggests that you begin with increasingly demanding walks before you actually start jogging.

"Jogging should then begin with short runs of 25 to 30 yards, alternating with walks of about the same distance," he continues. "The running pace should be held in check; in fact, at first it should not exceed the walking pace by much. From then on, one may gradually increase the running portion of the training session, remembering to keep the pace at a modest level."[2] Table 2 will help you establish a good pace.

Health and Safety

Since jogging places added strain on the feet, the American Podiatric Medical Association has the following recommendations for joggers:[3]

1. *Wear good shoes.* Properly-fitted jogging shoes should provide cushioning and support for both heel and arch. There should also be ample room to move the toes. Worn-out shoes should be discarded, since they can affect your running style. Patched shoes are also a no-no, except in a temporary situation.
2. *Keep feet clean and dry.* If perspiration causes friction and irritation while wearing socks, switch to a soft, thick pair. Give the shoes a chance to air and dry out between runs. Foot powder is recommended for both feet and shoes.
3. *Cut toenails properly.* Since the toenail is there to protect the toe, do not cut the toenail into the quick or leave the nail long and jagged so that it catches on shoes and socks. So cut the toenails straight across. When bathing or showering, scrub the toenails in a forward and backward motion. Use a firm brush to keep cuticles back and to prevent calluses and debris from irritating the toes. Jogging can aggravate infected or ingrown toenails.
4. *Muscle fatigue and spasms.* Stretching exercises and warm-ups can often prevent further strain on overworked and underconditioned muscles and tendons. If pain begins to subside during slow, easy exercises, then continue

Table 2
WALK-JOG-RUN PACE

			Time for Various Distances (Min:Sec)				
Pace	Speed mph	55 yds.	110 yds.	220 yds.	440 yds	880 yds	1 mile
Slow Walk	3	:38	1:15	2:30	5:00	10:00	20:00
Moderate Walk	4	:28	:56	1:52	3:45	7:30	15:00
Fast Walk	4.5	:25	:50	1:40	3:20	6:40	13:20
Slow Jog	5	:22	:45	1:30	3:00	6:00	12:00
Moderate Jog	6	:19	:38	1:15	2:30	5:00	10:00
Fast Jog	7	:17	:33	1:05	2:09	4:17	8:34
Slow Run	8	:15	:29	:57	1:54	3:47	7:34
Moderate Run	9	:13	:25	:50	1:40	3:20	6:40
Fast Run	10	:11	:22	:45	1:30	3:00	6:00
Competitive Running	11	:10.5	:21	:41	1:22	2:44	5:27
	12	: 9.5	:19	:38	1:15	2:30	5:00
	15	: 7.5	:15	:30	1:00	2:00	4:00

This chart should be used to help anyone follow the basic jogging program provided here or any other exercise program that involves walking, jogging or running. If the distance a person is walking, jogging or running is known, timing over these distances will determine speed.

Source: "Jogging/Running Guidelines," President's Council on Physical Fitness and Sports.

the routine. If pain becomes worse, you'd better rest or see a podiatrist or other professional.

5. *Injuries.* After you have been injured, cold packs can often provide temporary relief. If there is continued pain and swelling, you should see a professional.

6. *Corns and calluses.* These obstructions, which develop on the skin as a protection for deeper structures in the foot, indicate pressure, friction and imbalance. Eliminate the cause of the irritation. Again you may need professional help.

"Research has shown that running more than five days per week increases the injury rate by 50 percent," says the Podiatric Association. "It is quite important to stretch the calf muscles because the muscles in the back of the leg need continual stretching, whereas the muscles in front of the thigh and leg may need strengthening exercises."[3]

The Association goes on to say that flexibility exercises can help to minimize injuries. Unfortunately, many joggers and marathon runners emphasize strengthening and endurance training, which often lead to shortened muscles and decreased flexibility, along with subsequent muscle imbalance, arch pain, shin splints and strained muscles and ligaments.

Writing in *Jogging,* David E. Corbin, Ph.D., Associate Professor in Health Education at the University of Nebraska in Omaha, says that the jogger's most feared adversary is the automobile.[4] He quotes Joe Henderson, longtime editor of *Runner's World,* as saying that "always imagine that every driver is out to run you down." As a special precaution, Dr. Corbin recommends that you try to keep away from traffic. If you do run adjacent to a road or highway, run towards oncoming traffic and veer off the road as a vehicle approaches. It is also advisable to observe traffic laws and to not run abreast with other joggers in a heavily trafficked area. If you are wearing headphones, you need to be especially alert for traffic and menacing dogs. Running at night is not advisable, unless you are wearing reflective material, such as 3M's Scotchlite. And it is not too helpful if you are wearing reflective paint or whatever only on your shoes. Running at night in high-crime areas is also asking for trouble.

Speaking of man's best friend, a vicious dog can put a damper on any run or jog. If you generally run the same route, says Dr. Corbin, perhaps you and the neighborhood dogs can get to know each other sufficiently so that you can "peacefully coexist." You can sometimes avoid a confrontation by jogging on the side of the street away from the dog. Chemical sprays are inconvenient to carry, so some joggers prefer wearing a small chain around their waist. By rattling the chain, you can often scare the dog away. When jogging with your own dog, a stray dog will generally avoid you and concentrate on your dog but will generally not attack it, Dr. Corbin adds. He quotes a Swiss doctor as saying that about a dozen of his patients have been treated for scalp wounds after they were attacked by birds while jogging. You might avoid pesky birds by painting a pair of eyes on the back of your running hat. Otherwise, says Dr. Corbin, if you have run into any belligerent birds, perhaps you should change routes until the mating and nesting seasons are over.

Joggers, especially those out of condition, should be wary of jumping into a running or jogging program at a high altitude, according to William J. Bowerman and W. E. Harris, M.D., in their book, also called *Jogging.*[5] Obviously, some people acclimate to higher altitudes better than others but, in any event, this can increase the burden on the respiratory and circulatory systems. Most people can eventually adjust to the lower amount of oxygen that is available.

"The subject of the effects of vigorous exercise on the performance of athletes, and even on their health," was a concern years ago at the Olympics in Mexico City, the authors add and is still an unknown. "Physiologists, coaches, physicians frankly admit that they do not completely understand the complicated physiological changes that take place at higher altitudes."[5]

They say that some controlled research with athletes shows that the physical mechanism needs at least six weeks to adjust to a change to high altitude. After that, they continue, the athlete can perform up to his customary level of effort without undue strain or uncomfortable effects. As an example, they continue, a runner who has consistently run a mile in 4:00 to 4:03 minutes in Eugene,

Oregon, elevation 375 feet, can put out the same effort in Mexico City if he has conditioned himself properly at 6,000 feet.

For seasoned joggers, they add, jogging while in the high country will probably be fine. But for those out of condition who are planning a visit to Chile or Tibet, better wait until you return home to resume your jogging. "So, for joggers who move from one altitude to another, the advice is simply to remember the principles of the activity: Measure your ability, limitations, needs and goals and adjust the jogging program to fit them," they maintain.[5]

Benefits of Jogging

A study done some 20 years ago indicated that ten minutes of jumping rope was as beneficial to the cardiovascular system as jogging. But M. T. Buyze, et al, writing in *Physician and Sportsmedicine,* disagree with this research.[6] They studied 25 previously sedentary volunteers, who trained five times a week for six weeks. Those who jumped rope exercised for 10 minutes; the joggers worked out for 30 minutes. These researchers found that the joggers increased their oxygen consumption by 13 percent over the six weeks, while those jumping rope only improved oxygen intake by 1 percent.[6] The latter group also had more injuries and more members who gave up before the study ended.

If you want to take your small child with you as you jog, the Walkabout may be an ideal solution. Disappointed that a busy schedule kept him from spending enough time with his small son, Travis, a competitive runner from Yakima, Washington, developed the three-wheeled stroller, which is an all-terrain vehicle that goes across sand, through gravel and on trails, reports *The New York Times,* January 25, 1988.[7] Because of the demand for his invention by local friends, Phil Baechler, the 39-year-old inventor, has quit his copy editing job and he and his wife, Mary, now operate Racing Strollers, Inc.

The Walkabout, which has a hand brake and a wrist strap to keep it in check, can be folded up and put in a closet. It measures 47 inches long and 28 inches wide and is suitable for children up to four years of age or those who weigh up to 50 pounds. It and the Baby Jogger, an earlier and larger model, sell for $239.95. A stroller for twins sells for $319.95. (For a brochure, call 509-457-0925.)

It may be premature, but researchers at the University of Toronto, Canada, believe that they are on to something concerning the value of jogging in minimizing jet lag. According to Nicholas Mrossovsky and Peggy A. Salmon, a single three-hour exercise on a wheel in a cage permitted hamsters to adjust to a severe case of jet lag within a day and a half. Hamsters who did not exercise needed eight days to recover, says *The New York Times,* November 26, 1987.[8]

During the experiment, artificial light kept 20 hamsters on a daily rhythm. Then the animals were given a schedule in which the time was advanced eight hours, as though they had taken a long flight east. Half of the hamsters were kept busy when the new schedule required it; the controls generally slept.

"We are not quite sure whether it is the running itself, or that the animal is kept awake when it shouldn't be awake or the excitement," Dr. Mrossovsky told the *Times.* "Now what we should do is to vary things, the amount of exercise and so on."[8]

Some Negatives About Jogging

And now for the bad news about jogging. In an earlier book, *Program Your Heart for Health,*[9] I quoted J. E. Schmidt, M.D., as saying that jogging can damage the sacroiliac joints, the joints of the spine, the veins of the legs, the abdominal rings in men, the uterus and breasts in women. In addition, he says, jogging can give you a "dropped" stomach, a loose spleen, floating kidneys and fallen arches.

He goes on to say that the sacroiliac joint, which is located between the sacrum (the end of the spinal column, which is fused into one bone) and the hipbone, is the "soft underbelly" for the jogging assault. The border of the hipbone is attached to the sacrum by ligaments or tough bands of tissue; these joints, although sturdy, are under constant stress when jogging. This is because the weight of the body above the hips bears down upon the top of the sacrum, through the spine, which sits on the sacrum.

"Even without undue violence, as that inflicted by jogging or lifting weights, the sacrum frequently tends to sag and thus loosens its linkage with the hipbones, causing the familiar sacroiliac pains, especially in women," says Dr. Schmidt. "To this normal and often damaging pressure upon the top of the sacrum, now add the ballistic impact or thump of the lower end of the spine each time the foot of the jogger hits the ground. It is not unlike splitting a log by driving a wedge into it with a sledge hammer."

He adds that jogging contributes to a herniated (or slipped) disc in the same manner that it strains the sacroiliac joint—by pounding the disc with a hydraulic impact at each footstep of the jogger. Veins are also at risk because they do not have the same elasticity as the arteries, since their walls are thin and prone to dilation.

"Considering that the veins of the leg support a column of blood of considerable height, it is not surprising that dilated and varicose veins are common. . . . With every step, a column of blood several feet high pounds the veins of the legs like a battering ram. The repeated impacts encourage phlebitis. Moreover, if clots or crusts are present in the veins (they usually adhere to the inner surface), the impact may release them into the bloodstream and cause them to be swept into the heart and lungs."[9] (Although he does not mention it, is it possible that blood clots are the reason why many joggers, especially young athletes, drop dead while jogging? Invariably, we learn that the victim had just been given a clean bill of health by his physician.)

For women, continues Dr. Schmidt, jogging puts a special strain on the uterus, which is a rather loosely fixed, pear-shaped organ between the rectum and the bladder. Normally, it falls over the top of the bladder, but for women who have given birth, it may slip off its perch and either sag downward or roll backward, pressing against the rectum. In either case, he adds, the displacement produces a "bearing-down" discomfort and other symptoms. Because of the compactness and weight of the uterus, jogging militates in favor of abnormal displacement, he says.

Jogging also contributes to sagging breasts in women, he adds. Since the breast contains no muscles or ligaments—it is basically a sac filled with milk glands, ducts and fat—a network of slender fibers provides tenuous support for the soft interior of the breast. While jogging, he says, the breast acquires substantial movement and these fibers or miniligaments snap easily. Thus, the breasts flattens and droops, like a partially deflated balloon.

Men are susceptible to an inguinal hernia. Because of the male anatomy, he adds, there are in the lower part of the abdomen two thinned regions that under provocation, such as internal pressure, may open and permit a part of the intestine, or some other organ, to slither through, causing the hernia.

"Jogging, although it accelerates the heartbeat, may do the heart more harm than good," Dr. Schmidt concludes. "The heart is a massive organ that is not particularly well anchored, considering its weight. It is held in place by little more than the connecting arteries and veins. In some plane and automobile crashes, where the movement of the body is suddenly stopped by a collision, the heart often breaks through the chest wall and remains suspended grotesquely outside by its blood vessels, like an old light fixture detached from the ceiling or wall and hanging awkwardly by its wires."[9]

Although jogging does not result in such a traumatic or dramatic picture, the tug on the major blood vessels with every thump of the jogger's step is both severe and undesirable, Dr. Schmidt remarks. Thrombi or blood crusts on the inner surface of the blood vessels, especially the coronary blood vessels, may be shaken loose and carried to smaller heart blood vessels. Here they can cause a serious blockage—the classic heart attack, he says.

In view of this somewhat ominous picture, should you jog? Of course, if that is your pleasure. However, you should wear the proper shoes and do the warmup exercises discussed in chapter 8. And learn the recommended technique for jogging. A short, steady pace—slightly more than walking—can minimize the chances for an injury or serious health problem. Those who are overweight who pound their feet into the pavement as they run are asking for trouble. "Word-of-mouth" publicity is generally a great way of publicizing or advertising something, and this may have been responsible for converting more joggers and runners to walking. After all, when you have heard a jogger's detailed litany of all the shin splints, bone spurs, back aches, etc., that have plagued him in recent years, you generally begin reflecting on a less strenuous routine. In that light, a brisk walk around a beautiful lake doesn't seem half bad.

References

1. *Jogging/Running Guidelines* (Washington, D.C.: The President's Council on Physical Fitness and Sports, undated).

2. John La Place, Ph.D., *Health*, Fifth Edition (Englewood, N.J.: Prentice-Hall, Inc., 1987), pp. 98–99.

3. *Your Podiatrist's Jogging Advice* (Washington, D.C.: The American Podiatric Medical Association, undated).

4. David E. Corbin, Ph.D., *Jogging* (Glenview, Ill.: Scott, Foresman and Company, 1988), pp. 38–39.

5. William J. Bowerman and W. E. Harris, M.D., *Jogging* (New York: Grosset & Dunlap, 1978), p. 33.

6. M. T. Buyze, et al., "Jumping Rope: Is it Better than Jogging?" *Physician and Sportsmedicine* (Vol. 14, November 1986), p. 65.

7. Barbara Lloyd, "Joggers' Kids Can Roll Along," *The New York Times* (January 25, 1988), p. C11.

8. "Jog Away Jet Lag? Maybe," *The New York Times* (November 26, 1987), p. B12.

9. Frank Murray, *Program Your Heart for Health* (New York and Atlanta: Larchmont Books, 1978), pp. 278–280.

Chapter 4

Racewalking

Although people have been having walking races for over 400 years, the sport of racewalking did not begin in earnest until the beginning of the 20th century, according to the North American Racewalking Foundation in Pasadena, California. During the 1908 Olympic Games, athletes from around the world competed in a 50 kilometer walking race, roughly 31 miles.[1]

American interest in racewalking began to decline during World War II, and by the 1960s the sport in America was almost extinct, the Foundation continues. It remained for a handful of athletes, including U. S. Olympic Bronze Medalist Larry Young, to carry on the racewalking tradition and compete against the Europeans.

However, racewalking is now again fashionable, and racewalking clubs are springing up across America. Many of the members are former joggers who, for whatever reason, have become disenchanted with running and are now perfecting their style and skill as racewalkers.

"Racewalking turns regular walking into an enjoyable, challenging sport," adds the Foundation. "Like tennis and golf, racewalking involves technique; unlike these other sports, its technique is based on skills you already possess."[1]

When properly done, says the Foundation, racewalking is a rhythmic, flowing movement and, by developing the upper and lower body evenly, the racewalker develops systematic balance and coordination. And, unlike other forms of exercise, racewalking offers minimal orthopedic stress. Since the sport is making a comeback, the Foundation urges young athletes to get involved, since the better ones can qualify for national teams and compete internationally. For the masters walkers (those 40 and older), there are the World Games and championships in the United States and abroad.

As outlined by the rulebook of the Amateur Athlete Federation, racewalking involves a progression of steps in which there is unbroken contact with the ground. In addition, the athlete's supporting leg has to be straight at the knee when in the vertical, upright position. The familiar hip movement was created to increase stride length, and the heel-toe action propels the athlete forward. The shortened arm swing provides both speed and balance.

"At major competitions," explains the North American Racewalking Foundation, "racewalk judges enforce the contact and straight-knee rules. Competitors are given two warnings if they have lost contact with the ground (running) or have bent knees (creeping). Three warnings and the competitor is disqualified."[1]

Racewalking and Health

Since no one had studied body composition, physical work capacity, pulmonary function, blood chemistry and other variables for racewalkers, Barry A. Franklin, Ph.D., Assistant Professor of Physiology at Wayne State University School of Medicine, Detroit, and three collaborators decided to examine the physiological and selected psychological characteristics of nine racewalkers when compared with distance runners and other athletes of similar age. He was assisted by Krishna P. Kaimal, M.D., Chief of Cardiology at the University Medical Center, Lafayette, Louisiana, and Assistant Professor of Medicine at Louisiana State University School of Medicine, New Orleans; and Thomas W. Moir, M.D., and Herman K. Hellerstein, M.D., both Professors of Medicine at Case Western Reserve University, Cleveland, Ohio. Their study was published in the September 1981 issue of *The Physician and Sportsmedicine*.[2]

Except for a slightly lower aerobic capacity, the researchers found that the physiological and psychological profile of the racewalker is quite similar to that of the marathon runner.

"As in an earlier study of marathoners, the scales signifying neuroticism and depression were within normal limits," the team reports. "The walkers in this study were not more withdrawn than other athletes or nonathletes, as has been previously reported for distance runners, but also has been recently refuted. Indeed, the walkers were found to be almost identical to the population average on the measure of introversion-extroversion used in this study."[2]

The researchers add that the racewalkers had a mean total cholesterol count of 169 and that the total cholesterol ratio was remarkably low. These findings are similar to those previously reported for distance runners, and are compatible with a low incidence of coronary heart disease when matched with statistics from the familiar Framingham study.

Franklin and colleagues go on to say that recent studies by G. H. Hartung, et al. suggest that high-density lipoprotein-cholesterol differences among marathon runners, joggers and inactive men (65, 58, and 43 mg/100 ml, respectively), "are primarily the result of training mileage rather than dietary factors."[2]

Racewalking Technique

In the December/January 1988 issue of *The Walking Magazine,* a reader from Massachusetts asked about the difference between racewalkers, striders and pacewalkers.[3] The magazine reported that striders walk briskly, using whatever armswings they prefer, and that they are not required to keep one foot on the ground at all times or straighten the knee before tee-off. Pacewalking is brisk walking with a generous armswing.

The best way to learn racewalking is to seek the guidance of an experienced racewalker, says Gary Westerfield in the June/July 1987 issue of *The Walking Magazine*.[4] He is the coach of the national women's racewalking team. Westerfield says that beginning racewalkers may feel discomfort in their shins from holding the toes up as they plant their feet. He recommends that you try to land on the side of the foot, keeping only the big toe up, to establish the proper rocking motion.

"Once your foot strikes the ground, your leg is in the support phase, and should straighten fully," he says. "Think of your leg as a lever operating against the ground, with the heel as its fulcrum. Rocking over the support leg maintains forward momentum. If your knee is bent, the stride is not only illegal, but inefficient because the tiring work of supporting the body is taken up by the large muscles of your thigh (quadriceps). . . . Only the muscles around your knee need be contracted to keep your leg straight."[4]

To get the most efficient armswing while racewalking, Westerfield recommends that the arms should be kept at 90° angles and that they should work like pendulums. Pump your arms so that your hands are roughly six inches behind your hips; on the follow-through, your hands should reach about mid-chest.

To offset the head bobbing of normal walking, racewalking levels out this up-and-down body movement with hip and shoulder adjustments that result in a smooth, flowing motion, Westerfield explains.

There is more to the technique of racewalking than this, but the refinements can be learned from a professional coach, using practice sessions at home. With proper coaching, you should move from fast walker to racewalker in a matter of months, Westerfield insists.

In spite of its frantic appearance, racewalking is actually a smooth, efficient pace that enables the athlete to move at from five to twelve mph for relatively long periods of time, Westerfield explains.

In a later issue of *The Walking Magazine,* Gordon G. Hill, who is co-founder and race director of the Florida Suncoast Racewalkers Club in St. Petersburg, says that the more acceptable speed range is from five to ten mph, and that the ten mph walker is rather rare. He points out that the world record for the one-mile racewalk is 5:46.6 or 10.54 mph.[5]

It is Hill's belief that there is too much stress on technique, and the benefits of racewalking are often overstated. When the athlete realizes that nutrition, body weight and training mileage are equally as important as proper form, the hype is replaced by discipline, effort and attitude, which are the true benefits of any aerobic exercise, Hill says.

Judging by the way that racewalkers twist and turn, the uninitiated might assume that there is considerable pain. But there is negligible pain, usually in the beginning stages, says Julie Kellam Morrison in the December/January 1988 issue of *The Walking Magazine.*[6] She is editor of *Running Journal* and lives in Concord, North Carolina.

"If racewalking were painful, I wouldn't do it," she says. "I experienced some soreness when I first began racewalking, particularly in the shins. This happens to many beginners. But with practice, the muscles in this area get stronger and the pain goes away."[6]

She quotes John Gray, author of *Racewalking for Fun and Fitness,* as saying that exaggerated hip and arm action might overwork the middle of your body, bringing on a cramp in your side. In that case, he says, slow to a stroll and bend slightly forward, gently rubbing the sore area as you move along.

For more information about pacewalking, contact Dr. Jonas at PaceWalkers of America, Box QQ, East Setauket, New York 11733.

References

1. Promotion leaflet from the North American Racewalking Foundation, Pasadena, Cal.

2. Barry A. Franklin, Ph.D., et al., "Characteristics of National-Class Race Walkers," *The Physician and Sportsmedicine* (Vol. 9, No. 9, September 1981), pp. 101–108.

3. Alice Harvey, "Racewalk vs. Pacewalk," *The Walking Magazine* (December/January 1988), p. 8.

4. Gary Westerfield, "Feel the Need for Speed?" *The Walking Magazine* (June/July, 1987), pp. 72–74.

5. Gordon G. Hill, "Racewalking at 10 MPH," *The Walking Magazine* (December/January 1988).

6. Julie Kellam Morrison, "Is It as Weird as It Looks?" *The Walking Magazine* (December/January 1988), pp. 72–74.

7. Ray Floriani, "Going for the Long One," *New York Running News* (June/July 1984), pp. 30–32.

8. Kit Bradshaw, "Getting Started at 40-Plus," *The Walking Magazine* (October/November 1987), pp. 74–75.

9. Nancy Harris, "WCA Slates Racewalking Summer Camp," *The Walking Magazine* (April/May 1977), p. 16.

10. Steven Jonas, M.D., and Peter Radetsky, *PaceWalking—The Balanced Way to Aerobic Health* (New York, NY: Crown Publishers, Inc., 1988), pp. vii, 38–44, 199.

Chapter 5

Running

Although many people assume that the modern-day marathon is a rather recent event, the history of this long-distance race goes back to September 490 B.C., when Pheidippides, a Greek messenger, ran from the Plain of Marathon to Athens to announce the Greek victory over the invading Persians.

The battle started when Darius I, the Persian King, dispatched an army and fleet to seize the Greek islands of the Aegean Sea. Darius' troops, including some 25,000 men on horseback as well as others on foot, disembarked on the beach at Marathon in northeastern Attica and moved to the west edge of a great marsh in the northwest part of the plain, where they camped. To counter the threat, Miltiades, the Athenian general, marched with 10,000 hoplites (heavy-armed infantry) to Marathon. In the meantime, the Athenians' fastest runner, Pheidippides, was sent to Sparta to ask for assistance. He made the 140-mile journey by the next day, which obviously sapped his energy for his final run. Since the Spartans were busy celebrating the festival of Apollo Carneius, they told Pheidippides that it would be about a week before they concluded their religious holiday and could join the fray. However, the Athenians did welcome 1,000 Plataeans from Boeotia, who joined their encampment at Marathon.

Learning through Ionian spies that the Persian cavalry for some reason was not in camp, Miltiades attacked and routed the Persians. During the battle, the Persians lost seven ships and 6,400 men, many of whom perished in a swamp. As the Persians set sail in retreat, Miltiades, afraid that they would attack Athens, sent Pheidippides to Athens to spread the word. This was another 25 miles (40 kilometers) for the already fatigued runner, who had just completed the 280- to 300-mile round trip to Sparta (historians debate between 140 and 150 miles for the one-way trip). As he reached Athens and blurted out the news, Pheidippides collapsed and died. His warning was unnecessary, since the Persians, smarting from their decisive defeat, had already high-tailed it back to Asia.[1]

When the Olympic games were revived in 1896, it was decided to include a race of about 25 miles to commemorate Pheidippides' famous run. The current marathon distance of 26 miles, 385 yards was established when King Edward VII wanted to watch the start of the 1908 Olympic race from his home, Windsor Castle, which was 26 miles from the Olympic stadium in London. The 385 yards were added to the marathon so that the race could end at the

King's royal box. This converts to 42.2 kilometers. The official distance (for purists it is actually 42.195 kilometers) was adopted as the international standard in 1924.[2]

The Olympic Games

The original Olympic games were held every four years as part of a five-day religious festival for over 1,100 years, from 776 B.C. to A.D. 393, according to the *Reader's Digest Book of Facts*.[3] They were abruptly terminated in the final year by Theodosius I, the Christian Emperor of Rome, who said they were too pagan. The Games did not appear again until 1896, and they have been held every four years since, except for breaks during the World Wars.

In the original games, married women were not allowed to watch their husbands compete, and women were prohibited from competing in the games. The Greeks felt that the presence of wives would defile Greece's oldest religious shrine, according to *The Encyclopedia Americana*.[2] This ruling would certainly have sent a feminist group into an outrage, if such an organization had existed, especially since young girls could attend the games. This was also an ironic ruling, since the shrine that was off-limits to married women was dedicated to a woman, the fertility goddess Rhea, who was the mother of the supreme god, Zeus.

"The penalty for women who broke the rule was to be thrown from a nearby cliff," continues the encyclopedia. "Only once is a grown woman known to have watched the Games and lived. She was a widow named Callipateira, who dressed up as a male judge in order to watch her son, Pisdorus, compete. When he won, she was so overjoyed that she threw off the judge's robes. She was not condemned to death, because her father, brothers and sons had all performed gloriously in successive Olympics. Instead, a new law was passed requiring all judges to appear like some of the athletes: naked."[2]

The encyclopedia goes on to say that winning a victor's crown in the ancient Olympics had more in common with an election than with today's standard method of awarding first place to the racer with the best time. In those days, there was no timekeeper, and crossing the finish line was no guarantee that you would be declared the winner. The judges considered rhythm, style and grace just as important as beating out a competitor. After each race, the judges would debate for several minutes before casting a secret ballot. And then the winner would be announced.

Credit for the modern Olympic Games goes to Baron Pierre de Coubertin, a Frenchman, whose passion for world peace ignited a resumption of the Games, according to Raymond Krise and Bill Squires in *Fast Tracks—the History of Distance Running*.[4] The Baron suggested a revival of the Games at a lecture delivered at the Sorbonne in 1892. At first ridiculed, the idea blossomed and the revived Games were soon a reality.

"Coubertin then convened a Congress on World Peace at Paris in 1894," the authors explain. "The Olympics plan was the Baron's major, but not sole, program through which to achieve global stability and harmony. Skepticism stemmed from delegates thinking the idea too good and simple to be practical, but the Olympics finally catalyzed the Congress into action. A date was set—1896—and a place was set—Athens. Then the Olympic fever hit hard. Frenchman Michel Breal argued that the new Games should pay homage to the old by instituting a new race, the marathon, to honor the great Greek *hemerdroni,* as personified by Pheidippides. Breal put up a silver cup as prize for the winner of the first marathon and, for the first time in history, men and at least one woman began training to run 25 miles in competition: thus did poetry and imagination give birth to concrete fact."[4]

The modern Olympics began on April 6, 1896 at 10 a.m., Krise and Squires continue. But the American delegation, consisting of Tommy Burke, Jimmy Connolly, Bobby Garrett, Artie Blake and Ellery Clark, all from Boston, may have invented on-the-spot some new four-letter words. Forgetting that the Olympic Games would be run by the Greek calendar, the Americans arrived on what they thought was April 1, which was actually April 12 or 13, ten minutes before the start of their events. Jimmy Connolly was so ticked off that he had no time to prepare for the Games that he promptly triple-jumped 44 feet, 11¾ inches, making him the first Olympic champ in the modern Games.

Tommy Burke, who was just as angry but had had a little more rest than Jimmy, won the 100 meters with a 12-flat blast, the authors say. Then he ran 400 meters on the 333-meter dirt Olympic track in 54.2 to record another win. In all, the first American Olympic team received nine silver medals out of the ten events the small team entered. (They didn't all finish second, the authors add, because first prize in the 1896 games was a silver, not a gold, medal.) Composed of men from the greater Boston area and sponsored by the Boston A.A., with enthusiastic support from its president, George V. Brown, this U.S. team dominated the first Olympics and established an American tradition of track and field supremacy. Competing as a member of the English team, Edwin Flack, an Australian, won the only two running events not taken by the Yanks. For the 800 meters, Flack ran 2:11. For the 1,500, he recorded 4:33.2.[4]

The modern Olympic marathon began at 2 p.m. on April 10, 1896, with 25 official entrants, according to Krise and Squires. The runners were joined by a somewhat apprehensive Greek woman, Melopene, who eventually finished the race at approximately 4:30. The official distance was 24.9 miles. Unfortunately, the Americans did not fare so well in this event. Their best hope, Bostonian Arthur Blake, who had actually never run such a long-distance race, had to slow down after fourteen miles, even though he had closed in on the Frenchman, Lemesieux. The Frenchman was eventually hit by the bicycle ridden by his coach, which obviously slowed him considerably.

At 21 miles into the first modern marathon, the authors add, a little Greek shepherd, Spiridon Loues, overwhelmed Edwin Flack and chugged on to victory after a two-mile shootout that sent the Australian to the hospital.

"It was a hot time in old Hellas that day," the authors continue. "Loues needed police to push the manic crowds out of his way for the last two miles. Sixty thousand rabid spectators anxiously awaited him in the Olympic Stadium. When Spiridon hit the Olympic track the multitude did not merely explode, they nova-ed. King George I of Greece somehow managed to remain in the royal box, but Prince George and Prince Constantine leaped onto the track to accompany their humble countryman to the finish line. The classic democratic ideal of a commoner standing above an aristocrat on the game field was here incarnate.''[4]

Needless to say, the 24-year-old shepherd was an instant hero, the authors add. Since he was a happily married man, he turned down a wealthy Greek merchant who proffered Spiridon his daughter in marriage and a dowry of one million drachmas. It is assumed that he may have accepted free food, clothing and barbering for the remainder of his life, although he insisted that he wanted to remain an amateur athlete. However, there are no records indicating that he ever ran again.

The authors go on to say that Spiridon's training bore almost no resemblance to modern techniques. However, since he was a water carrier for the sheep, this probably helped Spiridon to develop an excellent aerobic capacity by walking 15 miles each day beside his mule. The shepherd trained mainly by faith, they continue. He dreamed that he would win the marathon and restore Greek glory as his sacred duty. And the day before the race, he did nothing but pray before holy pictures and icons. He also fasted. On the day of the race, he ate a whole chicken. That, say the authors, may account for the pained expression on his face as he ran the marathon.

If you think that cheating during a marathon is of recent vintage, consider the plight of another Greek, Spiridon Belokas. Although finishing third, he was later disqualified when it was discovered that he had hitched a ride in a horse-drawn carriage during the race, the authors report.

The First American Marathon

Since the Boston and New York City marathons are so widely publicized, it might be assumed that these are the oldest marathons in the United States. But that distinction goes to Stamford, Connecticut, which was the beginning of the first U.S. marathon on September 19, 1896, five months after the revived Olympic games and seven months before the Boston Marathon, the second oldest American race.

As reported by Stamford's *Daily Advocate* on Monday, September 11, 1896, "the Connecticut Marathon, a Grecian foot-race, will start from Stamford and is one of the greatest sporting events ever held on this Continent."[5] The sponsors were the prestigious Knickerbocker Athletic Club of New York City, a gentleman's club that charged the then-extravagant sum of $50.00 to join. In addition to the annual track and field events, the New Yorkers decided to add the marathon and a discus competition to the 1896 games.

"The contest which is attracting the most attention, and for which entries are being received from all over the United States, is the 'Marathon' race, a counterpart of the old-time race from Marathon to Athens, a supreme test of endurance," said *The Daily Advocate*. "The distance was 25 miles. H. S. Corniab, who is manager of the games, after carefully examining the country surrounding Williams Bridge, selected Stamford as the starting point for the big race. In the first place, it is just the right distance from Columbia Oval, where the race will end, and, in the second place, the road from here to Williams

Bridge is just about as hilly as the Greek course."[5] (Columbia Oval, where the other games were being held, is in the Bronx, New York. The location is sometimes confused with Columbus Circle, which is in mid-Manhattan, near the entrance to Central Park.)

The newspaper reported that, with the kind permission of Capt. G. L. Fitch of Company C, the athletes will use the company room at the armory to dress for the contest, and Chief Bowman "has undertaken to see that they are allowed to 'depart in peace'."[5] On the day of the race, the athletes and their assistants arrived in Stamford by train around 11 a.m. and proceeded to the armory.

In addition to the marathon, the newspaper reported that "there will be chariot-racing, throwing the discus, contests of markmanship and a dozen other exciting events which will help towards making the Knickerbocker's meeting the most memorable ever held in America."[5]

According to the Stamford newspaper, the contestants began at West Park, then ran down South Street and turned up on Richmond Hill Avenue. From there they ran through Mianus and up Put's Hill to Greenwich. After passing Lenox House, the runners proceeded to Port Chester (New York), Rye, Mamaroneck, Larchmont, New Rochelle, Pelhamville (now Pelham) and Mount Vernon to Williams Bridge. Regular commuters on the Metro-North railroad line or the Amtrak to Boston will note that the newspaper failed to mention Harrison, which is located between Rye and Mamaroneck.

Before the race, the Stamford newspaper said that, "the steepest hill of all is encountered just before reaching the grounds, and it is doubtful if many will be in a condition to run up it. When this point is reached, the progress of the other games will be suspended to give the spectators a chance to see the distance runners complete their 25 miles by going twice around the quarter-mile track. The first three men to finish will receive gold, silver and bronze wreathes (sic) respectively, mounted on oak panels; and every man completing the course will receive a souvenir medal."[5]

Because of the deadline required for the newspaper to publish its afternoon edition on time, the September 19 issue of *The Daily Advocate* was unable to print the results of the race. But it did give a lot of local color by describing the runners arriving in town and preparing for the race.[6]

The newspaper listed the names of 26 participants; runners lived in Connecticut, New York, New Jersey and Massachusetts, although some athletes lived in one place and represented athletic clubs elsewhere. As an example, the two contestants who lived in Stamford—E. H. Baynes (in charge of local arrangements) and John Cliffe—represented respectively the Knickerbocker Athletic Club in New York and the Manchester Harriers in England.

As reported by the *Advocate,* the crowd assembled at the junction of Main and South Streets in Stamford, where the runners appeared at 12:20 p.m. The throng extended along both sides of South Street almost to Willow Street. Teams lined both curbs and people squeezed in wherever they could to get a view of the muscular-looking set of men, stated the newspaper.

"They lined up on the Main Street walk, across South Street, a line that had to be partly doubled, there being so many of them," added the newspaper.

"After being checked off by starter Whitman (W. B. Whitman of the Knicker-bocker Athletic Club) and standing for a number of cameras to be snapped upon them, they were given the word at 12:25 and were off. They started in an easy lope, passing between the rows of wagons like a pack of hounds just let out of leash. They soon disappeared around the bend near Richmond Hill Avenue and were lost to sight."[6]

Each runner was supposed to be accompanied by a cyclist from the Harlem Wheelmen, in case there was an accident, but, unfortunately, not enough of the cyclists turned up before the race began. The ones who did followed behind the pack. "The surviving runners will probably appear at Columbia Oval about four o'clock," the newspaper predicted.[6]

The next edition of the paper reported that the marathon was won by J. J. McDermott with a time of 3:25:55 3/5.[7] This contrasts with the winning time of 2:58:50 (also reported as 2:58:30), set by the Greek shepherd at the Olympic games that had recently occurred. A New York laborer and a native of Ohio, McDermott, 24, was a member of the somewhat lowly Pastime Athletic Club, whose initiation fee was a measly $3.00.

Historians have reported the number of participants in the Stamford marathon between 28 and 30. The September 19 issue of the Stamford newspaper listed 26 names, and the number of finishers has been variously reported from ten on up. In the wrap-up story on the marathon, *The Daily Advocate* gives the names of seventeen finishers, although the times for the last six runners were not available. The last recorded time was for Samuel Waters of the Williamsburgh Athletic Association, who finished in 4:30.[7]

By contrast, the 1987 New York Marathon was won in 2:11:01 by Ibrahim Hussein.[8] A native of Kenya, he lives and trains in Albuquerque, New Mexico. He also won the Boston and Honolulu marathons close to his New York win.

In summing up the results of the Stamford marathon, historian Pamela Cooper says that, "It was all a disappointment and rather an embarrassment to the Knickerbocker Club, which had expected a marathon world record. . . . And so, from that time to this, the first American marathon has been depreci-ated. The current New York City Marathon, which traces its roots to the Stamford-to-Columbia Oval marathon, frequently presents inaccurate informa-tion and disparaging statements about this event."[9]

But, she continues, the Stamford race was of significance because it brought the long distances out of the categories of exhibitionism and pseudo-sport and into the realm of legitimate athletics. She goes on to say that, in the 19th century, gentlemen's sports clubs had established an athletes' bureaucracy that controlled the standardization of equipment, distances and procedures, as well as accurate record keeping on the events. And, she adds, confining the marathon distance to 25 miles was at least an attempt to legitimize the race.

"Further," she says, "this marathon brought the amateur long distances, and the idea of road races, into public awareness. The last American record of 2:52:24 for 25 miles had been set on a track in 1884. The English record of 2:33:44, again on the track, dated from 1881. In both England and America, distances over ten miles had been neglected for years."[9]

Marathon Records

Since the late 1800s, male and female runners have continued to chip away at the marathon times. A two-hour marathon doesn't seem to be too far away.

In the 15 years from its inception in 1897 to 1911, the Boston Marathon was variously won by a student, a blacksmith, a carpenter, a clerk, a plumber, a farmer and a mill hand, according to Richard Benyo in *The Masters of the Marathon*.[10] All of those winners were either in their late teens or early twenties.

Record times for women have also continued to slide since Melopene came in at 4:30 during the 1896 Olympic games. Take Rosa Mota, the spirited Portuguese marathoner, as an example. On September 12, 1982 at the European Championships, she came in first at 2:36:04. On August 29, 1987, at the World Championships in Rome, she was again first with a time of 2:25:17. Her best time until then was 2:23:29 at the Chicago Marathon, on October 20, 1985, which was only good for third place.[11]

Priscilla Welch, from England, at age 42, won the 1987 New York City Marathon in 2:30:17. This time was a New York City women's masters record and would have been good enough to place her eighth in the men's masters field. Grete Waitz, an eight-time winner of the marathon, was unable to compete because of a stress fracture, which also prevented her from competing in Rome. But she was on hand as a commentator for ABC.[12]

On June 4, 1988, 8,260 women (a record) participated in the L'Eggs Mini Marathon, a 10k (6.2 miles) race mostly through Central Park in New York City. Also a record number was the 6,169 women who finished the race.[13]

The race was won by 32-year-old Ingrid Kristiansen of Norway, who, because of flight delays, had endured a 16-hour trip from her home the day before. The second finisher was Lisa Martin of Australia, who had won in 1987.

"Kristiansen was the favorite, and her time of 31 minutes 31 seconds was her fastest ever in a road race," reports *The New York Times*. "Martin finished in 32:04. The L'Eggs best time, over a slightly more difficult course is 30:59:8 in 1980 by Grete Waitz of Norway, who won the Stockholm Marathon yesterday [also June 4]."[13]

The world record for the 10k is 30:13:74, which was set by Kristiansen in 1986. She is the fastest woman in history in the marathon and 5,000 and 10,000 meters.[13]

"Behind [Kristiansen in the L'Eggs Mini], some of the world's most celebrated distance runners were jockeying for position," says the *Times*. "Francie Larrieu Smith of Dallas finished third in 32:10, her fastest ever; Mary Decker Slaney of Eugene, Ore., fourth in 32:18; Anne Audain of New Zealand, fifth in 32:33; Margaret Groos of Nashville, Tenn., sixth in 32:43 and Joan Benoit Samuelson of Freeport, Me., seventh in 33:05. Smith is a three-time Olympian, Slaney a former world champion and record holder, Audain a four-time Olympian, Groos the winner of the United States Olympic marathon trial five weeks ago, and Samuelson the 1984 Olympic marathon champion."[13]

It was an especially good race for Slaney, who was coming off of Achilles tendon surgery, and Samuelson, who had recently had back and leg problems.

Another Popular Race

A familiar race in some 16 cities, both here and abroad, is the Manufacturers Hanover Corporate Challenge Series, which is a 3.5-mile road race for employees of corporations, businesses and government and financial institutions. Begun in 1977 in New York City, the 1988 race attracted 108,000 runners from approximately 5,200 companies. The 1989 calendar included races in Miami; New York City (3 races); Albany, N.Y.; Philadelphia; Los Angeles; Chicago; Syracuse, N. Y.; Boston; Buffalo, N. Y.; San Francisco; Atlanta; Long Island, N. Y.; Morristown, N. J.; London, England; Dublin, Ireland; and Oslo, Norway. The locations are generally the same and are related to cities where Manufacturers Hanover does business. In addition to Manufacturers Hanover, the events are co-sponsored by *The New York Times;* Perrier, Greenwich, Conn.; AVIA Athletic Footwear, Portland, Ore.; *Fortune* magazine; American Airlines, DFW Airport, Tex.; Advil, New York, N.Y.; Paleta International Corp., Brooklyn, N.Y.

The races are usually staged in the business or financial district of the host city, usually after work on a week night. Companies can enter an unlimited number of runners, and the winning teams are flown to New York for the championship race. Details about the races are available from Manufacturers Hanover Corporate Challenge, 270 Park Avenue, 34th Floor, New York, NY 10017; tel., 212-808-8100.

Proper Running Technique

During 1985–1986, approximately 800,000 Americans finished some sanctioned road race, according to *An Introduction to Running: One Step at a Time,* published by the President's Council on Physical Fitness and Sports.[14] For 1985 alone, the National Running Data Center listed 95,377 marathon finishers.

"Running continues to retain its standing as one of the more popular forms of aerobic exercise," the publication says. "Surveys show that more than 26 million adult Americans are running regularly. Most run a mile or two at a time, two or three times a week, to improve their overall fitness levels. Many run for competitive purposes, testing their ability against fellow runners in fun runs and road races throughout the year."[14]

Although most sports require speed and power, this is not the case with running. Therefore, the following suggestions from the President's Council will help you to develop a comfortable, economical running style:

1. Run in an upright position, avoiding excessive forward lean. Keep back as straight as you comfortably can and keep head up. Don't look at your feet.
2. Carry arms slightly away from the body, with elbows bent so that forearms are roughly parallel to the ground. Occasionally shake and relax arms to prevent tightness in shoulders.
3. Land on the heel of the foot and rock forward to drive off the ball of the foot. If this proves difficult, try a more flat-footed style. Running only on the balls of your feet will tire you quickly and make your legs sore.

4. Keep stride relatively short. Don't force your pace by reaching for extra distance.

5. Breathe deeply with mouth open.

As for gear, the council recommends a pair of sturdy, properly-fitted running shoes. Training shoes with heavy, cushioned soles and arch supports are better than flimsy sneakers or racing flats. Although weather will generally dictate the type of clothing to wear while running, a general rule is that you should wear lighter clothing than temperatures might seem to indicate, since running generates a great deal of body heat.

"Light-colored clothing that reflects the sun's rays is cooler in the summer, and dark clothes are warmer in the winter," says the booklet. "When the weather is very cold, it's better to wear several layers of light clothing than one or two heavy layers. The extra layers help trap heat, and it's easy to shed one of them if you become too warm."[14]

Some type of head covering is advised when it is cold or when it is hot and sunny, the President's Council adds. Wool watch caps or ski caps are ideal for winter wear; some type of tennis or sailor's hat that provides shade and can be soaked in water is suggested for summer. Properly dressed, you can run in almost any kind of weather, although it is not a good idea to run when it is extremely hot and humid. On those days, schedule your runs in the early morning or in the evening.

"Don't wear rubberized or plastic clothing," adds the booklet. "Such garments interfere with the evaporation of perspiration and cause body temperatures to rise to dangerous levels."[14]

Before beginning a running program, get a physical check-up. Few beginning runners are capable of running continuously for any distance, cautions the booklet, so begin by walking. It may take several years before you are in shape, especially if you have not had a regular exercise program.

"The 'walk test' will help you determine where to begin," says the booklet. "If you can comfortably walk three miles in 45 minutes, it's okay to start running. Or, more precisely, alternately running and walking. If you can't pass the test, walk three miles a day until you can. In the beginning you should alternately run and walk continuously for 20 minutes. Speed is not important, but the amount of time is. It takes about 20 minutes for your body to begin to realize the 'training effects' of sustained, vigorous exercise."[14]

The booklet adds that no one can tell you exactly how far you should run/walk at the beginning of your training. Each of us is different and exercise capacity will vary even between people of the same age and similar build. A good rule of thumb: After your warmup, walk briskly until you are moving easily. Run at a comfortable pace until you begin to become winded or tired or both. So walk until you are ready to run again. Repeat this cycle until your 20 minutes are up, advises the booklet.

To keep in shape after beginning a running program, the President's Council recommends at least five workouts per week, with three workouts weekly the absolute minimum. To help you develop the right pace, use the "talk test." In other words, you should be able to carry on a normal conversation while running or walking. If you are too winded to talk, you are probably going too fast.

After eight or ten weeks of training, you should be able to run the full 20 minutes at a reasonable pace, says the booklet, although this may be a little longer for older runners. After you have mastered this plan, then extend your running to 30 minutes.

To prevent injuries and soreness, always complete the required warmup exercises before running and cooldown exercises after. Some of these are given elsewhere in this book. In addition, the President's Council recommends these:[14]

1. *Achilles tendon and calf stretcher.* Stand facing a wall approximately three feet away. Lean forward and place palms of hands flat against the wall. Keep back straight, heels firmly on floor, and slowly bend elbows to hands, and tuck the hips toward the wall. Hold position for 30 seconds. Repeat with knees slightly flexed.

2. *Back stretcher.* Lie on back with knees bent and arms at sides and palms down. Slowly pull right knee toward chest, keeping the left foot on the floor. Hold position for 30 seconds. Repeat with opposite leg.

3. *Thigh stretcher.* Stand arm's length from the wall with left side toward the wall. Place left hand on the wall for support. Grasp right ankle with right hand and pull foot back and up until heel touches buttocks. Lean forward from waist as you lift. Hold for 30 seconds. Repeat with opposite hand and foot.

4. *Modified hurdler's stretch.* Sit on floor with one leg extended straight ahead. Bend other leg at knee, placing heel against the inside of extended leg. Slowly bend forward, sliding hands along extended leg. Bring chest toward knee and keep back straight. Hold for 30 seconds. Repeat with opposite leg.

5. *Straddle stretch.* Sit on the floor and spread the legs at a comfortable width apart. Keeping the back straight, slowly bend forward, sliding your hands along the floor until you feel a stretch on the inside of your legs. Beginners can bend knees slightly. Hold for 30 seconds. Return to starting position. Slowly stretch forward over right leg, bringing your chest toward your knee until you feel a stretch in the back of your leg. Hold for 30 seconds. Return to starting position and repeat second step of exercise to the left side.

6. *Leg stretcher.* Sit in same position as in preceding exercise. Rest left hand on left thigh and grasp inside of right foot with right hand. Keep back straight and slowly straighten right leg, letting it raise to about a 45-degree angle. Hold position for 30 seconds. Repeat with other leg.

The key to all warmup and cooldown exercises is to *move slowly*. Muscles will respond more favorably to a gentle tug, rather than sudden jerks. After all, you are not tightening piano wires. In watching some runners perform their warmup exercises, in quick jerky fashion, one wonders how much damage they are doing to their muscles before they begin the race. This unnecessary abuse might well be a prelude for injuries later on in the race.

In addition to these flexibility exercises, some runners will benefit from strength exercises, such as pushups, bent-knee situps or lifting weights, all done *slowly*. It's the quality of the warmups and cooldowns, rather than the quantity.

Earlier it was mentioned that if you can't talk comfortably while you are running, you are probably moving too fast. Bernard Gutin, Ph.D., Professor of Applied Physiology and Education at Teacher's College of Columbia University, New York City, adds another dimension. He told *Men's Health* that if you're running slowly enough to be able to talk, but too fast to sing, your pace is just about right.[15]

As you approach a hill, don't charge up it like Theodore Roosevelt but, instead, save your energy so that you can run faster *down* the hill, reports Susan Kalish, editor of *FitNews*, a publication of the American Running and Fitness Association.

"When you run up a hill," explains Kalish, "your body uses 35 percent more energy than it does on a flat surface. If you run fast up a hill, you make your body work even harder—leaving you drained for the rest of your race. Instead, run up the hill at your normal pace, but use shorter strides and lean into the hill to make the climb easier."[16]

As you reach the top of the hill, she continues, increase your speed so that you can run fast downhill. Obviously, this permits you to take advantage of gravity, which helps to propel you down the hill; it works against you as you are climbing.

However, cautions Kalish, do not run so fast that you lose control and lose your balance. As you move downhill, lean back slightly, keeping your arms relaxed, and try to increase your horizontal stride length. This allows you to keep control yet maintain speed, she adds. To perfect this suggestion, practice on grassy areas. Of course, she continues, running fast uphill—but not during a race—will make you stronger at any speed. Just do it during practice runs.

Running and Health

As you get older, your training must obviously change, points out Mike Tymn in *Runner's World*.[17] He quotes Frank Shorter, who had just turned 40, as saying, "You can't train the way you did when you were 23. It just isn't going to work. All you do when you're 23 is go out the door, turn left, turn right, and go as hard as you can until you start to break down. Then you take a day or two of easy running to heal up. But that's not what happens when you get to be a master."[17]

The key for the older athlete,. says Tymn, is to analyze the way you mix hard days and easy days throughout the week. "I don't mean alternate hard-day/easy-day training," he explains. "That's for runners in their 20s and early 30s. I mean *hard–easy–easy–easy* days for 40-year-olds and even more easy days for older runners. In fact, those over 60 should probably do no more than one hard day a week."[7]

A letter writer to *The Runner* asked Bill Rodgers how often he should run a marathon during the year. Rodgers replied by saying that, at the height of his career, he raced only four or five marathons annually. He advised the reader to select one or two marathons—three at the most—that he felt he could excel in.[18]

Writing in *The New England Journal of Medicine,* A. Luger and colleagues found that runners who trained more than 45 miles per week had blood levels three times higher than normal of cortisone and ACTH, two stress hormones.[19] These elevated levels might result in osteoporosis and a suppression of the immune system, the researchers say. Runners who had a moderate training program of 15 to 25 miles weekly showed rather small elevations of these hormones.

The constant foot-pounding that runners experience does not necessarily lead to degenerative joint disease, according to a study conducted by Richard Panush, M.D., an arthritis researcher and marathon runner at the University of Florida Health Science Center, Gainesville.[20] His study involved seventeen long-distance runners and eighteen non-runners, age 50 to 74. Eight of the runners were marathoners, who averaged 27 miles a week and had been running for an average of twelve years. The average age was 56 for the runners and 60 for the non-runners. All volunteers were male, since not enough females could be found for the study.[20]

"In all respects, there were no statistically significant differences between the two groups," Dr. Panush says. "In fact, there were a few quantitative differences that were not statistically significant that actually favored the runners. Their joints seemed to move a little bit better. They were a little bit more limber."[20]

Although he adds that running does not prevent or improve osteoarthritis, he did say that, "I think what we can say is that within the limits of this study, putting a normal joint through a normal range of motion is not deleterious."[20]

If you want to save your joints from pounding, you might adopt a form of Groucho Marx's close-to-the-ground scurry, advises Thomas McMahon, Ph.D., Professor of Applied Mechanics and Biology at Harvard University, Cambridge, Massachusetts.[21] This approach emphasizes the role of your thigh and buttock muscles as shock-absorbing springs, and helps to spare your knees, hips and back. So, he says, bend your knees a little more and take longer steps—"but don't run with a cigar in your mouth." An added dividend, this posture requires more energy so that you burn up about 25 percent more calories.

Psychological Aspects of Running

Although running is excellent exercise and it has many health benefits, it can become a psychological crutch if overdone, according to Connie Chan, Ph.D., an Assistant Professor at the University of Massachusetts, who is herself a runner. She began her study after noticing the mood changes in some runners who had to stop temporarily because of injuries. Dr. Chan's study involved 40 runners who had to give up running for two weeks to recuperate from an injury, and 40 athletes who continued to run a minimum of 30 miles a week for the same period, according to *The New York Times.*[22]

At the end of the two weeks, both groups of volunteers were given a battery of standardized psychological tests that evaluated mood, depression and self-esteem.

Those prevented from running were significantly more depressed, anxious, tense and confused, she says. They were significantly less vigorous and suffered from greater overall mood disturbances than those who continued to run. For those who had to stop running, she adds, they imagined their bodies had fallen apart after two weeks of no running, and substitute exercises such as swimming, biking and hiking had not provided many of them with the psychological benefits of running.

Dr. Chan explained that an addiction is something that you cannot do without; even if it's unhealthy for you, you continue doing it. "Running can fit this description," she said.[22]

"For the joggers in the study," reports the *Times*, "running had become their only coping mechanism for reducing stress, combating depression and elevating mood. In this regard, the runners are not psychologically healthy. They put all their eggs in one basket. Nothing else satisfies them. When they are deprived, they are devastated.[22]

Dr. Chan points out that since all joggers and runners are likely to suffer running injuries from time to time, the compulsive runners should be cognizant of their dependence on running, so that if they have to stop for a time, they will recognize how important that loss can be to their mental health, concludes the *Times*.[22]

Alayne Yates, Ph.D., and Catherine Shisslak, Ph.D., both runners, became aware of the problems faced by some compulsive runners while working at the University of Arizona Medical Center, Tucson. While doing research at the sports medicine clinic, they noticed that when some runners were told to stop running for a time because of an injury, it was as though they were told they would have to cut off their legs, reports *Medical Tribune*.[23]

This led them to begin a study of compulsive runners and patients with eating disorders, such as anorexia nervosa and bulimia.

Commenting on one phase of the research, Dr. Yates says that "it demonstrates a definite correlation between a person who has a ritualistic preoccupation with running and one who has a preoccupation with food. Both are likely to come from high-achieving middle-class families, are often obsessive-compulsives by way of striving for high achievement, are introverted, have trouble expressing anger, and are narcissistically obsessed with details about their bodies."[23]

Dr. Yates goes on to say that the excessive compulsive, ritualistic styles exhibited by obligatory runners and patients with eating disorders are amazingly similar, in that the obligatory runners sound just like eating disorder patients in describing their rituals.

Dr. Shisslak estimates that about five percent of steady runners could be classed as compulsive runners. And they are likely to continue running in the face of adverse conditions in spite of obvious negative consequences.

According to Dr. Yates, the addictive runners are "predominantly middle-aged men who are locked into compulsive athleticism. If they are unable to exercise, they become severely anxious or depressed. No matter how well they perform, they remain dissatisfied with their achievement; there is no 'good enough' performance. When injured, they may minimize or deny pain and continue to run as if running were the whole source of health and satisfaction."[23]

Dr. Yates goes on to say that, for the most part, these people do their activity alone; in fact, it can serve as a way for them to avoid intimacy and contact with other people. They're very concerned about the narcissistic state of running. They exclude other things in their lives and become more and more involved with their running. Soon, everything else may be gone from their lives. Like people with eating disorders, many obligatory runners pursue their compulsion with a grim asceticism. They may lead monastic lives in many cases, thinking they can prove themselves through denial."[23]

Although much is yet to be learned about the compulsive runner, and this addiction apparently affects a small number of athletes, it does illustrate the importance of having a backup form of amusement, whether sports oriented or not, if and when injuries keep you temporarily sidelined. If the addiction gets out of hand, perhaps professional help is in order.

Although Drs. Yates and Shisslak are both avid runners, they have received considerable flack as being anti-running. Dr. Shisslak has, in fact, run in the New York City Marathon. But, as they explain, this problem affects only about five percent of all runners. A healthy analysis of why some runners are compelled to continue running with injuries might very well prevent these same runners from having debilitating illnesses that could prevent them from running again. Obviously, it is counterproductive to continue running so that injuries do not have time to heal.

Grete Waitz is quoted in *Health* as saying that, "Fear of failure is my biggest problem."[24] She is not alone, since 90 percent of 300 NCAA Division I athletes tested in one study were either afraid of failing or succeeding . . . or both.

Fear of failure is rather easily understood, but a fear of succeeding seems rather odd. However, these latter athletes can be apprehensive about fame, responsibility and social pressure, says Sharon Colgan, Ph.D., who conducted the study at the United States International University, San Diego, California.

If you do not have an understanding coach who can help you through this anxiety, says Dr. Colgan, then meet the problem head-on yourself. "Knowing the cause of the anxiety will help you work through it," she says.[24]

A certain amount of confidence, determination, eccentricity or whatever you want to call it can mean the difference in whether or not you will win or lose a race. In the September 1987 issue of the *Journal of Sports Medicine*, D. C. Nieman and D. M. George report that the leading male distance runners, whether amateurs or world-class, were more emotionally stable, happy-go-lucky, more submissive, more socially reserved and sensitive than the slower runners.[25]

Running and Immunity

According to several recent studies, the rigors of racing and training for a marathon may suppress the immune system, thus leaving the athlete prone to illness. The conclusions may be of significance to HIV-infected (AIDS) patients who are trying to boost their immune systems with exercise and strenuous activity, according to *Medical Tribune*.[26]

One study, reported at a 1988 meeting of the American College of Sports Medicine in Dallas, Texas, involved 1,800 runners who participated in the 1987 Los Angeles Marathon. Statistics were compiled from questionnaires returned by the athletes. Part of the study concerned whether or not the runners had a cold or flu within a week following the race. The controls were 134 runners who trained for the marathon but, for a variety of reasons, did not participate.

"The study found that 13% of the marathoners got sick, compared with only 2% of the runners who stayed on the sidelines," reported *Medical Tribune*. "Moreover, during the two months before the winter race, 43% of the runners in training reported infectious episodes; those who trained more than 60 miles a week were twice as likely to report being sick as their counterparts who logged less than 20 miles a week."[26]

David Nieman, D.Sc., Associate Professor of Health Science in the School of Public Health at Loma Linda University, California, said that, "The immune system doesn't handle the marathon experience very well. Race exertion, especially the marathon, is a tough psychophysiological stressor to the system. These were not elite marathoners, more what I would call fitness marathoners."[26]

In another study, still underway at the Centers for Disease Control, Atlanta, Georgia, preliminary data reveal that runners who logged 25 miles a week had only 1.2 infectious episodes during the time the data were tabulated, compared with two to three colds annually for the general population.

"The most persistent risk factor was higher mileage," said Gregory Heath, D.Sc. of CDC. "Individuals who raced were at greater risk of an upper-respiratory-tract infection than those runners who did not race."[26]

Dr. Heath went on to say that when the immune system is at about 70 percent of maximum, there is a "small window of opportunity" where a cold or flu might take hold.

Dr. Nieman added that this "window" lasts approximately three to six hours, during which time the immune system is trying to recover from the stress of running, which might give viruses and bacteria a chance to gain a foothold.

Both Dr. Heath and Dr. Nieman told *Medical Tribune* that an ideal solution might be for marathoners to practice germ avoidance, such as proper hygiene and several days of limited social contact following a race.

"Our overall conclusion," concluded Dr. Nieman, "is that heavy training or race experience induces enough physical and psychological stress that it appears to increase the odds for infectious episodes."[26]

References

1. James R. Wiseman, "Battle of Marathon," *The Encyclopedia Americana* (Danbury, Conn.: Grolier, Inc., 1987), p. 295.

2. Joe Henderson, "Marathon," *The Encyclopedia Americana* (Danbury, Conn.: Grolier, Inc., 1987), p. 294.

3. *Reader's Digest Book of Facts* (Pleasantville, N.Y.: The Reader's Digest Association, Inc., 1987), pp. 340-344.

4. Raymond Krise and Bill Squires, *Fast Tracks—The History of Distance Running* (Brattleboro, Vt.: Stephen Greene Press, 1983), pp. 25-28.

5. "A Connecticut Marathon," *The Daily Advocate,* Stamford, Ct. (September 11, 1896), p. 1.

6. "Marathon Race Starts," *The Daily Advocate,* Stamford, Ct. (September 19, 1896), p. 1.

7. "Both Local Men Finished," *The Daily Advocate,* Stamford, Ct. (September 21, 1896), p. 1.

8. "New York Results," *Runner's World* (January 1988), p. 68.

9. Pamela Cooper, "The First American Marathon," *New York Herald* (September 20, 1896).

10. Richard Benyo, *The Masters of the Marathon* (New York: Atheneum, 1983), pp. 3, 29-31.

11. Bob Wischnia, "Coming Up Rosa," *Runner's World* (December 1987), pp. 40-42.

12. Rich O'Brien, "Show Stoppers," *Runner's World* (January 1988), p. 64-68.

13. Frank Litsky, "Late Starter Is the Earliest Finisher," *The New York Times* (June 5, 1988), pp. 2S; 4S.

14. *An Introduction to Running: One Step at a Time* (Washington, D.C.: The President's Council on Physical Fitness and Sports, 1987).

15. " 'Talk-Sing Test' for Best Workout Pace," *MaleGrams from Men's Health* (February 27, 1987).

16. Susan Kalish, *FitNews* (American Running and Fitness Association, Vol. 5, No. 12, December 1987), p. 1.

17. Mike Tymn, "The Ever-Changing Body," *Runner's World* (November 1987), p. 26.

18. Bill Rodgers, "Marathon Frequency," *The Runner* (December 1985).

19. A. Luger, et al., "Running: Training Affects Stress Hormone Levels," *The New England Journal of Medicine* (Vol. 316, May 1987), p. 1309.

20. Patrick Dyson, "UF Scientist Finds Long-Distance Running Not Limited to Degenerative Joint Disease," University of Florida Health Science Center Communications (June 7, 1985).

21. " 'Groucho Running' Saves Knees," *Prevention* (December 1987), p. 8.

22. Sandra Blakeslee, "Runners Warned of Mental Danger," *The New York Times* (August 28, 1985), p. D18.

23. William Arthur, "Compulsive Runner Profile: Grim, Void-Filling Ascetic," *Medical Tribune* (April 23, 1986), p. 36.

24. Catherine Gysin, "Anxious Athletes," *Health* (July 1986), p. 16.

25. D. C. Nieman and D. M. George, "Distance Running: Personality Linked to Success," *Journal of Sports Medicine* (Vol. 27, September 1987), p. 345.

26. Rick McGuire, "Running Immunity Ragged," *Medical Tribune* (November 24, 1988), pp. 5, 8.

Chapter 6

Walking

One of the most celebrated walkers of recent memory was Harry S. Truman, who served as President from 1945, following the death of President Franklin D. Roosevelt, until 1953. His familiar walking cane and 120 strides a minute were regular routines as he headed out of the White House, or wherever he was, at 6 A.M., leading his Secret Service detail on a merry chase.

"Whenever Dad and Mother, or Dad alone, came to New York, they stayed at the Carlyle Hotel," writes Margaret Truman in *Harry S. Truman*.[1] "He followed his usual routine, arising at dawn, and taking a 6 A.M. stroll. If he was in town alone, he developed the habit of dropping in on me for breakfast. This created problems until I gave him his own key. My children have inherited their grandfather's habits and insist on getting up by dawn's early light."

Before they were married, when she was in her early 20s, it was Bess Truman who was a notorious walker in Missouri. In the biography of her mother, *Bess Wallace Truman*, Margaret Truman recounts the story of how Bess set out from Independence to visit friends in the country along with Julian Harvey, a beau at the time; Mary Paxton, her closest friend; and Pete Harris, Mary's beau. It was a six-mile walk, three miles each way. When asked about the stroll, Bess remarked that it was a "minor jaunt at best." With that, the men asked her what she considered a real walk. "Oh, to Lee's Summit," she replied. That was a 25-mile hike. "You're on," the men said, and a few days later the foursome, with packed picnic lunches, were off to Lee's Summit.[2]

President Thomas Jefferson is reported to have said, "Exercise and recreation . . . are as necessary as reading: I will say rather more than necessary, because health is worth more than learning. A strong body makes the mind strong. . . . And walking is the best possible exercise."[3] Henry David Thoreau and William Wordsworth were also enthusiastic about walking.

Former President Richard Nixon's early walks are getting earlier at his retreat in New Jersey. Perhaps that is when he makes mental notes about books he is working on, such as the recent *1999*. At any rate, in her column in the *New York Post*, December 14, 1987, Cindy Adams reports that, "He's up at 4:30. Only on really weary days does he lie around in bed until maybe 5."[4]

Former U. S. Senator Lawton "Walkin' " Chiles (D., Fla.) made headlines during his 1970 campaign by walking from Century, in the northern part of the state, to Key Largo in the south (a distance of 1,003 miles), while sampling

70

voters' opinions on the issues.[5] Although his combat boots had to be resoled several times, he did not have any foot or ankle injuries. He considers walking "ideal" and still walks when time permits.[6]

"Walking is easily the most popular form of exercise," says *Walking for Exercise and Pleasure*, a booklet from The President's Council on Physical Fitness and Sports.[7] "Other activities generate more conversation and media coverage, but none of them approaches walking in number of participants. Approximately half of the 165 million American adults (18 years of age or older) claim they exercise regularly, and the number who walk for exercise is increasing every year."[7]

The booklet adds that walking is the only exercise in which the number of participants does not decline as they get older. In a national survey, the highest percentage of regular walkers (39.4 percent) for any group was found among men who were 65 or older.

"Unlike tennis, running, skiing and other activities that have gained great popularity fairly recently," adds the booklet, "walking has been widely publicized as a recreational and fitness activity throughout recorded history. Classical and early English literature seems to have been written largely by men who were prodigious walkers, and Emerson and Thoreau helped carry on the tradition in America. Among American presidents, the most famous walkers included Jefferson, Lincoln and Truman."[7]

Studies show that, when done briskly and on a regular schedule, walking improves the body's ability to consume oxygen during exertion; it lowers the resting heart rate; it reduces blood pressure; it increases the efficiency of the heart and lungs; and it helps to burn off excess calories, continues the booklet. This is valuable information for everyone, since obesity and high blood pressure are among the leading causes of heart attacks and strokes.

"Walking burns approximately the same amount of calories *per mile* as does running, a fact particularly appealing to those who find it difficult to sustain the jarring effects of long distance jogging," says the booklet. "Brisk walking one mile in fifteen minutes burns just about the same number of calories as jogging an equal distance in eight and one-half minutes. In weight-bearing activities like walking, heavier individuals will burn more calories than lighter persons. For example, studies show that a 110-pound person burns about half as many calories as a 216-pound person walking at the same pace for the same distance."[7]

Although a faster walking speed does not burn significantly more calories per mile, an increased walking pace does produce more dramatic conditioning effects, the booklet maintains. Those starting out in poor shape will benefit from a slow walking speed, while those in better health will need to walk faster and/or farther to improve their fitness. In addition, studies have shown that there are residual benefits to vigorous exercise. Even after a vigorous workout, your metabolism remains above normal for a time, which burns off more calories.

In some weight-loss and conditioning studies, walking has proven more effective than running and other more highly-touted activities, adds the booklet. The reason is that walking is virtually injury-free and it has the lowest dropout rate of any kind of exercise. Walking gives you a psychological boost and it helps you to sleep better. Smokers who begin a walking program often cut down or quit, especially since it is difficult to exercise vigorously if you smoke. It also encourages the smoker to improve his/her overall health.

Proper Walking Technique

In order to benefit from the exercise, you must walk briskly enough to increase your heart rate and cause you to breathe more deeply. The President's Council offers these tips for developing an efficient walking style:[7]

1. Hold head erect and keep back straight, abdomen flat. Toes should point straight ahead and arms should swing loosely at sides.
2. Land on the heel of the foot and roll forward to drive off the ball of the foot. Walking only on the ball of the foot, or in a flat-footed style, may cause fatigue and soreness.
3. Take long, easy strides, but don't strain for distance. When walking up or down hills, or at a very rapid pace, lean forward slightly.
4. Breathe deeply (with mouth open, if that is more comfortable).

Although walking is ideal exercise for the legs, heart and lungs, it is not a complete exercise program. Therefore, warmup exercises are essential. Those who walk and do not warm up sufficiently tend to become stiff and inflexible, often with short, tight muscles in the back as well as the backs of the legs. The President's Council recommends these warmups:[7]

Stretcher. Stand facing wall, arms' length away. Lean forward and place palms of hands flat against wall, slightly below shoulder height. Keep back straight, heels firmly on floor, and slowly bend elbows until forehead touches wall. Tuck hips toward wall and hold position for 20 seconds. Repeat exercise with knees slightly flexed.

Reach and bend. Stand erect with feet shoulder-width apart and arms extended over head. Reach as high as possible while keeping heels on floor and hold for ten counts. Flex knees slightly and bend slowly at waist, touching floor between feet with fingers. Hold for ten counts. If you can't touch the floor, try to touch the tops of your shoes. Repeat entire sequence two to five times.

Knee pull. Lie flat on back with legs extended and arms at sides. Lock arms around legs just below knee and pull knees to chest, raising buttocks slightly off floor. Hold for ten to 15 counts. If you have a knee problem, you may find it easier to lock arms behind knees. Repeat exercise three to five times.

Situp. Start with the situp that you can do three times without undue strain. When you are able to do ten repetitions of the exercise without great difficulty, move to a more difficult version, as follows:

1. Lie flat on back with arms at sides, palms down, and knees slightly bent. Curl head forward until you can see past feet, hold for three counts, then lower to start position. Repeat exercise three to ten times.
2. Lie flat on back with arms at sides, palms down, and knees slightly bent. Roll forward until upper body is at 45-degree angle to floor, then return to starting position. Repeat exercise three to ten times.

3. Lie flat on back with arms at sides, palms down, and knees slightly bent. Roll forward to sitting position, then return to starting position. Repeat exercise three to ten times.

4. Lie flat on back with arms crossed on chest and knees slightly bent. Roll forward to sitting position, then return to starting position. Repeat exercise three to ten times.

5. Lie flat on back with hands laced in back of head and knees slightly bent. Roll forward to sitting position, then return to starting position. Repeat exercise three to fifteen times.

The President's Council recommends that you begin your walking program by walking 20 minutes at least four or five times a week at a pace that is comfortable. If that is too strenuous or too easy, reduce or lengthen your walking time accordingly.

"As your condition improves," says the President's Council, "you should gradually increase your time and pace. After you have been walking for 20 minutes several days a week for one month, start walking 30 minutes per outing. Eventually, your goal should be to get to the place where you can comfortably walk three miles in 45 minutes, but there is no hurry about getting there. The speed at which you walk is less important than the time you devote to it, although we recommend that you walk as briskly as your condition permits. It takes about 20 minutes for your body to begin to realize the 'training effects' of sustained exercise."[7]

Health Benefits of Walking

According to a 20-year study of 17,000 Harvard alumni, a brisk two-mile daily walk can reduce your risk of having a heart attack by 28 percent or more, report Stephen Kiesling, Senior Editor, *American Health*, and E. C. Frederick, Ph.D., Nike Sport Research Laboratory, Beaverton, Oregon in *Walk On*.[8] The chief investigator of the study, Ralph Pfaffenbarger, M.D., of the Stanford University School of Medicine, adds that for every hour of walking you can expect to live an hour longer.

"You do not need a burst of energy to add years to your life," Dr. Pfaffenbarger says. "You do not need to run marathons. Walking is enough."[8]

Generally, the more you walk the less chance you will have of having heart problems, he says. The limit of improvement, he adds, is about 3,500 calories worth of activity per week, which is about equivalent to a 150-pound man walking 40 miles. If you burn more calories than that each week, "your risk of a heart attack actually rises to only 38 percent less—not 54 percent less—than a sedentary person's."[8]

For those who are overweight, the Rockport Fitness Walking Test can assess your cardiovascular fitness while not overtaxing your present physical state. It was developed by James M. Rippe, M.D., and his colleagues at the Exercise Physiology Laboratory, University of Massachusetts Medical School, based on studies of 168 men and 175 women. To take the test, you simply walk one mile, find out how long it took you and then measure your heart rate. Details about the test and the accompanying charts are available from The Rockport Walking Institute, P.O. Box 480, Marlboro, MA 01752; tel., 617-485-2090.[9]

"The revolutionary aspect of these findings is that now, after 50 years of research, we have a simple, highly accurate test of physical fitness that applies to adults of all ages and training levels," says Dr. Rippe. "The really exciting part of this is its ease and uniformity, and also its accuracy. Anyone can use it, because all you need is a flat measured mile, a watch, and a pair of comfortable shoes. Few people have a treadmill, and surprisingly few can run for twelve minutes, but almost everyone can take this test—young or old, fit or unfit."[9]

Previous fitness tests, such as the treadmill, the Cooper 12-minute run and the stationary cycle have limitations related to a person's vigor, ease, familiarity or injury risk, according to Dr. Rippe. The new Rockport test offers specific fitness walking programs to help those taking the test improve their cardiovascular health, he says.

Maximum total body oxygen consumption (max VO_2) has long been considered the definitive way of determining fitness, Dr. Rippe says. But measurements of VO_2 have been generally confined to the laboratory and required sophisticated techniques and highly trained technicians. That led to the need for a test that can be easily administered and understood, such as the Rockport Fitness Walking Test, he adds.

Writing in the October 1986 issue of *Physician and Sportsmedicine*, Dr. Rippe and his colleagues report that, although strenuous exercise such as jogging provides better long-term, aerobic conditioning, walking is ideal because it is easy to do and there is virtually no strain on bones, muscles and ligaments.[10]

In another issue of the same medical journal, Dr. J. Porcari and associates found that their volunteers raised their heart rates to effective conditioning levels by walking a mile at a fast clip. The study involved 300 people who were 50 or older.[11]

"Running burns up about 100 to 120 calories a mile no matter at what speed you run," reports George Sheehan, M.D. in *The Runner*.[12] "This is apparently due to a uniform running form. However, rapid walking burns up many more calories per mile than walking slowly. For instance, at three miles per hour you will use an estimated 72 calories a mile as opposed to 95 at four miles per hour and 128 at five miles per hour. This increased demand is in part due to changes in walking form at higher speeds."

He goes on to say that calories expended *per minute* of walking are lower than those required for a minute of running. A rule of thumb is that you have to walk twice as long to use up the same number of calories you use when running. So, he adds, walking one hour at four miles per hour is equal to 30 minutes of running at approximately seven miles per hour.[12]

"Calories expended *per mile* are a little less during walking than running," Sheehan continues. "However, use of hand weights can increase caloric demand appreciably. Walking four miles per hour with hand weights uses up more calories per mile than jogging at seven miles per hour pace."[12]

If you are too tired to do the chores around the house, perhaps a brisk walk will get rid of the fatigue, according to Harold Kohl of the Institute for

Aerobics Research, Dallas, Texas. He reports that those who complain the most about chronic fatigue are generally not physically fit, he says in *Prevention*.[13]

"The idea is to make yourself start doing whatever activities you can do," he says. "Start a garden. Walk around the block or a mall. Do some housecleaning. You don't have to run a marathon. Just doing a little bit may have obvious energy benefits compared to not doing anything."[13]

The American Podiatric Medical Association has determined the calories that are burned per mile for the various styles of walking. They are:[14]

Strolling, walking at 2 mph; this burns up between 100 and 120 calories.

Functional walking, 2 to 4 mph; 120 to 140 calories.

Brisk or fitness walking, 3.5 to 5.5 mph; 120 to 160 calories.

Weight-loaded walking, with weights or packs; 170 to 280 calories.

Climbing, stairs or hills; 150 to 300 calories.

If you are between 20 and 30 years of age, your heart rate during exercise should be between 150 and 170 beats per minute, according to Connie LaBuhn, a physical education instructor at California State University, Dominguez Hills, Carson, California.[15] From age 30 to 40, the accepted rate is between 135 and 150. For those over 40, the heart rate should be around 120 to 140.[15]

"That is after an initial warmup of five to ten minutes, depending on the activity," she says.[15]

You can actually slow down aging with exercise, LaBuhn maintains. And exercise provides a "natural high" and helps to alleviate tension because, as you work out, hormonal changes cause more adrenalin to be secreted. She adds that jogging, fast walking, swimming, cycling, dancing and other aerobic activities help to trim and tone your body.

"The person who has exercised is standing up straight and tall," she continues. "There is a bright shine in his eyes, a little more color to the skin. The skin tone is tighter. It's like comparing a piece of wilted lettuce and a fresh piece of lettuce."[15]

After a surgical patient has recuperated at home for six weeks, Steven D. Herman, M.D., Chief of Heart Surgery at St. Vincent's Hospital, Bridgeport, Connecticut, has them walking two miles a day. He urges them to begin a walking program on the second day after they are discharged from the hospital.[16]

After they have returned home, the patients are urged to begin walking about a city block, on level ground, two or three times a day. They gradually increase the distance and the only acceptable excuse for not walking is inclement weather. The exercise improves stamina and endurance, since the blood vessels become larger and more flexible. In addition, Dr. Herman says that the exercise helps the mind and body to relax and often relieves some of the anxiety experienced by postoperative patients.

"Most recuperating patients experience generalized weakness and fatigue when they first get home," Dr. Herman explains. "Sometimes they feel even more fatigue than before the operation, which can be frightening. This fear makes them avoid such physical activity. Usually, however, the cause of this weakness is the temporary loss of muscle strength from being inactive in the hospital, and from having normal eating and sleeping routines disrupted. It's almost always temporary and can be seen in anyone who has had major surgery, not just in heart patients."[16]

He goes on to say that what patients need to understand is that cardiac surgery corrects only the current condition that made the surgery necessary. "Major changes in lifestyle are essential to avoid further heart disease in the future," he maintains.[16]

During rehabilitation classes in the hospital as they recover from the surgery, Dr. Herman urges the patients to follow a well-balanced diet, to try to reduce stress, to make exercise a daily routine, to maintain normal weight and to stop smoking. These steps, he believes, go a long way in perhaps preventing another heart problem.

For the more experienced walkers, there are various walk-a-thons around the nation to raise money for various causes and to improve the fitness of the walkers. The 1988 March of Dimes "WalkAmerica" event on April 24 was expected to attract over 21,000 walkers. Proceeds help to improve the health of low birthweight babies. For details about the March of Dimes events in your area, contact Jennifer L. Howse, Ph.D., Executive Director, Greater New York March of Dimes, 233 Park Avenue South, New York, N. Y. 10003; tel., 212-353-8353.[17]

Walking can increase your high-density lipoproteins, the good kind of cholesterol, according to Timothy Cook, Ph.D., of the University of Pittsburgh, as reported in *Prevention*.[18] The study involved 35 postal carriers, who obviously do a lot of walking, and a group of sedentary men. The mailmen walked an average of five miles a day during a four- to five-hour period. The results showed that HDL cholesterol levels were significantly higher in the postal workers than in the sedentary controls. Half the mailmen carried a mail bag and half used a pushcart, but there was no difference in their HDL levels.

"I think HDL is more affected by chronic activity than by physiological (aerobic) fitness," Dr. Cook says. "You do lower your risk of disease if you are physiologically fit. But it seems also that you can reduce your risk by being moderately active each day—doing things such as walking."[18]

Scholl, Inc., decided to find out how far people in various occupations walked each day. They selected 110 volunteers from various occupations and recorded their work habits for a week using a pedometer. Some of the results, as reported in *American Health*, were:[19]

Hospital nurses: average of 5.3 miles per day
Security officers: 4.2
City messengers: 4.0
Retail salespeople: 3.5
Food servers: 5.3
Hotel employees: 3.2
Doctors: 2.5
Real estate agents: 2.4
Advertising/PR executives: 2.4
Architects: 2.3

Secretaries: 2.2
Newspaper reporters: 2.1
Bankers: 2.0

And the lowest averages:

Dentists: 0.85
Radio announcers: 1.1
Housewives: 1.3

"Sweat-suited and sneaker-footed, with pedometers clipped firmly at waists, they appear sometimes before dawn, and slip quietly through the shopping-mall entrance with a wave to smiling guards," reports *Time*, May 26, 1986. "Early-bird bargain hunters? Well, no. These are not sales stalkers but a growing breed of fitness faddists, the mall walkers."[20]

Although these strollers are there to walk instead of to buy (they hardly glance at the window displays), community-relations-minded shopping centers are openly courting the strollers. Some malls have measured courses and created walkers' maps.

"The quarter-mile circuit at the Northwoods Mall in Peoria, Illinois, even includes half a dozen stations for stretching and light calisthenics," says *Time*. "The Ward Parkway Shopping Center in Kansas City, a pioneer that has been welcoming mall walkers for 25 years, actually opens for three hours on holidays just to accommodate its habitual hikers."[20]

"I'm on my 600th mile," boasts Ruth Kaufman, 60, a member of the Galleria Mall GoGetters in Glendale, California. "I could have gone to San Francisco by now."[20]

Another mall walker, Glen Strait, 53, who had quintuple coronary bypass surgery three years ago, walks three miles every other day at the Aurora Mall in suburban Denver, Colorado, according to *The New York Times*, February 8, 1988.[21] He averages five mph and has stopped smoking, gotten his weight to almost normal and pulled his cholesterol count out of the danger zone.

"All my brothers have heart trouble and two have died from it," Strait says. "It runs in the family. When I came out of the hospital after the surgery, I didn't think I had many prospects. I certainly didn't think I would live to see retirement. I started exercising, I stopped smoking and I began eating right. Now I see a future. I've begun to think I might not die so soon after all."[21]

Walking for Diabetics

Walking is an ideal way for diabetics to manage their regimen and enjoy the exercise at the same time, says Nell Armstrong, R.N., M.S., in *Diabetes Forecast*.[22] Some of the more important safety precautions are:

1. Whether you have Type I or Type II diabetes, if your blood glucose is often in the 250+ range, get it under control before beginning a walking program. Unusually high blood glucose is worsened by exercise because there isn't sufficient insulin to lower it properly, Armstrong says.

2. Know the action time of your insulin and plan your exercise program with your doctor or diabetes educator accordingly. It is important to take into consideration the type of insulin, the timing of injections (and peak action time), exercise and meals.

"Even the same insulin can affect different people in different ways," Armstrong continues. "Careful record keeping, especially during the initial stages of your walking program, will help you and your physician map out a workable exercise, food and insulin combination. Walking one-and-a-half to two hours after meals will minimize the risk of hypoglycemia (low blood sugar)."[22]

3. Test your blood glucose more often during the early phase of your program, so you and your physician or diabetes nurse can make a knowledgeable decision about whether or not you need to reduce the insulin dosage.

4. If you are taking insulin, always have on hand some fast-acting carbohydrates for emergencies. If you experience signs of hypoglycemia during a walk, don't think you can hold out until you get home, cautions Armstrong. As you walk, you burn calories and continue to lower your glucose level so, at the first signs of low blood sugar, stop and take carbohydrate immediately.

5. When you have increased your pace and distance, the effects of exercise will last longer and hypoglycemia may not begin until several hours after walking, she says. Regular, vigorous exercise enhances metabolism, and glucose may continue to be burned at a higher than usual rate even several hours after exercising. For those exercising in the evening, more food at the evening meal or a bedtime snack or more insulin may be required.

6. If you walk alone, be prepared for any contingencies by carrying a visible diabetes identification—bracelet or necklace—and instructions for what to do in an emergency. Carry some change for making a phone call.

7. After the walk, check out any pressure spots caused by the shoe or debris in the shoe, Armstrong continues. Be aware of any injuries that you might not have felt. This is especially important for those with neuropathy.

8. Learn to take your pulse rate so that you can pace yourself while walking or exercising.

"Walking is one of the least injury prone aerobic exercises," continues Armstrong. "Any exercise program, however, should be approached with some thought and planning, especially when you have diabetes."[22] She recommends these precautions:

• Get your doctor's approval.

• Walk on the most absorbent surface you can find—sand, grass, dirt or specially prepared tracks.

• Wear shoes that provide support, have a roomy toe box and a snug heel, are flexible where your toes bend, and have arch supports and cushioned soles. Buy walking instead of running shoes.

• Exercise indoors when it is extremely cold or hot or very humid. Wear clothing that absorbs perspiration and permits air to flow through.

• Drink fluids (especially water) before and after walking to avoid dehydration.

Aerobic Walking

Relatively new as a way of getting couch potatoes out of the house is aerobic walking, which was developed by Casey Meyers, and which is discussed at length in his book, *Aerobic Walking*.[23]

A former fitness runner, Meyers suffered severe knee damage over five years ago and he began to experiment with an injury-free aerobic exercise that was natural, effective and sustainable. He determined that, by making a few changes in his walking gait, he could accelerate from the normal, brisk 15-minute mile to an aerobic 12-minute mile or faster.

"Aerobic walking provides cardiovascular and physical benefits equal to or better than jogging but with less risk of injury," Meyers said. "It also exercises more muscle groups and burns more calories."[23]

Since Meyers is convinced that regular running shoes hinder walking performance, he has designed a shoe for aerobic walking which is trimmer and lower in the heel and forefoot than a running shoe. It is also lightweight. The extra padding in running shoes prevents the aerobic walker from accelerating his or her pace and gaining the maximum benefit from the walk, he explained.

The techniques for aerobic walking are rather simple and center on the correct posture, including: 1) Hold posture erect with shoulders back and directly over the hips; 2) keep the head level, chin up and parallel to the ground; 3) bend arms to 90° angles at the elbows; and 4) pump with every stride.[23]

Meyers recommends that you start your walking program slowly and build up your performance gradually over several weeks or months. The initial goal should be to reach three miles per day at least four times a week.

Regardless of your age or physical status, walking offers dividends that cannot be compared to other athletic activities. For one thing, it's inexpensive. All you need are some comfortable shoes and clothes; style is not a consideration. Of course, if you feel the need to dress up, there are many brands of comfortable walking shoes and fashionable walking outfits.

References

1. Margaret Truman, *Harry S. Truman* (New York: William Morrow Co., Inc., 1973), pp. 440-441, 564, 573.

2. Margaret Truman, *Bess Wallace Truman* (New York: MacMillan Publishing Co., 1986).

3. Nell Armstrong, R.N., M.S., "Walking Fitness Afoot," *Diabetes Forecast* (1987).

4. Cindy Adams, *New York Post* (December 14, 1987), p. 32.

5. Paul Clancy, "Senator Walkin' Away," *USA Today* (December 8, 1987), p. 2A.

6. Senator Lawton Chiles, personal communication (December 23, 1987).

7. *Walking for Exercise and Pleasure* (Washington, DC: President's Council on Physical Fitness and Sports).

8. Stephen Kiesling and E. C. Frederick, Ph.D., *Walk On* (Emmaus, Pa: Rodale Press, 1986).

9. Richard A. Schwartz, "Physical Fitness Test Based on Walking Unveiled," (The Rockport Walking Institute, May 1987).

10. J. M. Rippe, et al., "Walking: Is It the Most Perfect Exercise?" *Physician and Sportsmedicine* (Vol. 14, October 1986), p. 146.

11. J. Porcari, et al., *Physician and Sportsmedicine* (Vol. 15, February 1987), p. 119.

12. George Sheehan, M.D., "Does Walking Work?" *The Runner* (December 1986), p. 16.

13. "Walking Away from Fatigue," *Prevention* (November 1987), p. 8.

14. Hal Higdon, "Walking Ways," *American Health* (December 1987), p. 26.

15. "Starting to Exercise Need not Be Hard or Dramatic," (University Relations, California State University, Dominguez Hills/Carson).

16. Joan Philips, "Surgeon Urges Two-Mile Walks Daily Six Weeks After Heart Surgery," New York: Makovsky & Company, Inc., November 13, 1987).

17. "WalkAmerica '88," (New York: March of Dimes).

18. "Walking Up Your HDL," *Prevention* (May 1987), p. 6.

19. Madonna Behen, "Work to Walk—Does Your Job Send You Striding?" *American Health* (January/February 1988), p. 30.

20. Anastasia Toufexis, "Make Way for the Mall Walkers," *Time* (May 26, 1986).

21. William Stockton, "Circling the Malls to Get in Shape," *The New York Times* (February 8, 1988), p. C11.

22. See Reference 3.

23. Casey Meyers, *Aerobic Walking* (New York: Vintage Books, 1987).

Chapter 7

Proper Nutrition Helps You Win

Although the quality of an athlete's training has a great deal to do with his or her performance, the nutritional status of the athlete can actually determine whether or not he will win or at least improve on his usual time and endurance. Except for routine walking, other forms of strenuous exercise such as jogging and running are so stressful that they deplete the body of essential nutrients. And improper nutrition not only erodes performance but also is often a major cause of injuries.

It was probably George A. Sheehan and James F. Fixx, two men addicted to tennis, who got the nation jogging and running after their popular books were published. Sheehan, a New Jersey heart specialist, was 44 when he turned to running. In a burst of anger about being called out in the middle of the night to see a patient, he broke a hand by smashing it against a wall. Running seemed to be the perfect antidote until he could play tennis again. Fixx was a 35-year-old magazine writer when he took up running seriously. After pulling a muscle while playing tennis, he turned to running to strengthen his leg muscles.[1] Fixx serves as a perfect example of the fact—which is under debate—that fitness and health are not synonymous, suggests writer Robert Lipsyte.[1]

"In 1984, when Fixx dropped dead at 52 while running, he proved that it is possible to run fast, frequently and be on one's last legs," says Lipsyte. "Fixx's autopsy revealed advanced atherosclerosis (hardening of the arteries), that progressive circulatory disease in which plaque attached to the inside of arteries eventually closes the blood vessels. A moment comes when the body needs a rush of oxygen-bearing blood that cannot be delivered. Fixx was fit when he died, but he was not healthy."[1]

Iron Deficiency

Another well known example of the relationship of nutrition to running is seen in the story of Alberto Salazar, the world-class marathoner. Even though he had performed erratically during the Olympics, Salazar was expected to dominate the 1983 Helsinki Games. Instead he finished eighth.[2]

Confused by the athlete's poor showing, Dr. Douglas Clement of the British Columbia Sports-Medicine Clinic in Vancouver, Canada, after reviewing Salazar's performance on television, suggested to the runner's coach that the problem was an iron deficiency. After Salazar was given a blood test, it was found that he had virtually no iron stores in his body. After a few weeks of iron supplements, the athlete was almost back to normal.

"There are two basic reasons why athletes, especially runners, need more iron than the general population," explains *Superfit*.[2] "Exercise makes it more difficult for an athlete's system to absorb this mineral, and it speeds up iron losses by the body. In addition, higher body temperatures and increased circulation can shorten the lifespan of red blood cells, which store iron, and this causes iron to become unbound and excreted in urine. Also, hormones released during exercise can make red blood cells more fragile. Iron is also lost in sweat, and if the mineral isn't replaced, the losses add up."[2]

The fitness magazine goes on to say that studies performed on runners show that their ability to absorb iron is 30 to 40 percent less than that of non-runners. This is because food passes through the runner's gastrointestinal tract more rapidly, giving the body less time to absorb the nutrients. The problem is more acute for women, who also lose iron in menstrual flow.

Women are supposed to get 18 milligrams of iron daily, but a number of surveys show that many women are not getting this amount. The average male needs 10 milligrams of iron daily, which increases to 13 milligrams if he is physically active.

Tell-tale signs of iron deficiency, according to Samuel Smith, Ph.D., a professor of biochemistry and nutritional sciences at the University of New Hampshire, are that your time drops off, you feel tired and draggy and it's harder to run.[2] A serum ferritin test, which will show how much iron is in your body, can be performed at a clinic for about $35.

"The solution is a conscious effort to get enough iron," adds *Superfit*. "This includes vitamin-plus-iron supplements and eating plenty of iron-rich foods, such as liver, red meat, spinach, legumes and molasses. Vitamin C enhances the absorption of iron, so it is important to get enough of that too. And the bit of iron you get from cooking in an uncoated, cast-iron pot or skillet can also be absorbed and used by your body."[2]

A 1986 survey released by the U. S. Department of Agriculture showed that American women of childbearing age have mean iron intakes of only 61 percent of the Recommended Dietary Allowance. Iron deficiency is regarded as second only to obesity as the nation's most common nutritional problem.[3]

Women between the ages of 19 and 50 are often iron deficient because of the low-calorie diets that many favor, according to Tom McDermott of the Beef Industry Council, Chicago. He points out that women of child-bearing age average 1,588 calories per day. Since the average American diet contains only about 7 milligrams of iron per 1,000 calories, this often leads to an iron deficiency in many women, he continues.

Iron in the diet is available as heme iron, which is found only in foods of animal origin, and nonheme iron, which comes from both animal and vegetable sources. As an example, the iron in meat, fish and poultry is between 50 and 60 percent heme iron. Unfortunately, some foods interfere with the absorption of iron: chelates such as tannin in tea; phytates in whole grains, brans and soybeans; polyphenols in coffee; phosvitin in egg yolk; and chelates in spinach and chocolate.

Iron is essential for good health because it:

1. Transfers oxygen and carbon dioxide to and from body tissues.
2. Assists in the synthesis of heme iron in immature red blood cells. Heme iron joins with protein to form hemoglobin, which is the red pigment in blood that carries oxygen.
3. Helps to convert beta-carotene into vitamin A.
4. Aids in the formation of purines as part of nucleic acids.
5. Helps to remove fats from the blood.
6. Assists in the synthesis of collagen, the protein that binds cells together.
7. Helps to produce antibodies that fight infections.
8. Aids in the production of enzymes that are involved in releasing energy from the cells. (For the iron content of some foods, see Table 3).

Speaking at a press conference in New York in 1983, distance runner Julie Brown reported that she had fewer injuries after switching from a diet that consisted mostly of wholegrain bread. Added protein had cut down on her injuries, she said.[4]

Vitamin-Mineral Supplementation

Jack Cooperman, Ph.D., Director of the Nutrition Education Program at the New York Medical College, Valhalla, New York, told the meeting that, "Despite a surplus of food in America, surveys have shown that many Americans are undernourished, and this certainly applies to those millions of individuals who engage in recreational athletics. They are not meeting their nutritional requirements because they do not get enough of the necessary vitamins and minerals from their diets."[4]

Another speaker was F. A. (Ferdy) Massimino, M.D., a California sports medicine physician, who won the grueling U. S. National Triathlon in 1982. The world-class triathlete, who was 34 at the time of the press conference, said that nutrition had definitely played a role in his success. "There's a tremendous amount athletes can do to improve their performance by looking at nutrition in a scientific way," he said. "However, I believe that we are in the dark ages when it comes to nutrition in sports."[4]

As an example, he said that a deficiency in one of the B vitamins will almost certainly impair absorption and metabolism of the others in the complex. Since the B complex vitamins work as a team, the function and synergy of the entire group is essential for optimum performance in sports and for good health, he added.

That, he explained, is why researchers often recommend supplementation with the entire B-Complex group instead of doses of individual B vitamins. And he stressed that it is essential to replace electrolytes and other minerals during strenuous exercise in order to maintain normal body metabolism.

Table 3
IRON CONTENT OF SOME FOODS

Meat	Milligrams Per 100 Grams (3.5 oz.)
Beef liver, fried	5.7
Hamburger, cooked, lean	2.7
Lamb chop, broiled	1.8
Shrimp	1.8
Chicken breast, roasted	1.04
Perch	0.92

Non-Meat	
Filberts (hazelnuts)	8.1
Pistachios	6.7
Cashews	6.4
Whole-wheat bread	3.2
Enriched white bread	3.0
Popcorn (popped with oil)	3.0
White beans, boiled	3.0
Pinto beans, boiled	3.0
Chickpeas, boiled	3.0
Spinach, raw	2.7
Raisins, seeded (Muscat)	2.6
Eggs	2.01
Soybean curd	1.8
Bean sprouts	1.6
Broccoli	1.1
Romaine lettuce	1.1
Avocado	1.0
Iceberg lettuce	0.57
Apple	0.18

Source: U.S. Department of Agriculture

During a four-month period in 1982 (June to September), Massimino trained 30 hours a week while experimenting with megavitamin and mineral supplementation. He then competed in two events, finishing tenth in the Ironman (he was the highest finisher over 30 years of age), and, four months later, winning the U. S. Triathlon Championship at Malibu.

In training for the event, his day began at 4 A.M. with a hearty breakfast of complex carbohydrates, vitamins (added vitamin C) and minerals. By 7 a.m., he was ready for a 2.4-mile swim in the ocean. After completing the swim in about 53 minutes, he changed clothes and began a 112-mile bicycle race. Following 5½ hours of continuous, high-intensity cycling, he again changed clothes and began the biggest challenge: a 26.2-mile marathon, which consumed another 6½ hours of high-intensity exercise by what he admitted was a somewhat ravaged body.

Dr. Massimino added that nutritional research in the past ten or so years had determined that individual requirements for the various nutrients vary considerably from one individual to another, depending on the person's circumstances, stresses and state of health or ill-health. For that reason, the so-called Recommended Dietary Allowances (RDAs) should serve only as guidelines rather than gospel, he states. Instead of an average human being needing an average amount of nutrients to get through life, we now recognize the existence of what Dr. Roger J. Williams called "biochemical individuality." Therefore, says Dr. Massimino, the following factors help to determine one's specific nutritional needs:

1. Genetics or heredity.
2. Physiological and psychological stress.
3. State of illness or disease.
4. Environment.
5. Physical activity, including sports.

Although Muhammad Ali's training and physical strength excelled in his fight against George Foreman in Zaire in 1974, it was obvious that the champion was not in peak condition. Ali admitted that he was suffering from hypoglycemia (low blood sugar), which he attributed to the cakes, pies and sweet rolls that had been suggested by his doctor for improved energy.[5]

Since joggers, runners and walkers are exposed to high amounts of toxins in air pollution, especially along streets and highways, they may need extra amounts of vitamin E to combat this stress, according to Dr. Roy Bruden, a psychobiologist.[6]

Writing in *Your Personal Vitamin Profile*, Michael Colgan, Ph.D. says that, at the University of Auckland, New Zealand, he and his colleagues could not find any athletes who had not used or were not using vitamin and mineral supplements.[7] In fact, he says, 84 percent of Olympic athletes use supplements. He adds that well-known coaches such as D. Talbot of Canada do not think that it is possible to succeed as an athlete without vitamin and mineral supplements.

Dr. Colgan reports that it has been known for 50 years that requirements for vitamin B1 (thiamine) increase when there is a high carbohydrate intake and a lot of energy is being expended, such as with athletes. Since this vitamin is necessary for sugar metabolism, many athletes are convinced that extra amounts of thiamine will inhibit fatigue during high-endurance events. He notes that winning Australian Olympic athletes do have higher intakes of vitamin B1 than the athletes who lose. But, he adds, the entire B-complex is important, since these vitamins work together as a team.

Extra vitamin C before a competition may offer a marginal advantage for those competing in endurance events, Dr. Colgan says, since extra vitamin C may be needed to keep the body from being depleted during exercise. Vitamin C aids in increasing adrenaline during exercise, which can give an athlete an added boost, and it helps the body to use fats as an energy source. This might help to husband glycogen so that it can be called on to increase stamina. The extra vitamin C before a competition may also benefit oxygen metabolism, but, for insurance, the athlete should also probably fortify himself with the B-complex as well as vitamins A, D and E, he continues.

Dr. Colgan goes on to say that nutrient studies which have only analyzed one vitamin or mineral at a time, rather than a complete nutrition program, are doomed to failure. For one thing, he adds, these studies often look for only short-term effects, and it may take time for benefits to surface. Also, these studies often use volunteers who take the supplements for only a few days or weeks.

"As we have seen," says Dr. Colgan, "the real purpose of nutrient supplements is to build a better body. Because of the principle of physiological dynamics, requiring the turnover of generations of cells, this process is slow. Deficiency studies provide excellent examples of the time scale involved. Diets very deficient in vitamin C, for instance, reduce blood C levels almost to nil within three weeks. It takes eighteen weeks, however, for enough cells to die and new, defective cells to grow, before the first degenerative signs of scurvy begin to appear."[7]

As we know, an athlete's performance is often calculated as to how efficiently he is using oxygen. This depends on how much blood you have and how many red or oxygen-carrying cells the blood contains. Dr. Colgan points out that good nutrition and regular training can increase blood volume and red blood cells by 25 percent.

"With the help of vitamin C," he explains, "new capillaries grow in the heart and skeletal muscles to carry the improved blood, and there is a huge improvement in performance. But the whole process may take five years. Between three and six months is the absolute minimum period before you can expect a nutrition effect to show in athletes. Studies of supplementation of athletes given for a few days or weeks are useless."[7]

Dr. Colgan says that vitamin and mineral supplements are an essential part of the diet of Soviet Olympic athletes, and he believes that multiple nutrient supplements during the past ten years have helped the East Germans to gain world supremacy in many events.

In 1975, Dr. Colgan and his associates at the University of Aukland devised a double-blind study involving four experienced male marathon runners. The runners were divided into two groups of two each, matched for age, marathon experience, previous marathon times and stage of training. Their ages ranged from 26 to 35. The first two were given individual vitamin and mineral supplements, while the two controls received a daily placebo, which looked and tasted like the vitamin-mineral combo but which had none of the nutrients. After three months, the two groups were switched. But at no time did any of the runners know exactly what they were taking. It later turned out that all of them thought they had been getting vitamins and minerals. At any rate, the four athletes were tested for improvements during 20-mile training runs or marathons during the six months the study was in progress.

"The athletes' times were considerably better when they were receiving the real vitamins and minerals," says Dr. Colgan. "The best runner improved his marathon time by two minutes eight seconds in the three months with placebos. With real supplements in the second three months, he improved a further eight minutes, 52 seconds, a significant advance."[7]

He goes on to say that both runners who received real supplements for the first three months improved rapidly, but when they were switched to placebos in the second three months, their performance fell off for one and did not improve for the other. The two athletes who were given real supplements during the second three months overtook the other two runners whose supplements had been replaced with placebos during that time. So, he concludes, even though three months of supplementation is really too short to be of significance, the results suggest that supplements have a definite effect in improving endurance performance.

Encouraged by this study, Dr. Colgan, who now lives in San Diego, California, and his collaborators designed a double-blind study using four weight-lifters to determine whether or not vitamin and mineral supplements affect strength.

This was also a six-month study and the weight-lifters were given various strength tests during that time. It was determined that the two lifters who took supplements for the first three months increased their strength quickly. At the end of three months, one athlete had increased his strength by nearly 60 percent; the other one by over 40 percent. The two weight-lifters on placebos increased their strength by only 10 to 20 percent.

During the second three months, however, when the placebos were switched to real supplements, they caught up with the first two weight-lifters, whose performance then slumped when they were taken off of the vitamin-mineral supplements.

Dr. Colgan designed still another double-blind study, this one involving ten male marathon runners, whose best times were between 2½ and 3 hours. They were matched for age, experience, and other factors and divided into two groups of five.

When the final results were tabulated, Dr. Colgan and his staff found that the runners taking the supplements increased their mean marathon time from 9 minutes, 44 seconds to 28 minutes, 25 seconds. Because of their training, three of the men taking placebos increased their time from 7 minutes, 1 second to 11 minutes, 20 seconds.

An added dividend, Dr. Colgan continues, was that the athletes taking supplements registered lower heart rates, lower blood pressure and lower cholesterol levels.

"In addition," says Dr. Colgan, "the supplemented athletes had 35 percent fewer minor injuries (52 as opposed to 70 in the placebo group), and 81 percent fewer infections (six as opposed to 28) than those on the placebos. The supplements not only improved performance, but very likely exerted a protective effect upon the body as well. The three types of measurement—improved performance, improved biochemistry and reduced illness and injury—all point to a decided advantage for those taking individual vitamin and mineral supplements. In top competition, where the edge on opponents is often very small, this advantage might make the difference between losing or setting a world record."[7]

Women who exercise may need twice the RDA for vitamin B2 (riboflavin), Daphne Roe, M.D., of Cornell University told a meeting of the American Chemical Society in St. Louis in 1984.[8] She has determined that women who exercise cannot maintain normal levels of this important B vitamin in their bodies if they consume only the RDA. Additionally, she says that even sedentary women may need 80 percent more than the RDA recommends.

Dr. Roe's observations are based on three human studies with active, sedentary and dieting women. There were twelve volunteers per study, and she determined their body stores of vitamin B2 by measuring the amounts of red blood cell enzyme that requires B2 to work.

"Riboflavin is essential to energy production, and its depletion, especially in women who exercise, may reflect an increased requirement by working muscles," Dr. Roe says.[8]

Thomas Kirk Cureton, Ph.D., Professor Emeritus and Director of the Physical Fitness Institute at the University of Illinois, Urbana, says that a survey conducted by him and Dr. Wilbur Bohm demonstrated that Olympic athletes and top Olympic coaches favored the use of vitamin C, the B-complex and vitamin E, in spite of some of the skepticism of attending physicians. Dr. Cureton adds that he and his staff have faith in the results of several years of longitudinal trial and error, systematically rotated, on wheat germ oil (which contains vitamin E) and then off for a period, then on placebos, and then on octacosanol (found in wheat germ oil), off again and on placebos, on nothing, and then on wheat germ cereal.[9]

Trace Minerals

Writing in *ACS Symposium Series 354,*, which evolved from a meeting of the American Chemical Society, Anaheim, California, in September 1986, Linda Strause, Ph.D., and Paul Saltman, Ph.D., of the University of California at San Diego, report that their interest in trace minerals and bone metabolism developed when they were introduced to the orthopedic problems of Bill Walton, the professional basketball player.[10] Although they do not mention it, racing back and forth on a basketball court could conceivably equate with the pounding that the feet take while running or jogging.

"Several years ago (Walton) was plagued by frequent broken bones, pains in his joints and an inability to heal bone fractures," Drs. Strause and Saltman say. "We hypothesized that he might be deficient in trace elements as a result of his very limited vegetarian diet."[10] (At one time Walton favored the so-called macrobiotic diet, which can be deficient in various nutrients if it is not properly planned).

In cooperation with Walton's physician, the San Diego researchers analyzed Walton's blood and found no detectable manganese. His serum concentrations of copper and zinc also were below normal.

"Dietary supplementation with trace elements and calcium was begun," the authors continue. "Over a period of several months his bones healed and he returned to professional basketball. In cooperation with several other orthopedic physicians, we analyzed serum from other patients with slow bone healing. Several of these patients also had abnormally low zinc, copper and manganese levels."[10]

Drs. Strause and Saltman go on to say that it is not surprising that trace minerals can affect the growth and development of bone, since deficiencies in these nutrients profoundly alter bone metabolism in animals, either directly or indirectly. When trace elements are not provided in the diet, they continue, this can lead to inefficient functioning of a certain enzyme or enzymes that require the transition nutrient as a cofactor. As an example, they add, copper and iron are required in the cross-linking of collagen, the connective tissue between bone, and elastins, which are tissue proteins.

As a result of their animal studies, the two researchers conclude that various trace minerals, especially manganese, may play a significant role in the development of osteoporosis.

In a recap of the Anaheim symposium, which appeared in *Science News,* Dr. Saltman recalled looking at X-rays of one of Walton's ankles that was not healing and exclaiming, "This guy has osteoporosis or an osteoporosis-type disease."[11]

Dr. Saltman adds that, although Walton was deficient in manganese, zinc and copper, he had lots of calcium, suggesting that the athlete "was not synthesizing bone well." In fact, Saltman continues, Walton had a remarkable imbalance of nutrients.

"Bone tissue is constantly breaking down and being reformed," says *Science News.* "So in another test the UCSD team measured the activity of cells responsible for the breaking down and laying down of bone tissue. Manganese-deficient rats broke down half as much bone as rats on a minerally balanced diet. Cells responsible for laying down new bone were inhibited even more . . . resulting in bone loss and increased porosity."[11]

Another symposium speaker, Jeanne Freeland-Graves of the University of Texas in Austin, says that the the RDA for manganese (2.5 to 5 mg daily) may be too low, because it takes at least 3.8 mg daily to prevent the body from depleting its stores of the mineral.

Constance Kies of the University of Nebraska says that three of the richest sources of manganese—wheat bran, tea and spinach—are actually unreliable sources, since the tannins in tea, the phytate and fiber in bran and the oxalic acid in spinach can inhibit the absorption of some minerals, including manganese. She says that preferred dietary sources are milk, meat and eggs.

Magnesium

Another mineral, magnesium, may play a significant role during exercise and when the body is under stress, according to several speakers at the Fourth International Symposium on Magnesium, which was held in 1986 in conjunction with the annual meeting of the American College of Nutrition in Blacksburg, Virginia.[12]

Dr. Gustawa Stendig-Lindberg of the Sackler School of Medicine in Ramat

Aviv, Israel, reported on a study of 43 healthy men who had hiked 40, 70 and 120 kilometers (8 to 22 hours), according to *Medical Tribune*.[12] There was no detectable change in blood magnesium levels after the 40km-hike, either following it or 72 hours later. And magnesium stores did not fall until 72 hours after the 70km-hike. However, there was a "significant drop" in serum magnesium immediately following the 120km-hike, and they had low magnesium stores when they were tested three months later.

In a study of marathon runners in Nebraska, continues the medical journal, Heinz Ruddel, M.D., of the University of Bonn, West Germany, and Kay Burta Franz, Ph.D., of Provo, Utah, report that serum magnesium decreased inversely to the increase of serum free fatty acids. They add that the anticipated drop in magnesium stores did not occur in a runner whose free fatty acids had risen the most. However, he had been taking magnesium supplements (370 mg per day).

"Drs. Ruddel and Franz consider it likely that the magnesium deposited in his bones during the premarathon period of supplementation had been mobilized during the exercise," says Mildred Seelig, M.D., M.P.H., the journal's reporter, who is herself an expert on magnesium and other trace minerals.[12]

The Nebraska researchers add that others have found that athletes with higher serum magnesium had a higher VO2 max, and that those who had taken magnesium supplements during training reported that they felt better during recovery after competition.

"These investigators recommend that athletes should receive at least 10 mM of magnesium as a daily supplement. This will allow sufficient magnesium to be deposited in bone to protect against a significant decrease in serum magnesium during long-term aerobic exercise."

In *Eat Better, Live Better*, we are told that the amount of magnesium that we can obtain from our food is dependent on the levels of calcium, protein, phosphorus and vitamin D in the diet.[13] The book adds that some magnesium is lost during the processing of foods.

"Good sources of magnesium such as whole grains, nuts, beans, leafy vegetables and milk should be eaten as part of a diet that is adequate in all other nutrients as well," says the publication, which is from Reader's Digest. "More magnesium is found in hard water than in soft."[13]

Calcium

B. Lawrence Riggs, M.D., of the Mayo Clinic, Rochester, Minnesota, is quoted in *Health News and Review* as saying that, "A famous researcher on osteoporosis once said that senile osteoporosis is a pediatric disease. By that he meant that we should begin preventive measures early in life. It's becoming increasingly clear that by increasing our exercise program we have a greater chance of maintaining bone mass and achieving peak bone mass. Nutrition is also obviously important. We recommend at least 1,500 milligrams of calcium daily during growth years and 1,000 mg a day for adult years as a minimum. Those at greater risk of developing osteoporosis should take more."[14]

In the same article, Evelyn P. Whitlock, M.D., who is in private practice in

Portland, Oregon, says that childhood and teenage years are the most critical in building a healthy skeletal mass. She adds that, since diet surveys show that many teenage girls are favoring soft drinks (high in phosphorus) over milk, we may be setting the stage for virtually all of the women of the next generation to develop osteoporosis. That is because a high-phosphorus diet depletes calcium.

While watching joggers, runners and other athletes during practice and in competition, it is obvious that many of them may be depleting calcium stores through their excessive intake of soft drinks. And, unfortunately, many athletes shun calcium-rich foods, which can help to keep their bones strong. For a listing of some calcium-rich foods, see Table 4.

What's the Best Diet for Athletes?

In an article in *FDA Consumer*, some nutritionists recommend that athletes follow a diet that consists of 30 to 35 percent of their calories as fat; at least 55 percent as carbohydrates; and the remainder as protein.[15]

As an example, the nutrition label for one slice of whole-wheat bread might read:

Protein: 2 grams

Carbohydrate: 14 grams

Fat: 1 gram

"Carbohydrates and protein provide 4 calories per gram and fat provides 9 calories per gram," says the magazine. "Therefore, one slice of this bread provides about 73 calories—8 from protein, 56 from carbohydrates, and 9 from fat. That means about 11 percent of calories come from protein, 77 percent from carbohydrates and 12 percent from fat."[15]

Detailed nutrient content of foods is available in *Nutritive Value of Foods*, Home and Garden Bulletin No. 72, published by the U. S. Department of Agriculture. For a copy write to the Superintendent of Documents, U. S. Government Printing Office, Washington, D. C. 20402.

FDA Consumer quotes Dr. J. R. Brotherhood as saying that there is no magic diet that in itself enhances performance. But, he adds, an incorrect diet will negate much of the hard effort on the training field.

Continues the magazine, "For the athlete, does good nutrition mean consuming more nutrients than non-athletes? Many athletes need more of some nutrients, but the same amount of others. Much depends upon the particular sport. Marathon running, competitive swimming or weight lifting require more calories than less demanding sports. Athletes engaged in these vigorous activities generally need more of the energy-providing nutrients, particularly carbohydrates. Because of increased fluid loss through perspiration, they also need more water and electrolytes (electrically charged chemicals within the body). . . ."[15]

Carbohydrates, protein and fat supply energy, but carbohydrates are the major source of energy during exercise, explains *FDA Consumer*. As an example, carbohydrates furnish the fuel for anaerobic exercise, such as sprinting, where muscles work faster than the heart and lungs can supply them with oxygen.

Table 4
CALCIUM-RICH FOODS

	Measure	*Calories*	**Calcium (mg)**
Dairy			
Cheese			
Blue	1 ounce	100	**150**
Cheddar, cut pieces	1 ounce	115	**204**
Feta	1 ounce	75	**140**
Mozzarella, made with whole milk	1 ounce	80	**147**
Mozzarella, made with part skim milk	1 ounce	80	**207**
Muenster	1 ounce	105	**203**
Parmesan	1 tbsp	25	**69**
Pasteurized process			
American	1 ounce	105	**174**
Swiss	1 ounce	95	**219**
Provolone	1 ounce	100	**214**
Swiss	1 ounce	105	**272**
Cottage Cheese			
Lowfat (2%)	1 cup	205	**155**
Creamed (4% fat)			
Large curd	1 cup	235	**135**
Small curd	1 cup	215	**126**
Milk			
Skim	1 cup	85	**302**
1% fat	1 cup	100	**300**
2% fat	1 cup	120	**297**
Whole (3.3% fat)	1 cup	150	**291**
Buttermilk	1 cup	100	**285**
Dry, nonfat, instant	¼ cup	61	**209**
Yogurt			
Plain, lowfat, with added milk solids	8 ounces	145	**415**
Fruit-flavored, lowfat, with added milk solids	8 ounces	230*	**345***
Plain, whole milk	8 ounces	140	**274**
Dairy Desserts			
Custard, baked	1 cup	305	**297**
Ice cream, vanilla			
Regular (11% fat)			
Hardened	1 cup	270	**176**
Soft serve	1 cup	375	**236**
Ice milk, vanilla			
Hardened, 4% fat	1 cup	185	**176**
Soft serve, 3% fat	1 cup	225	**274**

	Measure	*Calories*	**Calcium (mg)**
Seafood			
Oysters, raw, meat only (13-19 medium)	1 cup	160	**226**
Salmon, pink, canned, *including the bones*	3 ounces	120	**167****
Sardines, Atlantic, canned in oil, drained, *including the bones***	3 ounces	175	**371****
Shrimp, canned, drained, solids	3 ounces	100	**98**
Vegetables			
Bok choy, raw, chopped	1 cup	9	**74**
Broccoli, raw	1 spear	40	**72**
Broccoli, cooked, drained, from raw, ½" pieces	1 cup	45	**177**
Broccoli, cooked, drained, from frozen, chopped	1 cup	50	**94**
Collards, cooked, drained, from frozen	1 cup	60	**357**
Dandelion greens, cooked, drained	1 cup	35	**147**
Kale, cooked, drained, from frozen	1 cup	40	**179**
Mustard greens, without stems and midribs, cooked, drained	1 cup	20	**104**
Turnip greens, chopped, cooked, drained, from frozen	1 cup	50	**249**
Dried Beans			
Cooked, drained			
Great Northern	1 cup	210	**90**
Navy	1 cup	225	**95**
Pinto	1 cup	265	**86**
Chickpeas (garbanzos), cooked, drained	1 cup	270	**80**
Red kidney, canned	1 cup	230	**74**
Refried beans, canned	1 cup	295	**141**
Soy beans, cooked, drained	1 cup	235	**131**
Miscellaneous			
Molasses, cane, blackstrap	2 tbsp	85	**274**
Tofu, 2½" × 2¾" × 1" (about 4 oz.)***	1 piece	85***	**108*****

*These values may vary.
**If the bones are discarded, the amount of calcium is greatly reduced.
***Both of these values may vary, especially the calcium content, depending on how the tofu is made. Tofu processed with calcium salts can have as much as 300 mg calcium per 4 ounces. The label, your grocer, or the manufacturer can provide more specific information.

Source: Home and Garden Bulletin # 72, Human Nutrition Information Service, U.S. Department of Agriculture, 1985.

"The body burns both carbohydrates and fat during aerobic or endurance events (cross-country skiing or running a marathon)—activities in which muscles work slowly, permitting the heart and lungs to meet immediate demands for oxygen," continues the publication. "Initially, carbohydrates supply the bulk of this fuel, but the body obtains more of its energy from fat as aerobic activity continues."[15]

However, muscles do not perform at their best when fueled solely by fat, says *FDA Consumer*. Muscles also require glucose, a form of sugar that circulates in the blood, and glycogen, the form of carbohydrate in which glucose is stored in muscle and the liver. If the glycogen stores are used up, the athlete's performance is reduced. (Since the body requires glucose, many people equate this with eating sugar-rich foods. But the body is fully capable of converting proteins, fats and carbohydrates into glucose.)

"Because the body stashes limited quantities of glycogen—an average of 1,800 calories worth—athletes must continue to replenish their supplies by eating (complex) carbohydrates," says the magazine. "The body harbors enough fat, on the other hand, to supply an average of 140,000 calories. But athletes don't need a high-fat diet to maintain their fat reserves; calories in excess of body needs for carbohydrates, protein and fat are all stored as body fat."[15]

Effects of Sweating

As might be expected, those who exercise lose more water from sweating than does a sedentary person. While inactive people lose a quart of water daily to sweat, athletes engaged in strenuous exercise may lose two to four quarts (four to eight pounds) per *hour*.

The publication goes on to say that as little as 3 percent weight loss from sweating (4.5 pounds for a 150-pound person) causes fatigue and encumbers performance. If there are greater losses, this can lead to a decline in blood circulation, low blood pressure, hallucinations and heat stroke.

Because of the tension of athletic performance and excessive fluid loss, thirst may not always be a signal for a need for water. Therefore, *FDA Consumer* recommends these guidelines from the American Dietetic Association.[15]

1. Two hours before an event, drink three cups of water. Cold water (41°F.) is best, because it leaves the stomach and enters the system more rapidly than warm water.
2. Ten to 15 minutes before the event, drink two more cups of water.
3. Drink small amounts of water—one-half to one cup—at 10 to 15-minute intervals throughout the competition.
4. After competition or training, continue to drink water periodically until weight has been regained.

"To determine water needs, athletes should weigh themselves before and after training and monitor their water intake during the training period," continues the magazine. "For each pound lost, they should drink an extra pint of water."[15]

FDA Consumer quotes the American College of Sports Medicine as saying that runners should avoid large amounts of sugary drinks during races. These beverages decrease the speed at which water leaves the stomach. And athletes should also avoid alcoholic beverages to replace fluid, since alcohol increases fluid loss by stimulating urine production.

"When profuse sweating occurs, the body loses sodium and potassium; these are electrolytes that help maintain fluid balance, metabolize carbohydrates and protein, transmit nerve impulses, and contract muscles," says *FDA Consumer*. "While athletes who perspire profusely may need more sodium and potassium, they seldom require special supplements or beverages to get it. Many foods contain sodium and potassium. Moreover, a well-trained body conserves these minerals. During exercise-induced sweating the kidneys release less sodium; athletes acclimated to hot weather excrete less sodium in their sweat. Extra potassium is released into the blood when the body breaks down glycogen to produce energy."[15]

For athletes who sweat profusely, or who may not be acclimated to hot weather, sodium is available in salted snack foods, ham, pizza, and similar foods, or by adding salt to meals, according to Ann C. Grandjean, nutrition consultant to the University of Nebraska Athletic Department. She adds that potassium is available in apricots, dates, bananas, oranges and raisins.

Does a marathon runner get any benefit from being hosed down as he races? Carl V. Gisolfi, Ph.D., former president of the American College of Sports Medicine, and Professor of Physiology and Biophysics at the University of Iowa, Iowa City, says that drenching the marathoner only provides a psychological boost. The runner is already 100 percent wet from perspiration, he reasons and needs to ingest fluids, not have his skin cooled, reports *Medical Tribune*.[22]

"An individual performing prolonged exercise in a warm environment eventually will get to the point where, if he doesn't replace body fluids and if he's exercising at 60 to 80 percent of his maximum oxygen intake, he's going to be somewhat hyperthermic," Dr. Gisolfi told a sports seminar in New York.[22]

To prevent thermal injury, he adds that body fluids must be replaced, but that only water is necessary until after 90 minutes into exercise. Even after exercise goes on for hours, he continues, there is little evidence that electrolyte replacement is necessary. However, if the athlete becomes dehydrated during prolonged exercise, he may experience relatively low blood sugar and be hypoglycemic, Dr. Gisolfi insists.

Carbohydrate Loading

Some athletes have tried to boost their energy through so-called carbohydrate loading, but such a plan is potentially dangerous, explains *FDA Consumer*.[15] This can cause chest pain and passage of muscle protein in urine. Carbohydrate loading is especially a potential problem for adolescents, heart patients, diabetics and those with high blood fats, the magazine adds. The American Dietetic Association has proposed a modified version, in which athletes reduce their intake of complex carbohydrates (pasta, potatoes, etc.), but not total calories, one week before an event.

"Fatigue occurs, many experts believe, when glycogen supplies are exhausted," continues *FDA Consumer*. "Carbohydrate loading enhances endurance by packing muscles with higher than normal levels of glycogen. A regimen is followed that includes exercising to exhaustion one week before an event to deplete muscles of glycogen, then reducing carbohydrate intake and exercising moderately for three days, and finally 'loading up' on carbohydrate intake and exercising only lightly for four days before the event to replenish glycogen."[15]

Carbo loading was a diet publicized by Ron Hill, the British marathoner of the late 1960s, but Gayle Olinekova, herself a world-class marathoner, is not one of its devotees, she explains in *Go for It!*[16]

Carbohydrate loading would be a disaster for someone with hypoglycemia, such as herself, she says. It can also lead to constipation and dehydration, because carbohydrates need a lot of fluids to be digested and stored as glycogen. To compound the problem, she adds, the athletes who taper off their training prior to the event are not thirsty because they are not sweating and do not feel a need to drink. Thus, they may even be dehydrated by the time they enter the race. Since she is a vegetarian, she increases her fresh fruit and grain intake two to three days before a race, but she cautions that you cannot expect a burst of energy because of the extra carbohydrates.[16]

"Rigorous exercise substantially increases one's need for water, carbohydrates and fats, but only slightly for protein, vitamins and minerals," says Edward Frengille, Jr., a researcher in the Division of Nutritional Sciences at Cornell University, Ithaca, New York. "To help athletes reach peak performance, their daily diet should consist of 55 to 61 percent carbohydrates, 27 to 33 percent fat and 10 to 14 percent protein, along with ample quantities of water."[17]

While preparing for competition or a rigorous workout, Frengille suggests that athletes should limit their intake of salty foods beginning two days before. However, he warns that salt tablets can be dangerous. In the hours before exercise, he continues, fats and proteins should be limited because they take longer to digest than carbohydrates. Foods high in sugar and salt also are no-nos, although complex carbohydrates—cereals, bread, potatoes, pasta, etc.—are recommended. He also approves of skim milk, fruit, lean meat, poultry and fruit juices.

"While it's true that a calorie is a calorie when it comes to adding weight, a calorie is not a calorie when it comes to powering the body," says James McNair in *Power Food*. "Complex carbohydrates offer long-lasting energy; the same calories in simple carbohydrates or sugars are 'empty,' failing to keep the body going. Fats cause foods to taste great, but they add tremendously to the calorie count. By eating fat-free starches or complex carbohydrates with minimal fat added to enhance flavors, you could enjoy a far more filling and satisfying meal, using the same number of calories to provide better performance fuel."[18]

Individual protein requirements are dependent on the amount of lean body tissue present, according to Mackie Shilstone in *Feelin' Good About Fitness*. He is a nutritional consultant for a variety of professional athletes. Fat tissue requires very little protein to keep itself nourished, he says. However, blood, muscles and other metabolically active tissues must be maintained by a continuous supply of amino acids (links of protein) in order to function properly.[19]

"Protein in excess of the amount utilized by the body for daily maintenance and repair is not stored as such, but subsequently converted to glucose and/or stored as fat or excreted," he adds. "The adult requirement for protein may vary from individual to individual (depending upon the level of stress); however, a daily consumption between 50 and 56 grams—on the average—can be considered sufficient."[19]

Brad Hatfield, M.D., of the College of Physical Education, Recreation and Health, University of Maryland, College Park, says that, according to guidelines established by the American College of Sports Medicine, the best fluid to hydrate the body is water. Other fluids can skew the absorption process, he says.[20]

Dr. Hatfield goes on to say that drinks such as Gatorade are only necessary in the most unusual circumstances, such as if it is extremely hot or if the runner/jogger is out of shape. He also recommends that athletes stay away from candy bars, Cokes, etc., prior to exercise, since this can lead to insulin rebound and a sense of weakness. For those who must eat, he recommends whole-wheat bread, cheese and juice three hours before exercising.

As for carbohydrate loading, he says that it has been shown to be effective in increasing performance, but that it also affects the electrolyte balance of heart muscles, resulting in EKG abnormalities. For that reason, carbohydrate loading can be risky, he adds.

Writing in *Nutrition and Mental Illness*, Carl C. Pfeiffer, Ph.D., M.D., of the Brain-Bio Center in Skillman, New Jersey, suggests the following "optimum nutrition" for those who exercise:[20]

1. Chromium GTF, 3 tablets, morning and evening.
2. Vitamin C, 1,000 mg, morning and evening.
3. Dolomite, 2 tablets.
4. Vitamin E, 400 IU, morning.
5. Extra B1, B2 and B3.
6. Zinc (as gluconate), 15 mg, morning and evening.
7. Manganese, 10 mg, morning and evening.
8. Fresh fruit and vegetables; daily legumes.

For those who are not familiar with the Recommended Dietary Allowances for minerals, the Vitamin Nutrition Information Service, Nutley, New Jersey, recommends the RDAs shown in Table 5. Table 6 gives the VNIS RDAs for vitamins.

Judging by animal studies at the USDA's Vitamin and Mineral Nutrition Laboratory, Beltsville Human Nutrition Research Center, in Maryland, marathoners and other long-distance athletes may have more endurance and be more competitive if they have more chromium in their bodies. During the studies, rats that were fed chromium for five weeks depleted significantly less

Table 5

MINERAL SAFETY INDEX

From "Quantitative Evaluation of Vitamin Safety"
Pharmacy Times, May 1985
By John N. Hathcock, Ph.D.

Mineral	Recommended Adult Intake[a]	Minimum Toxic Dose (MTD)	Mineral Safety Index (MSI)
Calcium	1,200 mg	12,000 mg	10
Phosphorus	1,200 mg	12,000 mg	10
Magnesium	400 mg	6,000 mg	15
Iron	18 mg	100 mg	5.5
Zinc	15 mg	500 mg	33
Copper	3 mg	300 mg	33
		3 mg[b]	<1
Fluoride	4 mg	20 mg	5
		4 mg[c]	1
Iodine	0.15 mg	2 mg	13
Selenium	0.2 mg	1 mg	5

a. The highest of the individual Recommended Dietary Allowance (RDA)—except those for pregnancy and lactation—or the U.S. Recommended Daily Allowance, whichever is higher.
b. For people with Wilson's disease.
c. Level producing slight fluprosis of dental enamel.

muscle glycogen during strenuous exercise than the animals that were fed a low-chromium diet, said Richard A. Anderson.[23]

"These athletes prepare for competition by eating a high-carbohydrate diet to stockpile all the glycogen—the storage form of glucose—their muscle tissue will hold," Anderson reported. "But how fast the glycogen disappears during competition may determine who finishes first—or who finishes at all."

Vitamin E

Several recent studies have shown that vigorous exercise by marathoners, skiiers, mountain climbers and others who exercise to exhaustion, especially in polluted air, can experience damage to body cells if their vitamin E levels are too low.[24] As we breathe, molecular byproducts such as free radicals result in oxidative damage and can lead to such degenerative diseases as cancer, aging, arthritis, heart disease and cataracts. During strenuous exercise, we consume 10 to 20 times more oxygen than normally. And the more oxygen we use, the greater are the chances of cell damage from free radicals.

Lester Packer, Ph.D., of the University of California, Berkeley, points out

Table 6
VITAMIN SAFETY INDEX

From "Quantitative Evaluation of Vitamin Safety,"
Pharmacy Times, May 1985
By John N. Hathcock, Ph.D.

Vitamin	Recommended Adult Intake[a]	Minimum Toxic Dose (MTD)	Vitamin Safety Index (VSI)
Vitamin A	5,000 IU	25,000 to 50,000 IU	5 to 10
Vitamin D	400 IU	50,000 IU	125
		1,000 to 2,000 IU[b]	2.5 to 5
Vitamin E	30 IU	1,200 IU	40
Vitamin C	60 mg	2,000 to 5,000 mg	33 to 83
		1,000 mg[c]	17
Thiamin (B₁)	1.5 mg	300 mg	200
Riboflavin	1.7 mg	1,000 mg	588
Niacin	20 mg	1,000 mg	50
Pyridoxine (B₆)	2.2 mg	2,000 mg	900
		200 mg[d]	90
Folacin	0.4 mg	400 mg	1,000
		15 mg[e]	37
Biotin	0.3 mg	50 mg	167
Pantothenic Acid	10 mg	10,000 mg	1,000

a. The highest of the individual Recommended Dietary Allowance (RDA)—except those for pregnancy and lactation—or the U.S. Recommended Daily Allowance, whichever is higher.
Lower MTD's are identified for special circumstances:
b. For infants and also for adults with certain infections or metabolic diseases; 50,000 IU for most adults.
c. To produce slightly altered mineral excretion patterns.
d. For antagonism of some drugs; 2,000 mg for most adults.
e. For antagonism of anticonvulsants in epileptics; 400 mg for most adults. The RDA for vitamin B12, not included in the chart, is 2 mcg daily.

Courtesy of Vitamin Nutrition Information Service, Hoffmann-La Roche Inc., Nutley, New Jersey.

that the body has antioxidant defense systems such as enzymes and nutrients that protect us from oxidative cell damage. But he has found that for runners and cyclists the body's antioxidant stores are used up more quickly during exercise. An increase in certain nutrients, especially vitamin E, bolsters the antioxidant defenses and minimizes damage to our cells, he says.

In another study, which involved strenuous exercise by male college students, Satoshi Sumida and colleagues reported in the *International Journal of*

Biochemistry that vitamin E supplements also minimize cell damage from free radicals.[25]

Although many nutrition writers downgrade the need for vitamins and minerals for athletes, it is obvious from the material reviewed here that extra nutrients can benefit some runners, joggers and other athletes to counteract the stress of strenuous events and to minimize minor injuries and serious illness. Those nutritionists who fail to recognize the need for extra nutrients for some athletes have either not read the literature or are basing their convictions on limited trial studies. Of course, a detailed analysis of the special nutrient requirements for athletes would require another book.

References

1. Robert Lipsyte, "What Price Exercise?" *The New York Times Magazine* (February 16, 1986).

2. "Shortage of Iron Could Be a Problem for the Physically Active," *Superfit,* press release (May 9, 1985).

3. Frank Murray, "Iron Deficiency Poses Serious Health Problems," *Better Nutrition* (November 1987), pp. 8-9.

4. "Nutrition for the Recreational Athlete: The Fallacies, The Facts," press briefing, Waldorf-Astoria Hotel, New York, N. Y. (October 7, 1983).

5. Frank Murray, *Program Your Heart for Health* (New York: Larchmont Books, 1979), p. 139.

6. Ruth Adams, "Athletes Need Nourishing Food," *Better Nutrition* (June 1984), pp. 15-17.

7. Michael Colgan, Ph.D., *Your Personal Vitamin Profile* (New York: William Morrow and Co., Inc., 1982), pp. 97-112.

8. "Women Who Exercise Need More B-Vitamin," press briefing, The American Chemical Society meeting, St. Louis, Mo. (April 10, 1984).

9. Thomas Kirk Cureton, Ph.D. *The Physiological Effects of Wheat Germ Oil on Humans in Exercise* (Springfield, Ill.: Charles C Thomas Publishers, 1972).

10. Linda Strause, Ph.D., and Paul Saltman, Ph.D., "Role of Manganese in Bone Metabolism." ACS Symposium Series 354, *Nutritional Bioavailability of Manganese,* Constance Kies, editor (Washington, D.C.: American Chemical Society, 1987), pp. 46-55.

11. J. Ratoff, "Reasons for Boning Up on Manganese," *Science News* (September 27, 1986), p. 199.

12. Mildred Seelig, M.D., M.P.H., "Magnesium, Exercise and Stress," *Medical Tribune* (July 23, 1986), p. 42.

13. *Reader's Digest Eat Better, Live Better* (Pleasantville, N.Y.: The Reader's Digest Association, Inc., 1982), p. 45.

14. John Mitchell, "Osteoporosis: It Takes More Than Calcium to Preserve Bone Health," *Health News & Review* (January/February 1988), pp. 1, 10.

15. Doug Henderson, "Nutrition and the Athlete," *FDA Consumer* reprint (May 1987).

16. Gayle Olinekova, *Go for It!* (New York: Simon and Schuster, 1982), pp. 158-159.

17. Susan S. Lang, "Athlete's Body Burns Carbohydrates, Fats and Water," *Cooperative Extension News,* Cornell University (December 13, 1984).

18. James McNair, *Power Food* (San Francisco: Chronicle Books, 1986), p. 16.

19. Mackie Shilstone, *Mackie Shilstone's Feelin' Good About Fitness* (Gretna, La: Pelican Publishing Company, 1986), pp. 67-68.

20. Carl C. Pfeiffer, Ph.D., M.D., *Nutrition and Mental Illness* (Rochester, Vt: Healing Arts Press, 1987), p. 103.

21. Timothy J. McDonough, Associate Editor, Public Information, University of Maryland, personal letter (January 11, 1988).

22. James Trager, "Who Needs an Electrolyte Boost?" *Medical Tribune* (September 2, 1987), pp. 3, 14.

23. *Quarterly Report of Selected Research Projects*, United States Department of Agriculture/Agricultural Research Service (January 1 to March 31, 1989), p. 10.

24. Blitz, Caron, "Vitamin E Prevents Cell Damage Caused by Exercise," *Henkel News* (December 27, 1989).

25. Satoshi Sumida, et al., "Exercise-Induced Lipid Peroxidation and Leakage of Enzymes Before and After Vitamin E Supplementation," *International Journal of Biochemistry* (Vol. 21, 1989), pp. 835-838.

Chapter 8

Warmups and Cooldowns

Even though you may have chosen the ideal pair of shoes for your sport, and you are wearing the most comfortable and fashionable attire, you are still susceptible to injuries, pain, nausea, day-after soreness and other complications unless you warm up your body properly before a workout or competition and follow with a suitable cooldown afterwards. Just as trainers insist that a racehorse be given a cooldown period before it is returned to its stall, so must a jogger or runner gradually return his or her body to its preexercise state.

Unfortunately, many athletes give short shrift to a warmup and cooldown period, often jerking their muscles around and speeding up their warmup routines so that they do more harm than good. Muscle should be warmed up gradually, not as though you are jerking on a rope. Coaches, trainers and other professionals can suggest warmup and cooldown exercises especially for you. Also helpful will be local teachers of the Alexander Technique and the Feldenkrais Method. Although these techniques are usually tailored for performers such as ballet dancers, singers and actors, they can be especially useful for developing warmups that suit your body and personality. One of the advantages of these techniques is that the muscles are moved so slowly that you can hardly see the arm or leg moving. Obviously, a gradual warming up of muscles—although time consuming—will benefit greatly in the long run. Teachers of these techniques are listed under the names of those methods in local phone books. Or, for names and addresses of the nearest teachers, you can write to the North American Society for Teachers of the Alexander Technique, P.O. Box 148026, Chicago, Illinois 60614 (tel., 312-472-2404), or the Feldenkrais Guild, P. O. Box 11145, San Francisco, California 94101.

Since the body contains over 600 muscles (including the heart, a muscular pump), warmups and cooldowns can be somewhat complicated, depending on your sport or activity. If some of these hundreds of muscles are not properly warmed up before a workout or competition, it can spell trouble, not only for the immediate event but perhaps for months or years ahead. Improper warmup might easily end your jogging or running career and relegate you to being a Monday-Morning Quarterback. As you know, joggers and runners often explain to you in rather vivid detail the various injuries that have sidelined them. No doubt, better warmups, cooldowns, proper nutrition and other measures could drastically reduce the number of such injuries.

Why Warm Up First?

"An adequate warmup appears to prevent injuries (pulls and tears) to the muscles, tendons, ligaments and other connective tissues," explains Frank G. Shellock, Ph.D., Cedars-Sinai Medical Center, Los Angeles, California, writing in *The Physician and Sportsmedicine*.[1] "Muscle elasticity depends on blood saturation, so cold muscles, which have a low blood saturation, may be more susceptible to damage than warm muscles. In addition, the flexibility of the tendons and ligaments also appears to be affected by temperature. For these reasons it is recommended that athletes stretch only after warming up. Damage to connective tissue might occur if an athlete stretches excessively when the tissue temperatures are comparatively low. Although there are few objective experimental data to support the idea that warming up reduces the risk of injury, the evidence suggests that prudent physicians and trainers advise athletes to do some low-intensity, preliminary work before more strenuous activity."[1]

Dr. Shellock adds that the effects of temperature are probably more important in warming up than the acceleration of the respiratory and cardiovascular system and increases in hormone levels. In addition, he continues, an increase in temperature also reduces the internal viscosity of muscle protoplasm, which enhances the mechanical efficiency of the exercised muscles. Also, muscular contraction is accelerated when the muscle temperature (which increases as you warm up) is slightly higher than the body temperature.

"Conversely," he adds, "muscle temperatures below the normal body temperature increase muscle viscosity, making muscles sluggish and weak. Higher temperatures also facilitate the transmission speed of nervous impulses and increase the sensitivity of the nerve receptors. This allows an individual to move more quickly, and because coordination is believed to be augmented, more purposefully."[1]

The intensity and duration of the warmup period should be tailored to the athlete's capabilities and his or her sport, Dr. Shellock continues. For a regular athlete, a 15-minute jog may suffice. But for an Olympic-caliber athlete, 30 minutes of moderate to heavy running may be necessary while preparing for a 200-meter race. During a typical warmup, the rectal temperature should increase by from 1 to 2°C. And, he says, sweating is generally a good guide as to the effectiveness of a warm-up. On the other hand, a warmup that is too strenuous is counterproductive, since the athlete may be pooped before the event begins. The body generally returns to its normal temperature following about 45 minutes of rest. For additional information about warmups, contact Dr. Shellock at the Department of Cardiology, Cedars-Sinai Medical Center, 8700 Beverly Blvd., Los Angeles, California 90048.

Increased flexibility through stretching exercises may decrease the number of musculotendinous injuries, diminish and alleviate muscle soreness and enhance athletic performance, according to John E. Beaulieu, M.A., in *The Physician and Sportsmedicine*.[2] He adds that studies for various sports suggest that the more flexible athletes are usually the better performers.

Stretching Techniques

According to Beaulieu, the four most popular stretching techniques practiced by athletes are: ballistic; passive; contract reflex, a modified version of the proprioceptive neuromuscular facilitation technique; and static. He goes on to say that no one of these techniques is preferable to any of the others but that some of them contribute to a greater risk of injury. This is a capsule description of the four techniques:

Ballistic. Performed with a jerking and bouncing motion, this is the least desirable stretching technique. The tension created in a muscle with this method is more than double that of a slow, gentle stretch. When athletes stretch a muscle against this amount of tension, this increases the possibility of an injury to the muscles and tendons.

Passive: Also called partner stretches, this stretching uses external force to increase flexibility, Beaulieu continues. Normally, another person applies more pressure to the area that is being stretched. Unfortunately, he adds, when done carelessly or improperly, this can extend the muscles and tendons beyond their limits and can result in an injury.

Contract reflex: With this method, a muscle is isometrically contracted for five to ten seconds before it is stretched. It is assumed that the prestretch contraction causes the Golgi organ, which is that portion of the cell where proteins are packaged for transport, to fire and relax a muscle. Again, with these stretching exercises, injury can occur if they are done incorrectly.

Static: With the static method, the stretch position is assumed gradually and held for 30 to 60 seconds. Therefore, the contraction from the stretch reflex is slow and mild. "As the position is held," adds Beaulieu, "the tension from the stretch and stretch reflex contraction becomes strong enough to invoke the inverse stretch reflex, which signals the muscle to relax and be stretched farther safely. When this happens, the athlete gains greater flexibility. Compared to other techniques, static stretching produces the least amount of tension and is the safest method of improving flexibility. It should be used in athletic training, because when done correctly, the chances of musculo-tendinous injury are very low."[2]

He goes on to say that athletes who do not begin to stretch until their season begins will have minimal benefits—if any—for the remainder of their season. Therefore, a daily, year-round stretching program is recommended. If that is not feasible, at least begin those pretraining stretches a minimum of six weeks before the training season begins.

"The muscle groups should be alternated throughout the stretching routine," continues Beaulieu. "For example, if a routine begins with a mild hamstring stretching exercise, the next exercise should be for some other muscle group. Another hamstring exercise should come later and place a little more force on the muscle than the first. Spacing the exercises will prevent the possibility of exerting too much force on a muscle at one time, thus further reducing the chances of injury. Some shoulder and back exercises are exceptions."[2]

He adds that the stretching position should be assumed slowly and gently until tightness, not pain, is felt. Then hold it for 30 to 60 seconds. If exercises are held for less than 30 seconds, they will generally not cause the muscle to be relaxed, he says.

The Physician and Sportsmedicine recommends that runners and joggers wear sweats while warming up and stretching, and that an ideal prestretch warmup consists of a light jog for five to eight minutes, followed by 30 four-count jumping jacks. Also recommended is jumping rope for five to eight minutes.

In designing exercises for joggers and runners, Beaulieu does not recommend The Plow, which places too much strain on the lower back; touching the toes, which places too much stress on the spine and lower back muscles; throwing a leg up against a wall and bending, which is tailor-made for injuries; or pulling back on the leg, either from the front or back, which can damage the knee. For answers to additional questions on stretching, write to John E. Beaulieu, 615 West N St., Springfield, Oregon 97477.

"Runners particularly benefit from warmup exercises, as running incorporates only a limited range of movements," says *The Complete Manual of Fitness and Well-Being*.[3] "To warm up, use the swing through, body twists, body circles and wall stretch, which put the big muscle groups through a variety of motions. Gradually increase the duration of each exercise so that you give each muscle a stretch lasting 30 seconds or more."

The Manual adds that many athletes tend to overdo their beginning exercises before complete blood flow is realized through the muscles.

Following strenuous exercise, you need to gradually bring your body back to normal, otherwise the body can go into shock and muscles can shorten. This results in stiffness and loss of flexibility, the book explains.

Writing in *The Runner's Handbook*, Bob Glover and Jack Shepherd report that the cooldown, which should incorporate cardiorespiratory, cooldown and stretching, is basically a warmup in reverse.[4] The runners who skip a cooldown are more prone to injury because they haven't given their muscles sufficient time to relax, they continue.

After a run, suggest the authors, walk for about five minutes but avoid push-ups and sit-ups, which are usually part of the warmup routine. The cooldown further insures normal blood flow throughout the body and it helps to return your heart beat to under 100 beats per minute.

In addition, add Dianne Hales and Lt. Col. Robert E. Hales, M.D., in the *U.S. Army Total Fitness Program*, a five- to ten-minute cooldown prevents blood from "pooling" in your legs.[5] This, they say, deprives your heart and brain of oxygen and can result in dizziness and nausea. However, they believe that some stretching exercises repeated from the warmup will inhibit stiffness and soreness the following day.

Like many authorities, Allan Lawrence and Mark Scheid, in *The Self-Coached Runner*, believe that jogging in a slow fashion for one mile is a suitable warmup.[6] If you are running in spikes, then change into training flats, they suggest. And as you jog, make an effort to press your heels into the track to stretch the Achilles tendons.

It takes 15 minutes of vigorous exercise to increase muscle blood-flow and to raise muscle temperature to 103° F., the ideal level for peak performance, according to Richard Mangi, M.D., Peter Jekl, M.D., and O. William Dayton, ATC, in *Sports Fitness and Training*.[7] They remind athletes to warm up all of the major muscle groups in legs, arms, back, hips and trunk.

They go on to say that you should begin gentle stretching, followed by perhaps jogging, slow cycling or swinging your racquet if preparing for those sports. Push-ups and jumping jacks are next in order. Increase the tempo until you are perspiring, and you can conclude the warmup with some stretching exercises that you favor. The cooldown, which helps to remove excess lactic acid from the muscles, can conclude with a brisk walk, some simple calisthenics, your favorite stretching exercise and then a warm shower, they add. (Lactic acid is a colorless, syrup-like acid that is a waste product of sugar oxidation. A build-up of this acid can make you very tired).

During the warmup and cooldown, you can avoid getting overheated by wearing clothes that let you breathe, says Pekka Antero Mooar, M.D., Director of Delaware Valley Sports Medicine Center and Assistant Professor of Orthopedic Surgery at the Medical College of Pennsylvania, Philadelphia.[8] Sweatsuits are perfect, he adds, since they allow you to loosen up and break into a slight sweat.

"Another way to help yourself adjust and adapt to resuming your recreational sports during a winter break is to listen to your body when it talks to you," he continues. "If you're in pain, for example (your elbow, knee, back or shoulder hurt) then you've probably over-used your body. Don't ignore the pain; let it be your guide. Being over-confident and shrugging off pain and discomfort is risky because many individuals turn out to be suffering from problems which can become chronic ones if not checked out and cared for immediately."[8]

Saunas and Steam Rooms

After a strenuous workout, some athletes head for the sauna, whirlpool or steam room, but these therapies are not for everyone, according to Robert Kerlan, M.D., and Ronald B. Mackenzie, M.D., M.P.H.[9] An orthopedic surgeon, Dr. Kerlan is a consultant to the Los Angeles Kings, Lakers and Rams and the California Angels. Dr. Mackenzie is director of the National Athletic Health Institute, Inglewood, California.

Although these après-workout therapies are great for socializing, they are also great places for getting a bacterial skin infection, the herpes virus or a mild case of Legionnaires' disease if the hot tub is not properly maintained. The sudden temperature change as you enter a sauna or steam room can be fatal to someone with a heart problem. Changing from a hot-to-cold temperature and back and forth as you come and go can increase your heart rate by 60 percent, the same as moderate exercise, they say. In addition, as your body adjusts to a higher temperature, your blood pressure goes down. This can cause faintness in susceptible people. For someone over 50, with a mild heart condition or hardening of the arteries, the drop in blood pressure could precipitate a mild stroke, the authors continue. And pregnant women are urged to consult their physician before using a sauna, steam room or whirlpool, because remaining in this heat for over 40 minutes can possibly cause infant malformation.

For novices, the authors recommend that they spend six minutes or less in these devices; veterans should restrict their stay to 15 minutes. They advise that the temperature should not be over 190° in the sauna or over 120° in the steam room. If you feel faint, get out as soon as possible. In any case, afterward drink a lot of water or other liquid to replace the fluid you have lost and shower and shampoo to remove salts, acids, metals or chemical residues. Then apply a moisturizer to your skin.

Of course, these therapies are beneficial for those who do not have any health problems. In a dry sauna, you can sweat off 17 ounces of water and toxic metals in one session. At the same time you use up 300 calories. Warm heat also relaxes tight muscles and soothes sore joints. The whirlpool jets can massage away muscle soreness, they add.

"People with diabetes, vascular problems, hypertension, obesity, kidney dysfunctions, metabolic conditions such as hypo- or hyperthyroidism, or anyone on daily medication should consult with a physician before using a sauna or steam room," they report.[9]

They go on to say that those with very dry skin or a tendency to prickly heat or skin rashes should probably avoid these high-heat therapies. In addition, asthmatics can have difficulty breathing the hot, dry air. During a session in a sauna, you can lose almost two pounds of water, which should be replaced as soon as you get out.

References

1. Frank G. Shellock, Ph.D., "Physiological Benefits of Warm-Up," *The Physician and Sportsmedicine* (Vol. 11, No. 10, October 1983), pp. 134-139.

2. John E. Beaulieu, M.A., "Developing a Stretching Program," *The Physician and Sportsmedicine* (Vol. 9, No. 11, November 1981), pp. 59-69.

3. *The Complete Manual of Fitness and Well-Being* (Pleasantville, N.Y.: The Reader's Digest Association, Inc., 1988), pp. 106-107.

4. Bob Glover and Jack Shepherd, *The Runner's Handbook* (New York: Penguin Books, 1985), pp. 21-22.

5. Dianne Hales and Lt. Col. Robert E. Hales, M.D., *U. S. Army Total Fitness Program* (New York: Crown Publishers, Inc., 1985), pp. 17-24.

6. Allan Lawrence and Mark Scheid, *The Self-Coached Runner* (Boston: Little Brown and Company, 1984), p. 91.

7. Richard Mangi, M.D., Peter Jekl, M.D., and O. William Dayton, ATC, *Sports Fitness and Training* (New York: Pantheon Books, 1987), pp. 48-49.

8. Pekka Antero Mooar, M.D., "Spring into Training," Health Memo from The Medical College of Pennsylvania, Philadelphia, undated.

9. Robert Kerlan, M.D., and Ronald B. Mackenzie, M.D., M.P.H., "Temperature's Rising," *Shape* (September 1987), p. 26.

Chapter 9

You Haven't Got Time for the Pain

In a review of the clinical records of 1,650 patients seen between 1978 and 1980 by two sports physicians, 1,819 injuries were identified. Although men comprised 59.8 percent of the total patients, women under the age of 30 seemed to have the greatest risk of overuse running injuries, according to D.B. Clement, MSc., M.D.[1]

Dr. Clement and colleagues at the University of British Columbia in Vancouver found that the knee was the most frequently injured part of the body, accounting for 41.7 percent of the injuries. Although all anatomical parts of the body were equally susceptible to injury in both males and females, the least frequently involved areas were the lower back (3.7 percent) and the upper leg (3.6 percent).

"Patellofemoral pain syndrome was the most frequent disorder, accounting for 25.8 percent of all injuries," say the researchers. "Most patients had moderate to severe varus (bowleg) alignment and subsequent functional overpronation. Certain injuries were more frequent in one sex or the other, so we believe that our results should prompt other authors to differentiate incidence of injuries by sex in the future."[1]

The researchers listed the ten most common injuries in runners as:[1]

1. Patellofemoral pain syndrome.
2. Tibial stress syndrome (shinbone).
3. Achilles peritendinitis (heel).
4. Plantar fasciitis (foot).
5. Patellar tendinitis (kneecap).
6. Iliotibial band friction syndrome (pelvis).
7. Metatarsal stress syndrome (foot).
8. Tibial stress fracture (shinbone).
9. Tiabialis posterior tendinitis.
10. Peroneal tendinitis (nerves, muscles and blood vessels of the outer side of the leg).

Causes of injuries, as reported in an earlier study by S. L. James, et al., in the *American Journal of Sports Medicine* in 1978, were: 1) training errors; 2) anatomical factors; 3) running shoes; and 4) training surfaces. These Canadian researchers report that the training errors included high-intensity training without alternate days which were not so stressful; a sudden increase in training mileage and/or intensity without permitting the supporting structures of the lower extremities enough time to adapt to the increased work load; a single quite severe training session; a stressful competitive session, such as a 10K race or a marathon; repetitive hill running.

"Anatomical factors included leg-length discrepancy; femoral neck anteversion; quadriceps and hamstring insufficiency (poor flexibility and/or muscle dysfunction compared with the asymptomatic leg); genu valgum (knock-knees or bowlegs), varum (misalignment of a bone or joint) and recurvatum (curved or bent structure); excessive Q-angle (greater than 15 degrees); patella alta; tibial torsion; tibial varum; gastrocnemius/soleus insufficiency; lower leg-heel and/or heel-forefoot malalignment; pes cavus (a foot with an exaggerated arch, sometimes associated with claw toes); pes planus (flatfoot); and structural irregularities of the toes such as Morton's foot, hallux valgus (sideways turning of the big toe), and metatarsal adductovarus (plantarflexed first toe)," the researchers report.

They go on to say that factors implicating running shoes included inadequate heel wedging; soft, loose-fitting heel counters; inflexible soles under the metatarsal heads; narrow toe boxes; excessive lateral heel wear; improper application of sole repair material; and the removal or breakdown of orthotics.

Other factors contributing to injuries included hard surfaces, road camber (uneven terrain) and hills.

"Treatment consisted of combinations of modified rest (symptomatic reduction in training volume and intensity supplemented by weight training, swimming and cycling), ice massage, local physiotherapy, anti-inflammatory medication, soft and rigid orthotics, modification or change of shoe, and where indicated, surgery," according to the researchers. "Often running had to be stopped until symptoms disappeared or the injury healed. The runner could usually continue cardiovascular training by swimming or cycling," they add.

Writing in *Aches and Pains of Running*, Lowell Scott Weil, D.P.M., says that "runner's knee," a catch-all term for all knee problems associated with running, can be caused by a congenital malposition of the kneecap, looseness of the ligaments or a number of disorders related to the cartilage structures within the knees.[2] However, the most common cause of painful knees is excessive pronation of the foot, even though some pronation (the inward roll of the foot) is required for shock absorption. She adds that excessive pronation can be caused by tightness of the heel cord or running on angulated surfaces, such as running against the traffic when the right foot is forced into a pronated position.

Some solutions, suggests Dr. Weil, include rubber pads put in the arch of the shoe by the manufacturer; several layers of tissue in the arch area; over-the-counter arch supports; or a new pair of shoes.

"If the knee condition is severe, a neutral-position sports orthosis for the shoe may be necessary to control excessive pronation," adds Dr. Weil. "At the same time, graduated weight lifting should be started to strengthen thigh muscles. If symptoms persist past the self-treatment stage, a sports-medicine specialist should be consulted."[2]

Dr. Weil adds that some people are born with a tight Achilles tendon, which often causes them to walk with a bouncy gait as though they are walking on their toes. Such a problem causes both tendinitis and severe pronation, she says.

"Other people susceptible to Achilles tendinitis are those with a very narrow cord-like Achilles tendon," she continues. "Although we've yet to see a complete rupture of the Achilles tendon in long-distance runners, many do have chronic thickening and bumps around the covering of the tendon caused by microruptures or chronic inflammation of the tendon."[2]

The proper treatment, she says, is adequate flexing and stretching of the calf muscles and Achilles tendon. She recommends that runners push against a wall with the feet about three feet from it. Another exercise is to stand with the balls of the feet on a step and let the heels hang over, allowing the weight of the body to pull the heels down and stretch the Achilles tendon. Such exercises should be part of both the warmup and cooldown.

For those afflicted with Achilles tendinitis, Dr. Weil recommends that they buy running shoes that have the highest heel and the most flexible sole. Extra padding inside the shoe under your heel will also lessen the pull on the Achilles tendon, she adds.

"Local treatment consists of ice massage directly over the tendon area after running," Dr. Weil says. "Be sure to avoid low heels in street shoes. Don't attempt to run until you can walk without pain. And if the condition continues, see a sports-medicine specialist. Do not consider cortisone injection. Recent research indicates that cortisone around the Achilles tendon can create more harm than good."[2]

Shin splint tendinitis involves pain at the front and inside of the leg. Dr. Weil says that shin splints can be caused by running on hard surfaces, overstriding, muscle imbalance, or overuse of the muscles and tendons secondary to pronation. She reports that a change in training technique, a switch to a different running surface, or the use of a neutral-position sports orthosis will often help this problem.

Dr. Weil says that runner's heel is not as great a problem as it used to be, even though the heel makes 15,000 heel strikes at a force three times that of gravity during a 10-mile run. Shoe manufacturers have come to the rescue, she adds, by designing running shoes with a flared heel, good shock absorption, cushioning and heel elevation.

"However," she continues, "plantar fasciitis and heel spur continue to occur. Both are caused by pulling of a large ligament attached from the front of the foot to the heel and running along the arch. The condition can worsen if you have abnormal foot structure that causes overpull of the ligament. As for treatment, a large piece of foam rubber in the heel of the shoe sometimes relieves the condition. Otherwise, a sports orthosis is recommended."[2]

Ice cubes are ideal for applying to any sore area, Dr. Weil suggests. Have some water-filled Dixie cups in the freezer for emergencies. For sore knees and muscles, keep some water-soaked Ace bandages in the freezer, she says.

Following ice therapy, stretch a stiff or sore muscle to bring back range of motion. Although she does not discuss it, the stretching should be gradual and not jerky. Tight muscles will respond more quickly to a gentle stretching.

Dr. Weil, who is director of the Sports Medicine Center for the Dr. William M. Scholl College of Podiatric Medicine, and team podiatrist for the Chicago Bears, among others, is one of the few sports-medicine doctors to recommend that, if runners do not have a track, they should opt for asphalt or concrete rather than grass. She reasons that anyone running on grass can fall victim to unseen gullies and holes, rocks, and the like, which can be as damaging as harder surfaces. In addition, grass runners have to continuously look where they are running, which impedes their workout.

In his informative booklet, *Knee Pain and the Runner*, Ronald Green, D.P.M., says that there are so many complaints about "runner's knee" because the knee joint is a very complex structure, consisting of many muscles, tendons, ligaments, bursas, cartilage and other connective tissue.[3] The pain is usually around or under the kneecap, and it is usually most noticeable during or after a run. It is aggravated by hills, especially downhill, he says.

The medical term for this problem is chondromalacia patella, meaning a softening of the underside of the patella or kneecap. The diagnosis involves other complications, such as patellar tendinitis (tendinitis of the tendon coming into and away from the kneecap), patellar bursitis and other syndromes. Causes of this type of pain in runners, says Dr. Green, include an overstress syndrome brought about by stepped-up mileage or pace, a change in running shoes or running surface, or wearing worn-out shoes. Also, a previous knee injury that caused a loss of quadriceps muscle tone may have altered knee function, he adds.

"Often runners with knee pain have structural variations from the 'ideal' normal," continues Dr. Green. "Curving in of the leg bone (bowlegs or tibial varum) is common in runners, as is calcaneal (heel bone) varum. In either case, foot strike is toward the outside of the heel because the bone curves inward. As the weight comes down over the full length of the foot, body weight can't be maintained on the outside of the heel and the foot sags inward as the weight transfers inward. This causes the arch to come down more than it normally should (excessive pronation). When the foot excessively pronates, the entire leg and thigh turn inward as well, and this puts a 'torque' on the knee joint."[3]

Since the kneecap rides in a tendon, says Dr. Green, when the foot pronates and the leg turns in, the kneecap is unable to turn in tandem, so that it can slip slightly out of its bony groove on the leg and thigh bones. It slips a bit with each step, thus bringing on the aching pain.

In addition to echoing Dr. Weil's recommendations of cutting back on mileage and hill work, and applying ice packs before and after running, Dr. Green recommends specific quadriceps strengthening exercises using weights if there is no pain while running lightly. He recommends that the runner begin with three to five pounds of weight hung over the foot, and that the knee be held absolutely straight during the exercise.

"Lift the entire limb and hold for a slow count of 15," advises Dr. Green. "Repeat the exercise until the muscle is fatigued (there should be no burning or pain from the muscle). Adding a soft arch support or padding to the inside shoe may give some foot control and relieve mild symptoms.''

To prevent knee problems, Dr. Green recommends that runners regularly stretch the muscles in the back of the leg and thigh. If there has been a previous knee injury, a flexed-knee position may not be advisable. In addition, he says, follow these simple rules:

1. Don't increase mileage or pace more than 10 percent per week.
2. Don't wear worn-out running shoes.
3. If you're running on a slanted surface such as the side of a road, alternate sides every mile or so.
4. Alternate days of hard and easy training.
5. If you hurt, decrease your pace and mileage.
6. If this doesn't help—rest.

Runners who do not take sufficient time off following a marathon may be setting themselves up for injury or impaired performance, according to *Runner's World*.[4] Based on studies of highly trained male runners, researchers at Ball State University, Muncie, Indiana, and Ohio State University, Columbus, concluded that the ideal postmarathon recovery period is one week. They report that runners who rested completely, with no running for 6 days, recovered leg strength and work capacity more quickly than the athletes who jogged for 20 to 45 minutes during the first six days after the marathon. Swimming, walking, bicycling and other light workouts are permissible.

A runners' clinic conducted by William A. Grana, M.D., of the Oklahoma Center for Athletes, and Thomas C. Coniglione, M.D., of the St. Anthony Hospital Runner's Clinic, Oklahoma City, was established to evaluate and treat the problems of runners who run 20 or more miles per week. Of the 161 patients treated during the clinic's first year of operation, 49 had disorders of one or both knees; 15 had patellofemoral pain; 14 reported iliotibial band pain (this band is a group of hip-to-knee fibers that cover a fluid-like sac called a bursa; persistent pounding on slanted surfaces or overtraining can irritate the bursa); 20 complained of medial or lateral pain; and others had malalignment problems or other pre-existing problems.[5]

"We found the most common complaint to be iliotibial band pain, which occurred in 15 patients (18 knees, 30 percent), followed by patellofemoral pain, which occurred in 14 patients (16 knees, 29 percent),'' say the authors. "Other authors have noted this pattern of iliotibial band tendinitis as well as its association with training error, high running mileage and genu varum. Ten of the 16 knees with iliotibial band syndrome had a varum alignment, and 11 of these patients were running more than five miles each workout. Although Noble reported the need for surgery in such cases, our patients' symptoms were resolved with nonoperative measures, or they simply altered activity enough to relieve symptoms.''[5]

At one time doctors believed that chronic heel pain was due to bone "spurs,'' which were thought to be the result of calcium deposits. The current theory is that this pain is caused by tiny stress fractures, according to *Prevention*. With the aid of bone scans and tomography (varying depth X-rays), physicians are now able to determine the origin of heel pain. This procedure should help to eliminate unnecessary foot surgery, says Charles Graham, M.D., of the University of Texas Health Science Center, Dallas.[6]

"We know now that bone spurs usually don't cause pain, and so don't need to be removed," says Dr. Graham. "And for stress fractures, walking and stretching exercises and a heel pad in your shoe are all you need."[6]

If an orthopedic problem persists, it might be caused by an unsuspected malignant or benign tumor, according to a study by M. M. Lewis and J. F. Reilly reported in the *American Journal of Sports Medicine*.[7] In studying 36 athletes ranging in age from 10 to 46—who had initially reported torn ligaments, chronic sprained ankles and other problems—the researchers found that 18 of the patients had cancerous bone or soft-tissue tumors (Ewing's sarcoma, osteosarcoma, synovial sarcoma), while 18 had non-cancerous tumors (giant cell tumors of bone, chondroblastoma, and osteoid osteoma).

For some minor foot problems, podiatrists are now inserting a collagen gel under the skin as a semipermanent buffer to relieve pain, reports *Runner's World*.[8] Injected beneath the skin to form a cushion between the skin and bone, the implant lasts between 6 and 18 months, according to John Pagliano, D.P.M., former president of the American Academy of Podiatric Sports Medicine.

These implants are recommended for troublesome corns and calluses and other minor foot problems that often require surgery. The procedure is less painful and sometimes less expensive than surgery, explains Dr. Pagliano, although collagen inserts can range from $150 to $500, depending on the problem.

Writing in the *American Journal of Sports Medicine*, L.D. Lutter says that surgery can often alleviate heel pain but that it may not allow the athlete to return to a high-level performance.[9] After studying 182 athletes, Lutter recommends that those with heel pain should try rest, physiotherapy and orthotics before resorting to surgery.

A 29-year-old female runner asked *The Runner* how soon she could resume running following ligament reconstruction on her right ankle.[10] She was out of the cast and could walk with only minor pain. She was advised to continue walking and to forego any other exercises for the time being. In addition, it was suggested that she be checked for rearfoot imbalance to forestall the possibility of again rupturing ligaments.

Training errors were found to be the most common cause of injuries to runners in another study reported in the *American Journal of Sportsmedicine*.[11] The researchers reported 2.5 injuries per 1,000 hours of training for long-distance runners and 5.8 mishaps in sprinters and middle-distance runners.

Speaking at a sports symposium underwritten by Burroughs Wellcome Company in 1987, Ernest W. Johnson, M.D., Ohio State University, Columbus, said that rest is not the proper therapy for such problems as shin splints and tennis elbow.[12] Once X-rays or bone scans have ruled out a fracture, the inflammation is best treated with progressive resistance exercises and anti-inflammatory medications, he says.

Rest is not the proper procedure, he continues, because the pain will begin again as soon as activity is resumed. He believes that rest is one of the most overly prescribed treatments for athletic injury pain, and that it is really indicated only for injuries such as second- and third-degree ankle sprains and some stress fractures.

In addition to tennis elbow and shin splints, Dr. Johnson says that such injuries as first-degree ankle sprains and muscle pulls should not be rested. He recommends a combination of medications to reduce pain. This therapy may be required for two to six weeks or until the inflammation becomes pain free. For short-term relief, try aspirin and codeine, he says.

A surprising study reported in *Annals of Sports Medicine* and reviewed in *Runner's World* found that approximately half of the injured runners studied trained less than 20 miles a week.[13] As the training mileage went up, the injury rate went down. The study, involving 3,000 injured distance runners, was conducted by John Pagliano, D.P.M., and Doug Jackson, M.D.

As for running surfaces, the researchers found that 66 percent of the injuries occurred on paved road and sidewalk; 25 percent on dirt, grass and soft sand; and 9 percent on packed sand, track or other surfaces.[13]

It is easy to understand why runners are affected by so many injuries, reports *U.S. Pharmacist*, since a 150-pound runner subjects each foot to 120 tons of force over a one-mile course. Thus, in a 26-mile marathon, each foot, ankle and knee must endure over 3,000 tons of force, says the magazine.[14]

"When the knee flexes and extends on impact, the hamstrings and gastrochemius muscles stretch and absorb the impact," says the publication. "But when athletes overextend themselves, these muscles fatigue and no longer function as shock absorbers. Instead the energy of impact is taken up to a large part by the bones and stress fracture occurs. Stress fracture may also develop when bone resorption exceeds repair."[14]

Runner's knee, which affects from 25 to 40 percent of the patients visiting running clinics, can be caused by overweight, a deformed knee cap, malformation of the patellar surface of the femur or lower extremity malalignment, adds the magazine.

Blisters, which bring pain to many athletes, are often caused by ill-fitting footwear, says *U.S. Pharmacist*. This problem can be aggravated by nylon socks, the article continues. The problem can often be prevented by wearing two pairs of cotton or wool socks, with talcum sprinkled between the layers, or by using compound tincture of benzoin or Tuf-skin on the balls of the feet, heels and toes.

"One method of treating blisters is to puncture the blister with a sterile needle or pin at three or four distinct sites at the bubble surface, then allow the fluid to drain," advises the magazine. "Keep the blister top intact and allow it to serve as a natural barrier to help prevent infection. The area should be cleaned with 70 percent isopropyl alcohol prior to puncturing. An antibiotic ointment (e.g., neomycin-polymixin-bacitracin combination) may be applied, then the blister is covered with a sterile gauze dressing. A hole cut in a piece of moleskin and applied over the punctured blister may also offer added protection."[14]

For athletes who suffer from compartment ankle syndrome, the magazine recommends an orthotic device, a lateral heel wedge or a reinforced shoe upper with a rigid heel counter to keep the foot from pronating. For an acute injury, RICE (rest, ice, compression and elevation of the limb) is often prescribed. Muscle damage can appear within four to six hours, with irreversible damage within eighteen hours, says the magazine.

Pump bumps, which are tender, slightly red nodules that appear lateral to the Achilles tendon, are painful bursae that develop from an irritation on the bony prominence of the calcaneus caused by a poorly supportive padded heel counter in the running shoe, states *US Pharmacist*. Treatment includes ice, aspirin and stretching exercises. Within two to three hours, soak the area for 10 to 15 minutes in a warm bath, which should get rid of most of the pain. Achilles tendinitis is usually associated with uphill or downhill running or shoes with rigid soles, adds the magazine.

A New Jersey runner with bowlegs and bad ankles wrote to *Runner's World*, wondering whether or not his ankle problems could be corrected.[15] John W. Pagliano, D.P.M., responded by saying that ankle sprains often result from daydreaming: The runner's mind wanders and he steps off of a curb or trips over a hole. If the sprain is severe, try RICE for several days, Dr. Pagliano advises.

However, he continues, after years of sprains, the ankle ligaments stretch so that they no longer stabilize the foot the way they originally did. This results in chronic ankle syndrome, he adds.

Dr. Pagliano told the runner to have his orthotics checked, assuming they were fitted after proper biomechanical evaluation, and to find a sturdy, motion-control running shoe that is fully board lasted and has other stability features. Finally, he advised the runner to do exercises to strengthen his feet and ankles.

There has been considerable speculation in athletic circles that a buildup of lactic acid causes muscle pain. Lactic acid is a colorless, syrup-like acid that is found in muscle tissue as a waste product of sugar oxidation. It is produced by the fermentation of milk sugar (lactose) by lactobacilli, similar to the souring of milk. Lactic acid is also a byproduct resulting from the breakdown of glycogen to provide energy in the absence of oxygen. If lactic acid is permitted to accumulate in the muscles, perhaps because of poor circulation or prolonged exercise, muscle fatigue can develop.

However, the debate over the relationship between lactic acid and delayed-onset muscle soreness seems to have been put to rest by a study by James A. Schwane, Ph.D., University of Texas, Tyler, and colleagues at Oral Roberts University, Tulsa, Oklahoma.[16] In the study, blood lactic acid levels were measured before and during 45 minutes of treadmill running, once on a level surface and again at a -10 percent incline. In addition, blood lactic acid concentrations and subjective sensations of muscular soreness were evaluated for 72 hours after the exercise. Seven men were involved in the study.

"There is considerable indirect evidence against an association between lactic acid and delayed-onset soreness," say the researchers. "For example, lactic acid concentrations in muscle and blood return to resting levels within an hour after even exhaustive exercise, long before onset of the subjective sensations of soreness. Also, one would suppose that if lactic acid causes soreness, it would be throughout the body, even in nonexercised muscles, since lactic acid can diffuse from blood into muscles just as freely as from muscles into blood. This does not occur, however. Furthermore,'' add the researchers, ''exercise that involves extremes of eccentric muscle contractions (contractions in which muscles lengthen while developing active tension) is more effective at causing delayed-onset soreness than is exercise that involves concentric contractions (in which muscles shorten while developing active tension), despite the significantly greater metabolic cost of concentric contractions.''[16]

Another type of pain experienced by runners and joggers and others who exercise are the ''stitches,'' stomach pains that develop near the ribs. According to Gayle Olinekova in *Go for It!*, some of the causes are:

• Weak stomach muscles.
• Undigested food or gas in the intestine.
• Drinking very cold water when you are hot and sweaty.

''During one marathon, I developed stitches near the 11-mile mark,'' she reports. ''I was leading the race, but with those stitches, how to continue? Hearing once that sit-ups helped, I lay down in the middle of the road and banged out 40 sit-ups right there on the hot, sticky pavement. . . . Fortunately, the stitches disappeared and I continued on to win.''[17]

She has since developed a better cure:

1. Blow all the air in your lungs out while pushing your abdomen out.
2. Without breathing, suck your abdomen in.
3. Repeat several times.

This creates a vacuum pressure that eases gas and cramps, she adds. Eventually, you will be able to do this while exercising, without ever stopping. It also strengthens your stomach muscles and aids in elimination—try it first thing in the morning, she says. ''Actually, it's the same principle used in belly dancing—that's where I learned it,'' she adds.[17]

The Runner notes that a stitch is often caused by indigestion, incorrect breathing mechanics or poor fitness. If you can't get rid of the pain by slowing down, try this:[18]

1. Bend over, digging your fingers into the belly, just below the rib cage.
2. Inhale deeply and exhale through pursed lips to stretch diaphragm muscles.
3. Stretch the affected muscles by raising the arm on the affected side high over your head.

This should cause the stitch to subside so that you can continue running.

Overtraining, which as we have seen is a major cause of some running and jogging injuries, can also be a cause of depression, according to Richard Warner, M.D., who is in private practice in Boulder, Colorado.[19] Symptoms of this problem include lack of motivation, insomnia, diminished sex drive, reduced energy, decreased resistance to illness, poor appetite and loss of weight. He adds that some runners may be inclined to exercise energetically when they are elated or euphoric, and then cut back on their training when they are depressed. For these athletes, it makes sense to cut back on training, relax, look for other turn-ons in life and to reevaluate why they have a compulsion to overtrain.

However, Dr. Warner cautions, "Runners with these conditions should be careful about ascribing the cause of their condition to overtraining. There may be other causes."[19]

When it is time to seek professional help for a running problem, you need to choose a qualified health-care professional, rather than someone with questionable credentials. But the decision isn't easy, since you may require an orthopaedic surgeon, podiatrist, athletic trainer, chiropractor, nutritionist or other professional. It may be time to seek professional advice, according to Damien Howell, M.S., R.P.T., chairman of the Sportsmedicine Committee of the Road Runners Club of America, when:[20]

1. The discomfort is getting progressively worse.
2. The discomfort has plateaued at a level which is chronically affecting your performance.
3. The discomfort is more frequent and/or is present even when you are not running.
4. The discomfort is at a level of 3 or higher on a scale of 1 (no pain) to 10 (worst pain imaginable).
5. Attempts at self-treatment (e.g., new shoes, a change of surface or training) do not significantly improve the symptoms.
6. The discomfort is causing you to compensate and develop additional injuries.
7. The mental depression, denial or guilt you may be experiencing is pointed out to you by significant others.

Howell adds that a competent health professional should:

1. Examine you while you are motionless, walking and running.
2. Provide you with a specific diagnosis or a list of possible diagnoses.
3. Provide you with a possible cause of the diagnosis.
4. Counsel you about coping with possible withdrawal symptoms from not running, if abstinence from running is advisable.
5. Clearly explain how to prevent further injury during recuperation.
6. Advise you on training modifications to prevent recurrence.
7. Provide a multi-faceted treatment approach, since running injuries have multiple causative factors and, therefore, varied treatments.
8. Reexamine you after a therapeutic intervention and demonstrate to your satisfaction that the cause and/or injury has been adequately addressed.
9. Offer alternative treatment (including referral) if the first approach does not work.

References

1. D. B. Clement, M.D., et al., "A Survey of Overuse Running Injuries," *The Physician and Sportsmedicine* (Vol. 9, No. 5, May 1981), pp. 47-58.

2. Lowell Scott Weil, D.P.M., *Aches and Pains of Running* (Bethesda, Md: American Podiatric Medical Association with the American Running and Fitness Association, undated).

3. Ronald Green, D.P.M., *Knee Pain and the Runner* (Bethesda, Md.: American Podiatric Medical Association with the American Running and Fitness Association, undated).

4. "Marathon: The Day After," *Runner's World* (December 1987), p. 19.

5. William A. Grana, M.D., and Thomas C. Coniglione, M.D., "Knee Disorders in Runners," *The Physician and Sportsmedicine* (Vol. 13, No. 5, May 1985), pp. 127-133.

6. "Alternatives to Surgery for Foot Pain," *Prevention* (January 1988), p. 6.

7. M. M. Lewis and J. F. Reilly, "Athletes' Orthopedic Problems: Check for Tumors," *American Journal of Sports Medicine* (Vol. 15, July/August 1987), p. 362.

8. "Under Your Skin," *Runner's World* (November 1986), p. 16.

9. L. D. Lutter, "Heel Pain: Don't Rush Into Surgery," *American Journal of Sports Medicine* (Vol. 14, November/December 1986), p. 481.

10. "Foot Spasms," *The Runner* (December 1985), p. 14.

11. F. A. Pettrone, et al., "Injury in Runners, Gymnasts: Linked to Training," *American Journal of Sportsmedicine* (Vol. 15, January/March 1987), p. 168.

12. Kathy Bartlett, "Exercise, Not Rest, Is Best Treatment for Many Athletic Injuries," *Burroughs Wellcome News* (July 11, 1987).

13. Kate Delhagen, "Injuries: Where Does It Hurt?" *Runner's World* (November 1987), p. 18.

14. "Sports Participation Increases . . . and So Do Sports Injuries," *U.S. Pharmacist* (August 1987), pp. 62-68.

15. John W. Pagliano, D.P.M., "Bowlegs and Bad Ankles," *Runner's World* (November 1986), pp. 17-18.

16. James A. Schwane, Ph.D., et al., "Is Lactic Acid Related to Delayed-Onset Muscle Soreness?" *The Physician and Sportsmedicine* (Vol. 11, No. 3, March 1983), pp. 124-131.

17. Gayle Olinekova, *Go for It!* (New York: Simon and Schuster, 1982), p. 129.

18. "Stemming Stitches," *The Runner* (March 1987), p. 9.

19. Richard Warner, M.D., "Overtraining?" *Runner's World* (December 1987), p. 8.

20. Damien Howell, M.S., R.P.T., *Running Injuries* (Road Runners Club of America, undated).

Chapter 10

Athlete's Foot

During the early 1930s, an industrious advertising man coined the term "athlete's foot" to publicize a new patent medicine to fight fungal infections of the feet.[1] His campaign was so successful that, even today, we consider this fairly common complaint about as socially acceptable as leprosy.

Actually, there are two types of athlete's foot. The most common type, *intertriginous*, begins when cracks appear in the skin, generally at the base of the fifth toe and between the fourth and fifth toes. For the *squamous hyperkeratotic* type, the skin is red, scaling and thick, also between the toes. One or both feet may be infected and the irritation can spread to the soles of the feet.[2] Some athletes have reported that the infection has turned up around their toenails and even on their hands.

Also known as "ringworm of the feet" and "jungle rot," athlete's foot is caused by either a fungus (ringworm) or a bacterium. When caused by a fungus, the skin of the toes and feet may be dry and scaly and there may be itching. When the condition is related to bacteria, the skin can be smelly, painful and moist.

Contrary to its name, ringworm is not an infestation by a worm but a fungus of the Trichophyton family. In the case of athlete's foot, the culprit is *Trichophyton mentagrophytes*.[3]

Almost everyone has this fungus on their skin, but it is usually controlled by helpful bacteria, report Howard R. and Martha E. Lewis in *The People's Medical Manual*.[1] In susceptible people, the warm, dark, humid environment of the shoe and sock encourages the ringworm fungus to spread.

Although dermatologists disagree as to how one picks up the fungi or bacteria, the Lewises insists that athlete's foot is not necessarily contracted at public showers and pools. Of course, these areas are among the many that provide a warm, moist atmosphere for the organisms to grow. These authors also suggest that the dry, scaly skin may not be caused by athlete's foot but may instead be contact dermatitis, psoriasis or eczema. If the wrong remedy is used for the condition, a secondary infection more serious than athlete's foot might result.

Athlete's foot is slightly contagious, according to *The American Medical Association Family Medical Guide*.[4] It can be spread through contact with skin fragments shed by an infected person. However, this book also notes that irritation and itching between the toes may not be due to athlete's foot but to sweaty feet.

Prevention

Athlete's foot is generally related to hot weather, when the athlete is perspiring a lot, and if he/she is wearing tight shoes, report Gabe Mirkin, M.D., and Marshall Hoffman in *The Sports Medicine Book*.[5]

"Keeping the feet dry by exposing them to air or sprinkling them with powder is often helpful in preventing flareups," they maintain. "Showering and thorough drying of the feet as well as changing socks after your feet have perspired are basic rules that should always be followed."[5]

In addition to keeping feet dry, you can frequently prevent athlete's foot by thoroughly drying between toes and around nails following a bath or shower, suggests *The People's Medical Manual*.[1] Dust your feet regularly with a preventive, nonprescription foot powder, and sprinkle it in your shoes as well. This helps to curb the spread of the fungus. Alternate your shoes so that the pair not being worn can air out. In addition, do not wear tight, ill-fitting shoes and nonporous socks or stockings that prohibit air from circulating around the toes.

"Cotton or wool socks or cotton Peds help absorb moisture," says the *Manual*. "When you wear nylon or other synthetic stockings, insert small pieces of absorbent cotton or lamb's wool between your toes."[1]

For further protection, the Lewises recommend that you wear clogs when using public showers and pools. Footbaths or other measures to "sterilize" feet, shoes and socks are useless and may irritate the skin, they continue. This also applies to strong chemicals that are used to disinfect floors in bath areas.

"Avoid antihistamines, antiseptics or cortisone creams, which may intensify and prolong the infection. Organic mercurial antiseptics are among the common offenders. Other strong chemicals or salicylic acid ointments can lead to severe inflammation," they caution.[1]

For athletes who use foot powder, Raymond Dreyfack recommends that it be sprinkled inside the socks rather than in the shoes. This uses less powder and will generally be more effective, he says.[6]

Clean, dry shoes and socks and proper hygiene are probably the best deterrents to athlete's foot. As explained by Bob Glover, "The myth is that athlete's foot can be picked up in the locker room. But I spend half my life walking in and out of locker rooms in bare feet, and have never had more than a minor touch of athlete's foot. Lucky? I prefer to think that the condition is more a matter of your health care for your feet."[7]

Anti-Fungal Medications

Dermatologists and sports medicine experts are in disagreement as to whether anti-fungal creams and powders are effective. In some cases the athlete may be allergic to the preparation, or it might exacerbate the problem. Ointments often retain moisture at the skin surface and can actually aggravate the problem.

Physicians also prescribe antifungal tablets, which have to be taken for four to six weeks.

Since American consumers spend almost $85 million annually on over-the-counter antifungal remedies, an FDA/OTC advisory panel reviewed these preparations and made a variety of recommendations. The safe and effective OTC topical antifungal drugs are reviewed by Thomas A. Gossel, Ph.D., in *U.S. Pharmacist:*[8]

Iodochlorhydroxyquin. Originally used to treat amebic dysentery and to protect against traveler's diarrhea, this drug has been used to topically treat athlete's foot, jock itch and ringworm infections. A 3 percent concentration is recommended. Oral use of the drug is not recommended, since it might cause neurological symptoms.

Tolnaftate. A 1 percent powder dusted on feet and toes twice daily is said to reduce the incidence of athlete's foot in people who are prone to get the infection. There are generally no side effects, although some people can experience mild itching, dermatitis and irritation. The FDA/OTC panel does not recommend this drug for jock itch or ringworm. They suggest that the groin area is more sensitive than the feet, and that some patients might have adverse reactions. They also suggest that it would be futile to treat large areas of the body affected with ringworm with this drug.

Undecylenic acid and its salts. Since this acid is a normal constituent of sweat, it has been prescribed as an antifungal preparation since 1937. It is noted for its rather unpleasant odor, and it is generally used in combination with its zinc, calcium and copper salts. Zinc is said to serve as an astringent, thus curbing inflammation. The acid and its salts are available in powder, aerosol, ointment, solution and gel dosage forms. The powder form is the most popular since it is not as odorous.

"Sulzberger and Kanof evaluated its prophylactic use in athlete's foot," says Dr. Gossel. "Although the authors reported that undecylenic acid was an effective prophylactic against athlete's foot, the study contained several design deficiencies. There are no other studies that have evaluated the agent for possible prophylactic use."[8]

Originally used orally to treat psoriasis, undecylenic acid is said to cause irritation only rarely when used on the skin. The oral preparation has caused gastrointestinal disturbance, headache, fever, dizziness and hives in some patients. However, the FDA/OTC panel reports that the acid and its salts are effective when used topically in treating athlete's foot, jock itch and ringworm.

Povidone-iodine. The FDA/OTC panel has ruled that this combination is an effective antifungal treatment for athlete's foot, jock itch and ringworm. Various studies have shown that 10 percent povidone-iodine is recommended for a variety of bacteria, yeast and fungal infections. It is rarely toxic.

In addition, the panel has suggested that haloprogin, miconazole nitrate and nystatin, previously prescription drug ingredients, be approved as OTC medications for treating athlete's foot, jock itch and ringworm. The panel also approved these drugs for treating external feminine itching and superficial skin lesions caused by *Candida albicans*, a member of the yeast family.

The FDA/OTC panel also reported that the following antifungal preparations are either unsafe or ineffective:

Camphor
Candicidin
Coal tar
Phenolates
  Phenol
  Phenolate sodium
Resorcinol
Tannic acid
Thymol
Tolindate

Candida Infection

Writing in *The Yeast Connection*, William G. Crook, M.D., reports that the yeast germ, *Candida albicans*, is frequently at the root of many health problems affecting men and women.[9] For women, these problems include menstrual irregularities, vaginitis, pelvic pain, recurrent bladder irritation and a lack of interest in sex. For men, the problems include jock itch, athlete's foot, prostatitis and impotence. And in both sexes, the infection can cause fatigue, digestive complaints, headache, joint pain, mental confusion, loss of memory, irritability and other complaints.

Although three-fourths of his patients have been women, Dr. Crook reports that he suspects yeast connected health problems in men:

• Who are troubled by food and inhalant allergies.
• Who have been bothered by persistent jock itch, athlete's foot, or fungus infection of the nails.
• Who have taken repeated courses of antibiotics for acne, prostatitis, sinusitis or other infections.
• Who consume lots of beer, breads or sweets.
• Who crave alcohol.
• Whose wives or children are bothered by yeast connected illnesses.
• Who feel bad on damp days or on exposure to chemicals and/or tobacco.
• Whose sex drive is impaired.
• Who are troubled by fatigue, depression and other peculiar nervous system symptoms.
• Who are bothered by recurrent digestive problems, including constipation, bloating, diarrhea and abdominal pain.[9]

In addition to some of these symptoms, women can also be bothered by Candida infections if they are on birth control pills or antibiotics, have been treated with a Candida extract, or eat a lot of yeast-containing foods (such as cheese or beer). Both sexes can show more symptoms when they are around household molds, dried leaves and other sources of molds.

For those who are bothered by Candida infections, Dr. Crook recommends that these foods be avoided:

1. sugar and sugar-containing foods.
2. yeast, breads and pastries.
3. alcoholic beverages.
4. malt products.
5. condiments, sauces and vinegar-containing foods.
6. processed and smoked meats.
7. dried and candied fruits.
8. left-overs (unless foods are properly refrigerated, molds can form on them).
9. fruit juices, either bottled, canned or frozen; freshly prepared juices are an exception.
10. coffee and tea.
11. melons.
12. mushrooms, morels, truffles and other edible fungi.
12. cheese, cheese-containing snacks, buttermilk, sour cream and sour milk products.
13. yeasts.
14. B-complex vitamins, since they are often grown or originated from yeasts, and selenium products, unless they are labeled "yeast-free" and "sugar free."
15. antibiotics (penicillin, streptomycin, ampicillin, amoxicillin, Keflex, Ceclor, Septra, Bactrim, etc.).
16. peanuts, peanut products and pistachios, since they often contain mold.

Other diet recommendations are included in Dr. Crook's book.[9]

Obviously, there are many fine foods and substances included in this list. Therefore, they only need to be eliminated, hopefully, on a temporary basis by those bothered by Candida infections. For those athletes who are unable to find the origin of their recurring headache, athlete's foot, jock itch, irritation, fatigue, etc., you may wish to ask a professional about whether or not you may have a yeast infection.

Jock Itch and Other Problems

Jock itch, which is also called "crotch rot," "dhobie itch" and "gym itch," is a recurring rash, itching and scaling on the upper thighs, usually in men. It is caused by dermatophytic fungi, explains Dr. Thomas A. Gossel.[8]

"This infection is most common in men 18 to 40 years of age; it is rare in prepubertal children," continues Dr. Gossel. "Lesions typically take on a semicircle appearance rather than a ring-shaped feature, and their centers appear light brown from the resolving inflammation. Vesicles and pustules are uncommon. Several other diseases of non-fungal origin may also affect the feet and groin, producing similar symptoms. This may make diagnosis difficult. Such disorders include candidiasis, psoriasis, hyperhidrosis, allergic contact dermatitis, eczema and bacterial infections.[8]

Women athletes who suffer from vaginitis can generally trace the problem to foods and drugs mentioned earlier. While exercising they generally wear loose-fitting clothing. However, when they change to street clothes, they may wear tight-fitting jeans or slacks and pantyhose, which do not allow air to circulate in the groin area. This can sometimes precipitate an infection. Vaginitis can also signal the beginning stages of diabetes, since frequent urination associated with this disease can cause an irritation.

An Israeli-developed deodorant for bromodrosis (body odor) can eliminate perspiration odor for from four to 15 days with only one application, according to studies in the U.S. and abroad. Trade-named Lavilin, one formula is for underarms and the other for feet. Available in health food stores, the products utilize arnica, calendula and other natural, homeopathic substances.

"In our small sample we found, through culture and sensitivity coutns, substantial reduction in bacterial numbers for one to two weeks with just one application from almost all subjects," says Marc A. Brenner, D.P.M., and colleagues at the West Haven V.A. Hospital. "More importantly, clinically this (foot) cream has reduced odor and helped 98 percent of our subjects when used as directed. None of the subjects developed skin irritation or any other adverse reaction."[10]

References

1. Howard R. and Martha E. Lewis, *The People's Medical Manual* (New York: Doubleday & Company, Inc., 1986), pp. 65-66.

2. Randolph Lee Clark, M.D., and Russell W. Cumley, Ph.D., editors, *The Book of Health* (New York: Van Nostrand Reinhold Company, 1973), pp. 264-266.

3. Donald F. Tapley, M.D., et al., editors, *The Columbia University College of Physicians and Surgeons Complete Home Medical Guide* (New York: Crown Publishers, Inc., 1985), p. 448.

4. Jeffrey R. M. Kunz, M.D., *The American Medical Association Family Medical Guide* (New York: Random House, 1982), p. 256.

5. Gabe Mirkin, M.D., and Marshall Hoffman, *The Sports Medicine Book* (Boston: Little, Brown and Company, Inc., 1978), p. 122.

6. Raymond Dreyfack, *The Complete Book of Walking* (New York: Arco Publishing, Inc., 1979), p. 81.

7. Bob Glover and Jack Shepherd, *The Runner's Handbook* (New York: Penguin Books, 1987), p. 254.

8. Thomas A. Gossel, Ph.D., "Topical Antifungal Products," *U. S. Pharmacist* (June 1985), pp. 42-46.

9. William G. Crook, M.D., *The Yeast Connection* (Jackson, Tenn.: Professional Books, 1984), pp. 77-78, 194.

10. Marc A. Brenner, D.P.M., and Larry Daniel, D.P.M. "Hyperhydrosis and Bromodrosis, a New Plus for an Old Puzzle," *Current Podiatry* (November 1984).

Chapter 11

Diarrhea

During the 1976 New York City Marathon, Bill Rodgers ran the race in 2:10:09, which was just slightly off his American record. Later, when he was asked what was on his mind during the final moments of the race, with a new record in sight, he said that his first priority was to get to a bathroom.[1]

Diarrhea is a rather common complaint among runners and joggers. These watery stools are sometimes flecked with mucus. If there is blood and pus in the stool, this is known as dysentery. Acute diarrhea can last from one to three days, during which there may be from one to 20 evacuations in a day. Chronic diarrhea, without any known organic cause, is often associated with some kind of emotional disturbance.[2]

Causes

"Often diarrhea can be controlled by the elimination of fat from the diet, or of other foods, such as strawberries, shellfish and eggs, to which the individual may have become sensitive," report Randolph Lee Clark, M.D., and Russell W. Cumley, Ph.D., editors of *The Book of Health*. "Diet control alone, however, is not always sufficient to effect a cure of diarrhea. Rather, dietary control must be related to and based upon the particular condition that causes the diarrhea in the individual."[2]

When a person runs or jogs, the psoas muscles that bend the hips and lift the legs have to work harder than normal, and, after years of training, they become enlarged. Since these muscles are linked to the front of the lower spine, their bulky contractible sections are at the back of the lower abdomen, near the colon and rectum. As these muscles push up and touch the large intestine, this irritation often prods the bowels to move, resulting in jogger's diarrhea, jogger's trots or "the runs." If the athlete can hold out until after the race is over, the need to evacuate may subside.[3] Marathoner Grete Waitz is reportedly one of the many athletes who sometimes experience this problem.

Although some athletes complain of occasional diarrhea, abdominal cramps and bloating, others are bothered on a regular basis. The causes of diarrhea may be extreme bowel activity, lactose (milk) intolerance, food allergies, irritable bowel syndrome or infectious gastroenteritis, say Richard Mangi, M.D., Peter Jakl, M.D., and O. William Dayton, ATC, in *Sports Fitness and Training*.[4]

Exercise increases the activity of the gastrointestinal tract to such an extent that food and water are not properly digested, thereby causing diarrhea. The problem can be aggravated by alcohol, spices and fatty foods, and nervousness before a race.

"Sudden, uncontrollable cramps and diarrhea are common during prolonged strenuous exercise, much to the embarrassment of several world-class runners, who have been stricken on prime-time television," the authors report.[4]

Stomach cramps preceding the diarrhea begin 30 minutes or so after the start of the exercise, and the problem can last for several hours afterwards. Light meals 24 hours before an event or antispasmodic medication often control this problem, they add.

Excessive gas, bloating, cramps and diarrhea can be associated with lactose intolerance, which means that the athlete does not have the enzyme lactase to digest the lactose or milk sugar in milk. The avoidance of dairy products for a week or two before competition may solve the problem; however, since calcium from dairy products is needed for strong bones and teeth, these athletes should substitute foods rich in calcium (such as sardines, some nuts, and green, leafy vegetables) or take calcium supplements. The authors did not mention it, but health food stores sell several products designed to restore the necessary enzymes to the gut. Blacks and other nationalities that do not consume many milk products eventually lose the ability to digest milk. The lactase can sometimes be reintroduced to the gut by eating small amounts of cheese or yogurt and gradually introducing milk into the diet. If that does not work, LactAid or a similar product can usually work. Of course, the athlete may have sufficient lactase but may simply be allergic to milk.

Diarrhea and other stomach complaints are also associated with irritable bowel syndrome and infectious gastroenteritis, both of which need medical attention.

One way to avoid diarrhea, nausea, abdominal cramps and other gastrointestinal complaints is not to exercise too soon after eating, says Dr. Katherine Blanchette, sports medicine columnist for *The Dallas Morning News*.[5] In other words, allow ample time for gastric emptying and internal absorption of the nutrients to fuel the energy needed for running or jogging. For those planning to exercise heavily, she recommends that they eat at least three to four hours before exercising.

She quotes Dr. Jorge Rodriguez, a Dallas gastroenterologist, as saying that, for long-distance runners who are bothered by diarrhea, he recommends a high-residue diet consisting of fruits, cereals, bread and green vegetables. This type of diet, he says, allows more timely bowel movements and should avoid any problem with diarrhea. For patients who are chronically constipated, he recommends walking, jogging and other therapy.

In addition to milk intolerance, some runners have problems eating certain fruits and vegetables a day or two before the race, according to Allan Lawrence and Mark Scheid in *The Self-Coached Runner*.[6] They add that some race directors, thinking they are being helpful, mix the replacement drinks too strong, and the combination of too much sugar and stress may contribute to diarrhea. They suggest that runners drink water during the race and the replacement beverage afterwards.

Overtraining is a serious problem for beginners, amateurs and professional athletes, and this can cause a variety of symptoms, say Gabe Mirkin, M.D., and Marshall Hoffman in *The Sports Medicine Book*.[7] Beginners may overstress their out-of-shape bodies so that they become injured, tired and eventually give up their exercise program; seasoned amateurs and professionals overwork so that they are frequently injured and always fatigued. The authors say that these are some of the signs of overtraining:

- Constipation or diarrhea
- Headache
- Loss of appetite
- Unexplained drop in athletic performance
- Fatigue and sluggishness
- Loss of weight
- Swelling of lymph nodes in the neck, groin and armpits
- Absence of menstruation in women

Vitamin C

There is always a flap in the press about diarrhea being caused by too much vitamin C. Actually, that is simply a sign that your body has enough of the vitamin and you do not need any more for the time being. Vitamin C or ascorbic acid is a water-soluble vitamin, as are the vitamins in the B-complex, which means that you lose varying amounts in urine and feces. Dr. Robert Cathcart, III, a holistic physician in San Mateo, California, who can get rid of colds, hepatitis, monoucleosis and viral infections in a few days without the patient having to go to a hospital, may give 100 to 200 grams (100,000 to 200,000 milligrams) or more intravenously in a 24-hour period. For serious viral infections, he recommends that you titrate to bowel tolerance. In other words, take vitamin C at intervals during the day until diarrhea appears, then stop the vitamin C for awhile. Some people develop diarrhea on these megadoses; others do not. For those who don't, it means that the body used up all of the available vitamin C to fight the infection or stress before it reached the point where diarrhea might occur. If the vitamin C is to be effective, all body tissues must be saturated with the vitamin. Dr. Cathcart states that he can also successfully treat AIDS patients with vitamin C if the disease has not progressed too far.

One of the reasons that large amounts of vitamin C are needed is because human beings are among the few animals, birds and reptiles that do not make their own vitamin C. When animals are under stress, they manufacture enormous amounts of vitamin C to counteract the problem. Human beings lost the ability to synthesize vitamin C eons ago and, therefore, we must get the vitamin from our diet, as do guinea pigs and some apes. But the Recommended Dietary Allowance of 60 milligrams or so per day is hardly sufficient to ward off the various diseases and stresses that human beings face.

Another "old saw" in the press is that too much vitamin C will cause kidney stones. This notion has been dispelled many times but it continues to be discussed. Writing in the foreword to a book that Ruth Adams and I coauthored many years ago, which is now out-of-print, Frederick R. Klenner, M.D., said that, "The oxalic acid-kidney stone scare is another infamous chapter in the attacks on vitamin C. This big hoax, published in the general press and ladies' journals, as well as other monotonously repeated nonsense such as diarrhea on taking high daily doses of vitamin C, has been utilized for the propagation of little else than medical and news sensationalism. . . ."[8]

He goes on to say that, "After 28 years of research with really massive doses of ascorbic acid, I can state very emphatically that you will not develop a kidney stone by taking 10 or more grams of ascorbic acid each day. It is physiologically impossible for such a condition to develop. Kelli and Zilva reported that nutritional experiments showed that dehydroascorbic acid is protected *in vivo* from rapid transformation to the antiscorbutically impotent diketogulonic acid from which oxalic acid is derived. The only way oxalic acid can be produced is through splitting of the lactose ring."[8]

This happens above pH-5, Dr. Klenner explained. The reaction of urine when 10 grams of vitamin C are taken daily is pH-6. Oxalic acid precipitates out of solution only from neutral or alkaline solution—that is, pH-7 to pH-10, he continues.

"According to Meakins, stasis and a concentrated urine appear to be the chief physiological factors. With 10 grams or more of vitamin C each day, you have an excellent diuretic. The ascorbic acid-kidney stone story is a myth," he said.[8]

Other Causes

Diarrhea can be caused by athletes who become dehydrated and then gulp down large amounts of fluids too quickly, according to Mona Shangold, M.D. and Gabe Mirkin, M.D., in *The Complete Sports Medicine Book for Women*.[9] They add that some athletes also get diarrhea because they cannot degrade the carbohydrates they have eaten before exercising.

Menstrual cramps can be associated with diarrhea, nausea, and vomiting but Shangeld and Mirkin emphasize that women should not allow menstrual cramps or premenstrual discomfort to interfere with their exercising. Prostaglandin inhibitors, prescribed by a gynecologist, may alleviate the problem.

Writing in *The Runner's Handbook* (certainly one of the best books for runners) Bob Glover and Jack Shepherd report that diarrhea can be initiated by a change in diet, especially a sudden change to a vegetarian diet.[10] Increased exercise, and foods such as milk, wheat products, chocolate, nuts, raisins, fruits and vegetables can exacerbate the problem in susceptible individuals. Bowel problems can also develop from bacteria you have picked up in a foreign country that your body is not used to. In any event, prolonged diarrhea can dehydrate the body, causing fever, uncontrollable bowel movements and fainting. It can rob the body of essential vitamins and minerals which, of course, should be replaced.[10]

Remedies

"Always attempt a bowel movement before hitting the road," Glover and Shepherd suggest. "If you are planning a long run, or feel vulnerable, like the morning after downing lots of bad beer, be prepared by carrying along a wad of toilet paper. If the cramping becomes severe, stop and walk. Don't try to hold off too long; sometimes you can get away with walking into a restaurant and asking for a bathroom, but you can't count on this solution. The best bet is to look for a hidden spot, and go. . . ."[10]

Although it may not be practical for a competition, the following remedy for diarrhea, suggested by The Mayo Clinic, Rochester, Minnesota, could be useful if the problem develops while you are training out-of-town.[11] They recommend that you mix half a teaspoon of salt, the same amount of baking soda and four tablespoons of sugar in a liter of carbonated water. Use this as a supplement to a liquid diet of broth, weak tea and gelatin. To replace lost potassium, eat bananas and drink orange, apple and other fruit juices.

In his informative book, *Your Personal Vitamin Profile*, Michael Colgan, Ph.D. recommends the following for persistent diarrhea where there is no physical cause:[12] increase vitamin B3 (niacin) intake to 100 mg per day; add 400 mg of linoleic acid; and stop drinking coffee.

Bleeding

Blood in the stool can indicate the possibility of colon cancer, but, in the case of athletes, exercise causes a temporary constriction of circulation through the gut and blood may spill into the stool, says James Stewart, M.D., a Mayo Clinic researcher.[13] He goes on to say that blood flow in that area can drop by as much as 80 percent during heavy exercise, which can also cause diarrhea.

The loss of blood in the feces can contribute to runner's anemia, adds the article in *American Health*. In fact, iron-deficiency anemia among athletes has been associated with sweating, urinating iron out of the body, or the breakage of red-blood cells by the continuing blows to the feet. Since many runners believe that extra iron helps their performance, Lawrence McMahon, Jr., M.D. of the Yale Medical School recommends ferrous sulfate or gluconate supplements.[13]

Another Mayo Clinic researcher, David Ahlquist, M.D., points out that the circulating blood helps to eliminate waste products from the stomach, including stomach acids, according to Jim Ferstle in *The Runner*.[14] When blood flow is restricted to the stomach and gastrointestinal tract during exercise, stomach acids can hang around, thereby causing inflammation, irritation and bleeding into the stool. The stress of a marathon or a long race also can contribute to GI problems.

The author adds that the bleeding usually stops once the stress is over, and that a runner who has GI bleeding can usually solve the problem by cutting back on training. He says that runners who have recently run hard workouts, upped their mileage significantly (he gave one case history in which the runner was running 30 miles a week), or have run a marathon are the ones most likely to test positive for blood in the stool. This doesn't necessarily indicate any serious problems, but this can be checked out with a medical exam.

Jim Ferstle quotes John Cantwell, M.D., director of the Preventive Medicine Institute, Atlanta, Georgia, and a runner who has experienced rectal bleeding, as saying that, "If the runner is under 40 and retests negative once the high stress period is over, the likelihood of a serious intestinal disorder is diminished."[14]

If the physician suspects something more ominous, he will recommend a series of GI tests, including a digital examination of the rectum, an examination of the lower intestinal tract with a proctoscope, and a final exam with a colonoscope, which surveys the colon and large and small intestines. A barium enema is also generally part of the procedure.

In some instances, the athlete may be suffering from ulcerative proctitis, which is an inflammation of the rectum that is triggered by stress. Joan Benoit was afflicted with this problem prior to one of the Boston Marathons and also before the 1984 Olympic trials, according to *The Runner*.[14] The disorder is usually curbed with drug therapy.

Constipation

The opposite side of the coin, constipation, occurs when the feces become hard and dry and there is difficulty with defecation. Unfortunately, most people assume that they must have one or more bowel movements a day and they intervene with laxatives and other measures. Actually, some healthy people have only one, two or three bowel movements per week and that is perfectly normal for them. Constipation may result when there is too little undigestible residue or roughage in the diet to give the stool sufficient bulk or when the diet does not contain enough fluids (at least eight glasses of water a day). The regularity of meals also plays an important role, and a diet that is low in calcium, potassium and vitamin A can cause constipation, say Randolph Lee Clark, M.D. and Russell W. Cumley, Ph.D. in *The Book of Health*.[15]

"Constipation is usually relieved by adequate amounts of laxative foods in the diet," they continue. "Foods which stimulate bowel action are fats, fruits, vegetables and coarse cereals. Fruits contain a high proportion of undigestible cellulose, as well as sugars, acids and salts which have a chemically stimulating effect on the bowel. Undigested fat supplies a mild lubrication to the feces, while partially digested fats are mildly irritating and activate the bowels."[15]

They add that proper diet, adequate fluids, routine habits and the use of brewer's yeast, mineral oil, suppositories of glycerin or wetting agents and enemas are some of the ways to reestablish the defecatory reflex. Although they do not discuss it, mineral oil and enemas are notorious for removing important nutrients from the body. They also fail to mention that exercise is a great deterrent against constipation, assuming that the athlete does not have a serious gastrointestinal problem.

References

1. Bob Glover and Jack Shepherd, *The Runner's Handbook* (New York: Penguin Books, 1987), pp. 259–260.
2. Randolph Lee Clark, M.D., and Russell W. Cumley, Ph.D., editors, *The Book of Health* (New York: Van Nostrand Reinhold Company, 1973), pp. 464–466.

3. "Joggers' Diarrhea," *U. S. Pharmacist* (April 1986), p. 8.

4. Richard Mangi, M.D., Peter Jekl, M.D., and O. William Dayton, ATC, *Sports Fitness and Training* (New York: Pantheon Books, 1987), pp. 125–126.

5. Dr. Katherine Blanchette, "Diet, Emptying System Important for Running," *The Dallas Morning News* (April 7, 1988), p. 17B.

6. Allan Lawrence and Mark Scheid, *The Self-Coached Runner* (Boston: Little Brown and Company, Inc., 1984), p. 209.

7. Gabe Mirkin, M.D., and Marshall Hoffman, *The Sports Medicine Book* (Boston: Little Brown and Company, Inc., 1978), p. 33.

8. Frank Murray, *Program Your Heart for Health* (New York: Larchmont Books, 1978), p. 311.

9. Mona Shangold, M.D., and Gabe Mirkin, M.D., *The Complete Sports Medicine Book for Women* (New York: Simon and Schuster, 1985), p. 203.

10. Bob Glover and Jack Shepherd, *The Runner's Handbook* (New York: Penguin Books, 1987), pp. 259–260.

11. "Diarrhea: Replacing Fluids," *U. S. News & World Report* (May 19, 1986), p. 92.

12. Dr. Michael Colgan, *Your Personal Vitamin Profile* (New York: William Morrow and Company, Inc., 1982), p. 135.

13. "Elite Blood Loss: Culprit for Runner's Trots, Anemia," *American Health* (April 1985), p. 34.

14. Jim Ferstle, "GI Woes," *The Runner* (December 1985), p. 18.

15. Randolph Lee Clark, M.D., and Russell W. Cumley, Ph.D., editors, *The Book of Health* (New York: Van Nostrand Reinhold Company, 1973), pp. 464–466.

Chapter 12

For Women Only

Since the Recommended Dietary Allowances for vitamins, minerals, proteins and other nutrients are based on the nutritional needs of a healthy young man in his mid-20s, many nutritionists have wondered how these guidelines can be of any value to women, children, the elderly, those who are sick and even to men in other age groups. Actually, the RDAs were never intended to be individual interpretations; they were meant as guides for feeding large groups of people in an institutional setting. Considering that many Americans are continuing to be hooked on a junk-food diet, some concerned nutritionists suggest that perhaps some of the RDAs are too low and that, consequently, many people might benefit from food supplements as insurance against possible deficiencies. Since jogging, running and other strenuous forms of exercise deplete the body of nutrients, adequate nutrition is of special importance to athletes. And women are especially vulnerable to this added form of stress.

Women's Body Structure

Aside from the differing nutritional needs of men and women, there are obvious physiological differences. In his informative book, *The Sports Doctor's Fitness Book for Women,* John L. Marshall, M.D. says that, since most women have a wider pelvis than the average male to allow for childbirth, this means that when they run, most women have to shift their pelvis more in order to maintain a center of gravity over the weight-bearing foot. This results in greater hip movement and what appears to be a decrease in efficiency, according to Dr. Marshall and his coauthor, Heather Barbash.[1]

The wider pelvis also affects the position of the legs, Dr. Marshall adds. In women, the femur or upper bone of the leg has an obliquity in comparison to the male's. And since the femur leans in toward the knees, it causes some women to be knock-kneed. When women try to run with this condition, they could be putting unequal stress on their knees, pinching the outsides while stretching the insides.

Perhaps even worse, says Dr. Marshall, women are innately flexible, which not only makes their knees more mobile but also appears to go along with flat feet, which makes the toes turn out and the knees turn in even more. In addition, many women have weak thigh muscles that prevent them from holding their kneecaps in place. Consequently, many female runners complain of sore knees, excessive slipping of the kneecap and in some cases dislocations. This is often more pronounced in women in their 30s and 40s who have begun an active sports program following a decade of raising children or starting a career. This, says Dr. Marshall, is because they have not exercised to any great extent in many years, and their muscles are not properly conditioned to control their kneecaps and compensate for the angularity of their knees.

This problem can be circumvented, he adds, by shortening the stride and practicing running on the heels. Thigh muscle exercises are also a "must." And, he continues, there are mechanical aids, such as wedges in running shoes, that will keep the knees from turning in each time the runner's foot lands, or a patella (kneecap) alignment brace to keep the kneecap from slipping.

"The growth in popularity of running as a sport for women and the increased success of women runners prove that the female hip and leg structures, in the cases where they are disadvantages, are certainly not obstacles that can't be overcome."[1]

Menstruation and Hormones

Although stressful exercise can delay or disrupt women's menstrual cycles, this can generally be reversed and does not seem to affect fertility. As an example, Dr. Tenley Albright, a researcher at Harvard University (who won an Olympic gold medal for figure skating in 1956), Rose Frisch, Ph.D., another Harvard researcher, and their colleagues surveyed 2,622 women, aged 21 to 80, concerning how many children they had had. Most of the women had been on a college varsity team. Those surveys were compared with those of 2,776 women who had not been college athletes. There was no difference in the size of the women's families, Dr. Albright says.[2]

"Intense activity may mean women aren't apt to get pregnant, but our studies show there is no effect on fertility in the long run," Dr. Albright told *U.S. News & World Report.*[2]

The magazine article adds that any exercising woman who develops menstrual irregularities or stops menstruating should see a doctor to rule out thyroid disorders, hormone-secreting tumors, psychological stress and other disorders. And doctors recommend that women who are unable to become pregnant should cut back on their physical exercise.

"Scientists pretty much agree that the long-term benefits of exercise far outweigh any temporary side effects," continues the magazine. "And you don't have to run marathons. Albright says that even a couple of daily stretching sessions lasting as little as 7 minutes each can be beneficial. In short, if you were looking for an excuse to sit at your desk and munch on Snickers bars while your co-workers don their jogging shorts, you'll have to keep on looking."[2]

Researchers at the Veterans Administration Medical Center, Seattle, Washington, believe that high levels of cortisol, a hormone produced by the adrenal glands, may be linked to amenorrhea in female athletes, according to *Medical World News.*[3] However, the relation remains obscure, says William J.

Bremner, M.D., Chief of Medicine at the Medical Center and Professor of Medicine at the University of Washington.

Since animal and human studies have shown that elevated levels of cortisol can suppress the reproductive system, the researchers conducted a study of 71 women, ages 20 to 35, who did not smoke, were not on contraceptives or other hormonal therapy.

The researchers divided the women into three groups: 1) amenorrheic women who did not menstruate or who had had only one period in the year preceding the study; 2) women who had regular menses every 26 to 34 days; 3) a transition group, consisting of women who were amenorrheic when the study began but resumed menstrual function in six months. The controls were ten women who had normal menstrual cycles and who did not exercise regularly.

Fasting blood samples were taken weekly for four weeks, and there was no difference in cortisol levels for the women who had regular menstrual cycles, the transitional group and the women who did not exercise. In the amenorrheic group, however, cortisol levels were significantly higher. Of the nine women who had abnormally high cortisol levels, eight were in the group with abnormal menstrual cycles. All of the women in the transitional group, who resumed regular menstrual cycles after six months of regular exercise, had normal cortisol counts. Thus, Dr. Bremner concludes, "Hypercortisolemia indicates a higher risk for persistent amenorrhea."[3]

The medical journal adds that bone mineral content of the volunteers, measured by dual photon absorptiometry of the lumbar vertebrae, confirmed findings of earlier studies that women with exercise-related menstrual problems have lower mean bone densities than those who menstruate regularly.

Although exercise can relieve stress and anxiety, it can also promote them and can lead to menstrual difficulties, according to Mona Shangold, M.D., and Gabe Mirkin, M.D., in *The Complete Sports Medicine Book for Women*.[4] Although there are many factors, the emotional aspects of training and competition may aggravate the problem, they say.

They go on to state that exercise temporarily alters the production of several hormones, such as estrogen, progesterone, testosterone, prolactin, adrenaline and noradrenaline. After exercise, these functions generally return to normal in an hour or so.

"Women who exercise strenuously on a regular basis may develop some long-lasting hormone alterations, with the incidence rising as exercise is more strenuous, more prolonged, and more frequent," they add. "For example, women are more likely to develop a luteal phase defect when they increase their weekly running mileage. This minor disturbance may progress to a more serious condition: first, lack of ovulation with infrequent periods (in which the woman is still making estrogen but is not making progesterone), and then amenorrhea (with neither estrogen, progesterone, testosterone, [nor] prolactin . . .). Most of these changes return to normal independent of cause: 1) luteal phase defect, 2) infrequent periods without ovulation (progesterone deficiency), 3) total cessation of periods (estrogen deficiency)."

In addition to menstrual irregularities, some women athletes may also have heavy bleeding at regular intervals and bleeding between periods, menstrual cramps and premenstrual syndrome. These difficulties, say Drs. Shangold and Mirkin, should be analyzed by a gynecologist.

Unfortunately, women who exercise regularly are just as prone to menstrual complaints as those who are sedentary, according to Elizabeth Kaufman in *American Health*.[5] The Melpomene Institute for Women's Health Research in Minnesota queried 400 members concerning exercise and their menstrual patterns and found that the physically active were as prone to painful periods as the inactive women. However, 52.6 percent of the inactive women did report fewer menstrual complaints after they began exercising, and 41 percent of the women exercising vigorously reported relief.[5]

"Giving exercise a try is a good place to start," says Judy Mahler Lutter, president of the Institute. "But women shouldn't think something is wrong with them if exercise doesn't solve their menstrual problems."[5]

Although long-term studies have yet to be done, there is some indication that the Pill can affect athletic performance. In a column in *Runner's World*, Joan Ullyot, M.D., notes that one woman runner she knew of improved her time by going off of the oral contraceptive.[6] And she reports that British researchers found a 10 percent decrease in maximum aerobic capacity in a group of young women using the Pill. This returned to normal when they discontinued oral contraceptives.

Dr. Ullyot discusses the various forms of birth control and their usefulness to women athletes. Although convenient, the IUD can instigate cramps and heavy bleeding, which can cause anemia. The so-called barrier methods—diaphragm, cervical cap and condom—have no side effects, but the failure rate is rather high (from 2 to 25 percent). The remaining method is the rhythm method of periodic abstinence, or plotting your temperature chart to find out when ovulation has occurred. Testing cervical mucus is another way of determining ovulation. Sterilization, another option, is still questionable, since some women have reported cramping and severe premenstrual syndrome complaints.

"Once ovulation takes place you're generally safe until after your next period, so your time of abstinence (using the rhythm method) is reduced to the pre-ovulatory days," explains Dr. Ullyot. (If you're using barrier methods for birth control, the same techniques for determining ovulation can be used to enable you to dispense with the inconvenience for half of each month.)[6]

However, she continues, research by Dr. Jerilynn Prior and others has shown that many women runners have a shortened luteal phase in their menstrual cycle while they are training hard.

"This means," she adds, "that the time from ovulation to the onset of menstrual flow is reduced from the 'normal' twelve days to about eight. If you're using 'rhythm,' you may have fewer 'safe' days than sedentary women do."[6]

Although many factors are involved, some researchers report that a regular exercise program throughout a woman's lifetime may reduce her chances of getting breast cancer. In a study of 5,398 women, of whom 2,622 were college athletes, Rose Frisch, Ph.D., Associate Professor of Population Sciences at Harvard University, found that non-athletes had 2.53 times the risk of cancers of the reproductive system and 1.86 times the risk of breast cancer when compared with women who were athletes.[7]

Inactivity may be a major factor in the development of both colon cancer and breast cancer, according to data discussed at a meeting of the American College of Sports Medicine in Las Vegas, Nevada in 1987. Although much needs to be learned about this relationship, Steven N. Blair, M.D., Director of Epidemiology at the Institute of Aerobics Research, Dallas, Texas, says, "I would probably place this investigation (at the same point we were at) 30 to 40 years ago with cigarettes and lung cancer."[8]

Anorexia

Although we usually do not associate anorexia nervosa (self-starvation) or bulimia (self-induced vomiting after food binges) with women athletes, these are surprisingly frequent health complaints among some athletes. An article in the October 1986 issue of *The Runner,* describes "Ellen," who was a champion distance runner in high school.[9] After entering college, her performances nosedived, her kick failed her and her times rose alarmingly. The answer: She was starving herself to get thinner, thinking this would improve her performance.

"A recent Michigan State University survey shows that 32 percent of female college athletes use such potentially damaging weight-control techniques as self-induced vomiting, laxatives, diet pills or diuretics (water pills) in an effort to trim off pounds," the article says. "Of those who used these techniques, 83 percent admitted that they did so in hopes of improving their athletic performance."[9]

The study, which surveyed 182 college athletes, found that women participating in gymnastics (74 percent) field hockey (50 percent) and long-distance running (47 percent) most frequently used these dangerous methods of weight control. Although it was not discussed in the article, all of these procedures eliminate essential vitamins, minerals and other nutrients to such an extent that this can lead to anemia, irregular heart beats and a variety of complications. Laxatives and diuretics are, for that reason, dangerous to anyone, but certainly they are counterproductive for athletes.

"The stress of these methods may not have a negative impact on young bodies and sometimes performance might even improve," says Lionel Rosen, Professor of Psychiatry at MSU and coauthor of the study. "But when the individual gets a little older, the body will compensate for years of abuse and neglect."[9]

Treatment for anorexia nervosa generally consists of nutritional therapy, individual psychotherapy and family counseling, says *Facts About Anorexia Nervosa,* a publication of the U. S. Department of Health and Human Services, Washington, D. C.[10] Some of these patients require hospitalization, while others are nursed back to health in the family setting.

"But no matter where therapy is started, the most urgent concern of the physician is getting the patient to eat and gain weight," adds the publication. "This is accomplished by gradually adding calories to the patient's daily intake. If she is hospitalized, privileges are sometimes granted in return for weight gain. This is known as a behavioral contract, and privileges may include such desirable activities as leaving the hospital for an afternoon's outing."[10]

Self-help groups involving family members are critical in preventing the patient from having a relapse. Although men are sometimes affected by this problem, the majority of patients are women, who feel a need to be thin for cosmetic reasons or, as in the case of Ellen, to supposedly help athletic performance. Information on treatment centers, hospitals, and doctors specializing in anorexia can be obtained from:

American Anorexia Nervosa Association, Inc., 133 Cedar Lane, Teaneck, New Jersey 07666.

National Anorexic Aid Society, Inc., Box 29461, Columbus, Ohio 43229.

Anorexia Nervosa and Associated Disorders, Suite 2020, 550 Frontage Rd., Northfield, Illinois 60093.

Osteoporosis

Another health problem that affects men but is more pronounced in women is osteoporosis. The word means "porous bone," and this disease results in less bone mass and a greater likelihood that a bone fracture can occur. Osteoporosis is six to eight times more common in women than men, mainly because women generally have less bone mass to begin with and also because of the cessation of hormonal production after menopause. Approximately 200,000 Americans over the age of 45 suffer from broken hips due to osteoporosis each year, according to *Osteoporosis: Cause, Treatment, Prevention,* published by the U.S. Department of Health and Human Services.[11]

Bone, like other tissues in the body, is constantly being rebuilt, explains the publication. Old bone is torn down or resorbed and replaced with new bone. Living bone has a protein framework (the osteoid matrix) in which calcium salts are deposited. Actually, the bones and teeth contain about 99 percent of the calcium in the body.

"This process of bone resorption and remodeling serves two purposes: It keeps the skeleton well-tuned for its mechanical uses, and it helps to maintain the body's balance of certain essential minerals such as calcium," explains the publication. "The body keeps a relatively constant level of calcium in the blood, because important biological activities such as contraction of muscles, beating of the heart, and clotting of blood require quite constant blood levels of calcium. When the blood calcium level drops, more calcium is taken out of the bones to maintain the appropriate level. When the blood calcium level returns to normal, increased amounts of calcium are no longer taken from the bones."[11]

When youngsters are growing, the publication continues, bones are metabolically active, and calcium is deposited into the bones faster than it is taken out. This build-up of calcium into bone peaks at about age 35 in both men and women. It is at this time that "peak bone mass" is the densest and strongest, suggesting that we need to build up a strong bone mass by this time to carry us through the later years in which we lose more bone than is being replaced.

Some experts believe, says the publication, that the level of bone mass at this time may determine whether or not a person may later lose enough bone to fracture easily. If a young woman develops a high peak bone mass—possibly through increased calcium intake, moderate weight-bearing exercise and other lifestyle choices—she is probably less likely to develop osteoporosis.

"During a person's late thirties, after peak bone mass is attained, calcium begins to be lost from bones faster than it is replaced, and bones become less dense," continues the publication. "This occurs naturally and gradually in both men and women. In addition, in general, as both women and men age, their bodies begin to absorb less calcium from food. This begins at about age 45 for women and age 60 for men."[11]

Therefore, the factors affecting bone health can be summarized as: level of peak bone mass by age 35; rates of bone loss due to menopause and aging; certain systemic hormones (such as calcitriol, an active form of vitamin D; parathyroid hormone; and calcitonin); substances produced by the bones themselves; diet (especially calcium intake); intestinal and kidney function; and physical forces that act on the bones such as those caused by body weight and exercise.

Estrogen, the female hormone, seems to slow the loss of bone as well as to aid in the absorption of calcium by the intestine. After menopause, when the production of sex hormones is abruptly reduced, the health of the bones is naturally compromised. But this shutdown makes biological sense. When she is of child-bearing age, a woman needs a strong skeleton and a steady reserve of calcium for becoming pregnant and nursing children. After menopause, this protective reserve of calcium is not needed. Thus, as her estrogen level drops, her bones begin to contribute a larger share of calcium for the body's needs.

A number of studies have shown that American women between the ages of 25 and 74 are only getting between 450 and 550 milligrams of calcium daily. This contrasts with the RDA of 800 milligrams, and a recommendation of between 1,000 and 1,500 milligrams per day in food or supplements as a protective measure against osteoporosis. When the desired amount of calcium is not obtained daily, the body simply "goes to the bank" (the bones) to take what it needs. After years of the leaching away of calcium from the bones, they can eventually become almost like chalk, so that a fracture can happen simply by turning in bed. The suggestion that she "fell and broke her hip" may not be accurate. The brittle bone broke as she moved about, and then she fell. (Of course, brittle bones also can be broken during a fall.)

Therefore, a chronic shortage of calcium is a major cause of osteoporosis. In addition to the usual discarding of old bone, in which some calcium is lost, the mineral is also lost in urine and feces and, to a lesser extent, in perspiration. Although researchers are not convinced of the reasons, smoking and alcohol reduce calcium and vitamin D stores. The vitamin, which is obtained from the sun, from irradiated milk and a few other sources, as well as from supplements, is necessary for the absorption of calcium.

Other causes of osteoporosis, according to the HHS publication, include:

• Medications such as corticosteroids and heparin (an anticoagulant).
• Diseases such as hyperthyroidism, hyperparathyroidism, kidney disease and certain forms of cancer (lymphoma, leukemia and multiple myeloma).

- Impaired ability to absorb calcium from the intestine caused by diseases of the small intestine, liver or pancreas.
- Excessive excretion of calcium in the urine (idiopathic hypercalcuria).

Writing in *Complementary Medicine,* Nancy E. Lane, M.D., says that increases in calcium intake and exercise against gravity—running, aerobic dancing and brisk walking—should have the benefit of laying down more bone mineral.[12] Taken to the extreme, of course, this can have a detrimental effect. She says that some women marathon runners, who have exercised so extensively that they are amenorrheic, have been found to have bone density comparable to 50-year-old women. And these were women in their mid-20s! They were very lean (less than 10 percent body fat), had very low bone mineral levels and reduced amounts of estrogen.

Although there is no definite cut-off point at which running becomes dangerous to a woman's body, Dr. Lane says that in competitive runners this is believed to be about 50 training miles per week. Since each woman's body is different, the alarm signals will vary from woman to woman.

"You can run to a point," Dr. Lane continues, "and then your body will start to tell you to stop. Injuries will keep recurring; you will be tired. When you begin to lose weight and not perform well, you are over-stressing your body. If you have been able to run a 40-minute 10K, and although you keep training it becomes 42, 46 or 48 minutes, then you are overdoing it. I think the body can warn you long before there are any major problems. You have soft tissue over your injuries—tendinitis, muscle pulls, stress fractures—but I believe if you do not heed those types of injuries, you could eventually have damage to the joints."[12]

Sources of Calcium and Vitamin D

For a list of calcium-rich foods, refer to table 4 in the chapter on nutrition. Needless to say, dairy products are the richest source of dietary calcium. Three cups of milk, depending on the kind, can meet or exceed the RDA for calcium for the day. Cheese and yogurt are also excellent sources.

When a vegetarian tells me that she gets sufficient calcium from broccoli, kale, and the like, I suggest that she review the figures. As an example, to get the 1,000 milligrams of calcium per day that would hopefully prevent osteoporosis, she would have to eat about six cups of broccoli or about the same amount of kale. Or, to put it another way, she would have to eat over 13 broccoli spears.

Other vegetarians have told me, "Oh, I get my calcium from Tums." It's true that these antacids contain calcium carbonate, a reliable source of calcium, but, for an osteoporosis prevention program, you have to consume eight or nine of these tablets daily. Who knows what impact this amount of antacid would have on digestion, since these tablets are designed for another purpose, not as a source of calcium? Also, why take tablets that have a sweetening agent that you don't need? Or added flavors? Some antacids contain aluminum, which can interfere with the absorption of calcium. And some of these drugs contain talc, which could be carcinogenic.

When checking supplement labels, be aware of how many tablets it takes to get the amount of calcium you want. In addition, you may not be getting the amount of calcium listed on the label. For example, calcium carbonate is 40 percent calcium. Therefore, 100 milligrams of calcium carbonate contains 40 milligrams of elemental calcium, so that you need to know this when planning your calcium intake. Calcium lactate is 13 percent calcium (250 milligrams on the label actually converts to 34 milligrams of calcium). Calcium gluconate is 9 percent calcium.

Those who have difficulty digesting milk do not have the enzyme lactase to digest the lactose (milk sugar) in the milk. There are several ways this often can be corrected. For one thing, try a little yogurt or cheese at a time and gradually build up the amount you consume. This may reactivate the necessary enzyme. Some yogurts have lactase already. Also, eat yogurt or milk that has been treated with the enzyme. This enzyme is commercially known as LactAid and it can be bought at health food stores to add to your milk or yogurt at home.

The RDA for vitamin D is 400 International Units daily. It was added to milk many years ago to prevent rickets. For those who do not drink a quart of milk daily (which contains 400 I.U. of vitamin D), the vitamin is available in other dairy products, eggs, fish, and liver. A nice walk in the sun, providing the rays are not shielded by protective clothing, can also provide much of the daily requirement for vitamin D.

Although proper nutrition and other recommendations for preventing osteoporosis are well known, they may only benefit younger women, according to Shelley Kirk, exercise physiologist at the University of Southern California. In any event, the protective measures should begin before menopause, she told *Medical World News.*[13]

In checking ten women, 25 to 35 years old, who had been running an average of 33 miles per week for seven years, Kirk found that they had greater vertebral trabecular bone density and radial cortical bone density than age- and weight-matched sedentary controls. This did not hold true for eight postmenopausal runners, ages 55 to 65. Their vertebral bone density was almost identical to that of sedentary controls, Kirk says. But, she reports, exercising women in both age groups had greater levels of 25-hydroxy-vitamin D than did the controls.

Eating Well

In the April 28, 1988 issue of *USA Today,* it was reported that Joan Benoit Samuelson would be unable to repeat her championship participation in the 1984 Olympic games.[14] She withdrew from the 1988 Olympic Marathon Trials in Pittsburgh because of injuries that disrupted her training.

"Benoit won the 1984 Trials 17 days after arthroscopic knee surgery," reports the newspaper. "She gave birth in October and has had back, leg and hip injuries since January. The problems prevented her from running from late

January until late March. . . . Benoit, 30, has not run a marathon since 1985. She holds the second-fastest women's time of 2:21:21.''[14]

Writing in *The Nutritional Ages of Women*, Patricia Long reports that, ''Marathon runner Joan Benoit thinks nothing of having a cone of pistachio ice cream and calling it 'lunch.' ''[15]

Concerned nutritionists might wonder whether or not there is a connection between Benoit's recurring injuries and her diet. We, of course, are not told by Patricia Long what else Benoit eats, but the stress required to run a marathon requires a well-planned nutritional program. An ice cream cone would not supply enough vitamin D, vitamin C, iron, magnesium, protein, and other nutrients to keep a hummingbird alive, much less a marathon runner. Childbirth, of course, would contribute to the problem. If a pregnant woman is not getting sufficient nutrients for herself and the baby, the baby always wins out, because the fetus takes whatever nutrients it must have, leaving the mother to fend for herself.

Julie Brown, who a few years back ranked third in the world in women's marathon and second in the United States in road racing, says that proper nutrition is definitely related to performance. She reports that she can see the difference in her training since she switched from being a vegetarian to eating a well-balanced diet, adding that nutrition is responsible for the training highs and lows of athletes. Early in her career, she tried to subsist basically on whole grain bread and she was close to becoming anorexic.

''The injuries were coming more frequently when I was a vegetarian,'' she says. ''Now that I am getting more protein in my diet, I'm not getting injured as often. It has been my experience that most athletes don't eat well.''[16]

As insurance against possible deficiencies, Brown believes that vitamin supplements make good sense for athletes. When competing, she eats twice a day, with the largest meal at noon. Dinner is on the light side, as it should be for everyone, athletes and non-athletes alike. (Eating a heavy meal just before retiring is guaranteed to put on weight, since the digestive tract has to cope with a large amount of food while the body is inactive.) Brown's well-balanced diet consists of complex carbohydrates, fish, poultry and some meat. To avoid dehydration, she increases her fluid intake while running, especially water and fruit juice.

Like most women, many female athletes do not get enough calcium, iron and protein, says *FDA Consumer*, May 1987.[17] And athletes of both sexes, as well as many other Americans, may be deficient in vitamin B6 and folic acid, another B vitamin.

''To remedy these deficiencies, athletes should look to dairy products as a good source of calcium; meat, fish, legumes—peas and beans—and spinach for iron; red meat, poultry, potatoes, lentils, broccoli and bananas for vitamin B6 (pyridoxine); and such fruits and vegetables as spinach, beets, romaine lettuce and oranges for folic acid; and meat, eggs and dairy products for protein,'' recommends the publication.[17]

In one study, says *FDA Consumer*, adult male endurance runners consumed 20 percent of their calories as alcoholic beverages. ''Those 'empty calories,' like those in sugary sweets, have little nutritional value.''[17]

"The advice for feeding athletes has changed a lot since the time of Charmis of Sparta," concludes the publication. "We know that no single food or supplement provides a 'magic bullet' for an athlete's body. Thus, for the vast majority of athletes—from high school quarterbacks to middle-aged joggers, the modern-day advice is the same as that for the general public: Eat a well-balanced diet from a wide variety of foods in sufficient amounts to meet energy needs. When followed throughout life, such a meal plan will provide benefits long after an athlete's competitive peak has waned."[17]

Iron and Other Nutrients

Runners, both male and female, are at risk of developing iron deficiency anemia: 1) they lose iron at the rate of 0.4 milligram per liter of sweat; and 2) the runner's food passes through his or her digestive tract more quickly than the non-runner, providing less time for the iron to be absorbed from the diet, reports *Food & Nutrition News*.[18]

The newsletter adds that athletes who exercise strenuously can lose between 1 and 3 liters of sweat per hour. As an example, the RDA for iron for the male runner is 10 milligrams of iron because of the absorption problem. The RDA for iron for the female runner (or all women for that matter) is 18 milligrams daily. But she has to consume 23 milligrams of iron daily to prevent anemia. Women lose a great deal of iron in menstrual flow.

Iron deficiency anemia should not be confused with "sports anemia," continues the publication. This is a temporary condition that is found principally in military recruits during their first weeks of basic training, or when a previously sedentary person begins a daily exercise program. Sports anemia is temporary and is treatable; iron deficiency anemia can also be treated but it can be fatal.

Writing in *Today's Living*, Carlson Wade quotes Joan Ullyot, M.D., a world-class Master's (over 40) distance runner and member of the American College of Sports Medicine, as saying that, "Extra iron is a must for the athletic woman. The need for iron is especially noticeable in active women because of the high oxygen demand of running and other aerobic sports. Iron carries and binds oxygen in the blood and muscles. A chronic iron deficiency is common among women. . . . Even if you eat oodles of liver, spinach and egg yolks . . . you'll barely manage to keep up. And there may be more iron loss in active women because of high oxygen demands of exercise."[19]

Dr. Ullyot adds that many top runners have learned that unexplained slumps in their performances have been traced to a sudden iron deficiency. Consequently, she recommends that runners supplement their diet with at least a multiple vitamin-mineral formula with extra iron.

Wade quotes Doug Clement, M.D., codirector of the University of British Columbia's Sports Medicine Clinic and physician to the Canadian Olympic track team, as saying that 90 percent of the team's female runners were deficient in iron.

"Vigorous exercise in the absence of supplementation may be a reason for this deficiency, especially in joggers, runners and long-distance hikers," says

Dr. Clement. "Furthermore, heavy perspiring also can cause considerable iron loss. Since the oxygen-carrying capacity of blood is reduced with iron deficiency, fatigue is likely to occur earlier and last longer. Depression and insomnia also are common symptoms of iron deficiency."[19]

A study at Tufts University, continues Wade, reports that endurance exercise causes an excretion of large amounts of zinc, which is required for tissue repair, appetite, digestion and other uses. The researchers add that the blood levels of long-distance runners averaged 20 percent below normal levels for this important nutrient.[19]

Women athletes who develop amenorrhea eat less fat and fewer calories than other women, and they tend to run greater distances each week, according to Evelyn P. Whitlock, M.D., in *The Calcium Plus Workbook*.[20] In one study, women who had abnormal periods were running 42 miles each week, compared with an average of 25 miles per week for women with regular menses.

"Women between the ages of 20 and 35 who follow vegetarian diets and who exercise strenuously also have a higher prevalence of amenorrhea than those with more varied diets," she continues. "Women who are excessively thin and amenorrheic have the most bone loss. Luckily, not all women who exercise at these levels who reduce body weight in a moderate manner develop amenorrhea."[20]

Dr. Whitlock adds that, although women between the ages of 20 and 35 usually maintain a better balance of diet and exercise than older women, they still fall short of the ideal. As an example, she continues, women 20 to 35 generally consume only 75 percent of the RDA for calcium. But they consume one-and-a-half times their RDA for protein and at least 40 percent of their calories as fat.

Most younger women receive 200 International Units of vitamin D each day, which is often ideal except during pregnancy, adds Dr. Whitlock. Women who are in the sun for part of the day obtain some of their vitamin D when the sun reacts with oils and perspiration on the skin and the body converts this into usable vitamin D; other vitamin D comes from foods.

"Women between 20 and 35 also consume more alcohol than women in other age groups," says Dr. Whitlock. "At least 5 to 10 percent of women have more than two drinks per day. This is the threshold; women who have more than that lose calcium, which is likely to affect bone. This is also the age group in which most women have children (and pregnancy and lactation can also impact on the calcium stores of these women)."[20]

Dr. Whitlock goes on to say that one-third of the women between 20 and 35 diet at least once a month to lose weight. Over one-fourth diet for longer than a month. Further, 16 percent diet for two to five months; more than 10 percent diet for more than six months. Long-term diets that are inadequate in all nutrients can affect the health of the bones, she says.

"Most weight-loss diets provide adequate amounts of protein but are low in vitamins and minerals," Dr. Whitlock says. "One study which analyzed eleven popular weight-loss diet plans, including the Beverly Hills diet, the California diet, the Pritikin diet, the F-plan diet, the Stillman diet, and the Never-Say-Diet diet, found that not one diet provided 100 percent of the Recommended Dietary

Allowance for 13 vitamins and minerals. The nutrients most likely to be low were vitamin B1, vitamin B6, vitamin B12, calcium, iron, zinc and magnesium."[20]

Dr. Whitlock adds that another study reports that, after six weeks on a diet of 800 to 1,000 calories daily, women lost between 13 and 18 pounds. However, one-third of them developed menstrual irregularities. Surprisingly, after the women had been dieting for one month at these reduced calorie levels, their estrogen levels were the same as those seen in women in menopause. This could, of course, severely affect bone density.

Dr. Whitlock adds that at 1,200 calories per day it is virtually impossible to get the RDA for all vitamins and minerals; even a 1,600-calorie diet is suspect, she says. Therefore, at such low calorie levels, a vitamin-mineral supplement may be required to maintain adequate nutrient intake.

"Current research suggests that ultra-low calorie diets (500 calories or so) require increased protein during their course; to prevent muscle or lean tissue loss a woman on such a severe diet may need to consume double the RDA of protein," Dr. Whitlock cautions. "So far, no one is sure of the long-term detrimental effects on bone of a combination of high protein, low calcium and possible menstrual irregularities you would see in such extreme dieters. Those on ultra-low calorie diets should definitely be monitored by their doctors. In addition to not receiving the necessary amounts of nutrients, women who diet excessively or engage in excessive athletic training may experience menstrual difficulties or amenorrhea (total lack of menses . . .)."

Speaking at a meeting of the American Chemical Society in St. Louis in 1984, Daphne Roe, M.D., of Cornell University, Ithaca, New York, told the participants that women who exercise need twice the Recommended Dietary Allowance for riboflavin (vitamin B2). She adds that B2 is essential for energy production and that its depletion during exercise may indicate an increased requirement by working muscles. She adds that even sedentary women may need 80 percent more than the RDA for riboflavin.[27]

Riboflavin is available in eggs, milk, cheese, liver and poultry. The RDA is between 1.2 and 1.7 milligrams.

Women who smoke heavily are six times more likely to suffer a stroke than non-smokers, according to an eight-year study sponsored by the National Institutes of Health. The study, which involved 118,539 women aged 30 to 55, found that the risk of stroke increases steadily with the number of cigarettes smoked.[21]

The researchers add that, compared with women who do not smoke, women smoker's risk of stroke jumps:

- 2.2 times for those who smoke one to 14 cigarettes daily.
- 3.7 times for those who smoke over 25 cigarettes daily.
- 4.7 times for those who smoke 35 to 44 cigarettes a day.
- 6.2 times for those who smoke more than that.

Pregnancy and Running

Running during pregnancy should not be a problem for most women, providing you have been running for at least six months prior to becoming pregnant and your body is well conditioned to exercise, according to *Running Women—The First Steps*.[22] However, it is probably best to cut back as the pregnancy continues. Swimming is an excellent alternative, since it provides for physical conditioning while avoiding the pounding from the roads.

"Consult with your obstetrician as soon as you think you may be pregnant," suggests the booklet. "It helps tremendously if your obstetrician is exercise-oriented and supportive of your running endeavors. Obviously, if you notice any unusual spotting or discomfort, notify your OB. Otherwise, consult with your doctor first, wear a good supportive bra, non-restrictive clothing and be prepared to make many more 'pit-stops' while you're out running."[22]

A study published in the May 27, 1988 issue of the *Journal of the American Medical Association*, and elaborated on by Jane E. Brody in *The New York Times*, reports that moderate physical activity does not endanger the fetuses of healthy women as long as the woman has a normal pregnancy.[23] The investigators—Marshall Carpenter, M.D., an obstetrician; Stanley Sady, M.D., a physiologist; and Paul D. Thompson, M.D., a cardiologist—urged most pregnant women to continue jogging, swimming, cycling, playing tennis, and the like. They found that the heart rates of unborn children did not decline unless the pregnant women pushed themselves too strenuously while exercising. In cases where the fetal heart rate did decline, the drop only lasted from 2 to 12 minutes after the woman had stopped exercising, according to the research team from Brown University, Providence, Rhode Island. The researchers theorize that the reduced heart rate is caused by a reflex reaction rather than a reduced blood flow to the fetus.

The study team also reported that all the fetuses, even those that had a brief drop in heart rate, showed normal cardiac responses within a half-hour of the exercise session, the *Times* article continues. All of the babies delivered by the 45 women in the study were normal at birth, except for two babies with unrelated problems.

"Dr. Carpenter said the new study showed no ill effects on fetal heart rate at pulse rates of 150 and even higher," adds the *Times*. "But both he and Dr. Thompson cautioned women to be moderate about exercise and that they not try to push themselves to the limit."[23]

At the Hershey (Pennsylvania) Medical Center, John Botti, M.D., and Robert Jones, Ed.D., conducted a study of eighteen pregnant runners to determine whether or not exercise affected their developing fetuses, according to *Runner's World*.[24] After an initial 1.5-mile time trial, the women were tested every trimester as they ran on a treadmill or outdoor track.

"Women who continue to run almost until delivery, such as Joan (Benoit) Samuelson, usually report feeling better and regaining prepregnancy fitness more rapidly than women who do not run while pregnant," says *Runner's World*. "But until now, researchers knew little about the effects of the late-stage running on the mother and baby."[24]

After the Pennsylvania study was completed, the researchers reported that no harmful exercise-induced problems were noted in the children or their mothers. However, some of the women slowed significantly after the 32nd week, and they switched to walking and swimming. Althea Zanecosky, a nutritionist,

40-mile-per-week runner and 3:17 marathoner, ran successfully through her pregnancy and resumed her running less than a month after delivering a healthy girl.

"Pregnant women shouldn't assume that because of this study they can go out and run," cautions Dr. Botti. "These women—all of whom were trained runners—were monitored very carefully. And although the study was a success, we can't generalize that what is OK for one is OK for all. The patient who wishes to continue exercise should be evaluated by an expert."[24]

Mary Decker Slaney, the internationally-known runner, ran for the first five months of her pregnancy in 1986, she told *The Runner*.[25] She resumed running six days after the delivery of Ashley, and she continued her conditioning on a Nordic Track ski simulator. In her first race after becoming a mother, the Mercedes Mile in New York, she came in sixth, but she admits that she resumed high-intensity training too soon after giving birth.

During her pregnancy, Slaney complemented her running with weight machine workouts, supervised by her physician, Randy Lewis, M.D., of Eugene, Oregon. Dr. Lewis, also a runner, has delivered Alberto Salazar's two children, among others. He cautioned Slaney not to run in oxygen debt and to listen to her body. He also warned against overfatigue, since this can deprive the baby of everything it needs.

"I couldn't run normally the last four months of the pregnancy," Slaney continues. "The cramps would come and go, so after five months, I ran only every two or three days. Only a mile or so, and even that was walking and running. I also lifted light weights, did workouts on a Lifecycle and Nordic Track and ran in a swimming pool. I would do at least one of these activities every day. At a certain point I could only run a half-mile or even a quarter-mile. I'd get this awful pain, down below, where I was carrying. By comparison, Molly Salazar was able to run five or six miles a day almost until the day she gave birth."[25]

Slaney told the magazine that if she had that pregnancy to do over, she would do more sedate exercises, more fluid ones with not so much jarring. That, she believes, would allow her to run longer into the pregnancy.

"I think I made a mistake by doing exercises which included a lot of bounding, bouncing and hopping," she says. "After five months, I had a hard time running because I was carrying the baby low and that was causing a lot of cramping."[25]

Training and Temperature Regulation

According to *Women in Long-Distance Running*, published by the American College of Sports Medicine, women respond to systematic exercise training in almost the same manner as men.[26] In both cases, cardiorespiratory function is enhanced, as demonstrated by significant increases in maximal oxygen uptake. At maximal exercise, the booklet says, the amount of blood pumped per heart beat (stroke volume) and the total amount of blood pumped (cardiac output) are increased after training. At standardized submaximal exercise after training, cardiac output remains unchanged, heart rate decreases and stroke volume increases. Resting heart rate also declines after training. And, as with men, endurance training reduces relative body fat content.

"Long-distance running imposes a significant stress on body temperature regulation (thermoregulation)," continues the booklet. "There are differences between men and women with regard to thermoregulation during prolonged exercise. However, these differences are more quantitative than qualitative. For example, when women are exposed to the same thermal stress as men, they experience lower evaporative heat losses and their skin temperature and deep body temperature are higher when sweating begins. This may actually be an advantage in reducing body water loss as long as thermal equilibrium can be maintained."[26]

The booklet adds that women trained in long-distance running have often been more tolerant of heat stress than nonathletic women matched for age and body size. Therefore, it appears that trained female long-distance runners have the capacity to adequately deal with the thermal stress of prolonged exercise as well as the moderate-to-high environmental temperatures and relative humidities that often accompany these events.

Walking and Weight Loss

At the Rockport Walking Institute, researchers are conducting ongoing studies on the physiological benefits and biomechanics of walking. The Institute's prominent advisory board examines current walking research and assigns grants for ongoing research projects. In addition, the Institute sponsors educational literature on walking, corporate fitness programs, children's educational walking programs and a speaker's bureau of prominent physicians, athletes, authors, and the like. One of the educational projects developed by the Institute is *Rockport's Fitness Walking for Women,* by Anne Kashiwa and James Rippe, M.D., published in 1987 by G. P. Putnam's Sons/Perigee Books, New York. It is designed for women who want to take up walking and is oriented to such topics as losing weight, fitness during pregnancy, stress reduction, muscle toning, aerobic conditioning, and how to prevent injuries.

"Permanent weight loss involves adopting a lifestyle of good eating habits and moderate exercise," says Ann Ward, Ph.D., Exercise Physiologist and Research Director of the University of Massachusetts Medical School Exercise Physiology Laboratory, who helped with the exercises developed in the book. "This does not necessarily mean jogging or playing tennis every day, but simply increasing the daily amount of energy you expend."[28]

Dr. Ward adds that many people who want to lose weight realize the importance of exercise but don't know where to begin. That's where *Rockport's Fitness Walking for Women* provides a suitable starting point for women who want to lose weight, she says.

The program incorporates the Rockport Fitness Walking Test, which was developed by Dr. Rippe and his associates. It evaluates cardiovascular fitness based on walking and then makes suggestions concerning a walking program based on age and sex. In fact, the test has been adopted nationally by the

American Volkssport Association, the Denver Police Department, and the YMCA of USA Corporate Health Enhancement Program, among others.

"Fitness walking is an ideal exercise for weight-loss programs," says Dr. Rippe. "Most women are surprised to hear that walking 45 minutes a day, three to four times a week throughout a year will result in losing up to 18 pounds. Furthermore, fitness walking increases calorie expenditure, controls your appetite, helps maintain a resting metabolic rate and burns fat while increasing muscle mass."[28]

Dr. Rippe, who is Director of the University of Massachusetts Medical School Exercise Physiology Laboratory and Research Director of the Rockport Walking Institute, adds that, "When you go on a diet, up to 40 percent of your weight loss may actually be the loss of protein and muscle mass. Combining a regular walking program with a diet helps preserve lean muscle and selectively burns fat, which is precisely what overweight people should do."[28]

Sports Bras

A sports bra is recommended by Gayle Olinekova, the well-known athlete and nutritionist, for women runners because it helps to prevent chafed nipples, a familiar complaint. While running, women's nipples often become cold and erect, and can be irritated by a nylon or mesh shirt. Men can also have this problem, and women, she says, can borrow a solution from the male runners: cover the nipples with adhesive tape and petroleum jelly.[29]

What about sex before a race? Olinekova says this can rob men of needed vitamin E. This is not a problem for women, but sex before a competitive event does seem to inhibit their aggressive edge, she adds.

"Jogging can cause breast sagging and pain," say Kurt Butler, M.S., and Lynn Rayner, M.D., in *The Best Medicine*. "This problem can usually be prevented by wearing a sports bra which prevents lateral and spiraling motions of the breasts. The bra should not bind, but should be rigid enough to limit bouncing. It should have wide nonelastic straps, cotton cups, padded seams and covered metal fasteners."[30]

A study by Deana Lorentzen Ph.D. and LaJean Lawson tested eight brands of sports bras on 59 women as they were filmed while jogging on a treadmill at 6 mph.[31] They report that the Exercise Sports Top (Creative Sport Systems, $29.95); Lady Duke (Royal Textile Mills, $18.95); and the Freedom Frontrunner (Olga, $17) provided the least amount of breast movement in women wearing bra sizes A-cup to D-cup. The ideal bras did not have any irritating seams or fasteners next to the skin; they had firm, durable construction and nonslip straps. The researchers add that large-breasted women should select more rigidly constructed bras than women who are small-breasted.

Women who experience sore or bleeding nipples while running can usually solve the problem with a suitable sports bra, according to Christine E. Haycock, M.D., in *Physician and Sportsmedicine*.[32] Men can simply put band-aids over the nipples.

Writing in *Women's Sports & Fitness,* Cynthia Cummins quotes Dr. Lorentzen, who is Assistant Professor at Utah State University, as saying that a sports bra is as vital a piece of gear as is a tennis racquet or running shoes. And Gale Gehlsen of Ball State University, Ohio, recommends that all women wear supportive tops, regardless of their breast size.[33]

In their study, Lorentzen and LaJean Lawson of the University of Nevada, Reno, report that there is a considerable difference between the amount of vertical breast displacement of large-breasted runners when compared to other athletes. The A-, B- and C-cup athletes could use stretchier, more comfortable bras, Cummins says. However, the D-cup women need bras with rigid, more binding support.

The designers of sports bras approach the problem from two angles, says Cummins. One is to flatten the breasts to evenly distribute the mass across the chest (compression) and the other is to support each breast separately (encapsulation).

"Compression is a variation on the old bind-them-down-with-an-Ace-bandage solution," continues Cummins. "And former physical education instructor Vanessa George Goulden's answer to controlling her D-cup breasts was exactly that—until she designed The Exercise Suppotop (TES). TES is constructed with heavy, one-way stretch nylon/Lycra to minimize bounce and compress the breasts firmly against the chest. A rigid plastic strip in the top-seam keeps the breasts from bouncing up—and back down."[33]

Cummins reports that Jogbra, Inc. and Vanity Fair have both introduced new designs featuring encapsulation, as has Jembra. An advantage of the Jembra line, continues Cummins, is that there are 200 sizes, all custom-fitted. Custom-fitting is done in two different 15- to 45-minute sessions with a Jembra distributor. Unfortunately, the company only has about a dozen distributors nationwide.

In selecting a bra, Cummins says that raceback and cross-back designs prevent straps from slipping off the shoulder and provide maximum arm movement. The best encapsulation designs have nonstretch straps anchored to a nonstretch band toward the center of the back. Large-breasted women, she continues, should look for wide straps that won't dig into the shoulders. Actually, she adds, straps should never dig; they are there to hold the bra in place, rather than for supporting the breasts.

"To render cups comfortable and nonchafing, the best designs feature seamless cups or cups with seams that don't cross in the nipple area," says Cummins. "Nonstretch translates into support where the sides, back and bottom of a bra are concerned. A wide, nonelastic band at the bottom is generally very supportive and unlikely to ride up. And while front-closure designs offer convenience, they can chafe, and usually are not as supportive as back-closure styles."[33]

When trying on a bra in the fitting room, be sure to jump and jog to test it thoroughly, advises *Self*. With the help of Dr. Lorentzen and LaJean Lawson, by then a doctoral candidate at Oregon State University, the magazine rated eight of the leading sports bras, based on "hold," sweatproofing and suitability for various body types and sports activities. The eight with most to least hold in order, were: The Exercise Supportop; Lady Duke; Freedom Front Runner; The Sport Bra (Lily of France); Jogbra; Sports Bra and Exercise Mate (Cupid

Foundations); Actively Yours; and Olga's Christina SportsBra. However, even the lower-rated bras had qualities to recommend them, depending on the user's breast size and sports activity.[34]

It might be assumed that women who are walking might not need a sports bra, but this is not true, according to Terry Monahan in *The Walking Magazine*.[35]

"Most women are unaware that walking qualifies them for a sports bra—the underpinning of real jocks," says Monahan. "But walking creates the same breast movement as activities like running—possibly even more among fitness walkers, who combine a rapid stride with a vigorous arm-swing. Even for women who are satisfied with what they're wearing, the new sports bras warrant a closer look."[35]

Monahan quotes Christine Haycock, M.D., a New Jersey surgeon and outspoken advocate of support bras for active women, as saying, "If you went your whole life without a bra, you'd end up with your breasts down around your belly button."[35]

Monahan goes on to say, "The benefits of wearing a sports bra are the same for all women, regardless of age. Younger women are at the same risk for stretching breast tissue as older women and shouldn't consider youth sufficient protection against sagging. Older women, who may be stooped or round-shouldered, need a supportive bra to help compensate for their posture."[35]

In addition to providing good support, the best garments have moisture-wicking lining, seamless or covered seam cups, hypo-allergenic fabric, stay-put straps and covered hardware, says Dr. Haycock. And keep the sexy stretch bras in the bedroom. She adds that large-breasted women do not generally like the minimized profile bra, because they find the elastic all the way around their chest too confining. Older women may also find the compression style uncomfortable, especially if they have respiratory problems, says Dr. Haycock.

Monahan says that many of the suitable features for a sports bra are available in department stores. Therefore, each woman has to try on and determine which style is best for her.

References

1. John L. Marshall,. M.D., with Heather Barbash, *The Sports Doctor's Fitness Book for Women* (New York: Delacorte Press, 1981), pp. 21–22.

2. Joanne Silberner and Erica E. Goode, "Should Women Stop Jogging?" *U.S. News & World Report* (March 7, 1988), p. 72.

3. "Amenorrhea Linked to Hypercortisolemia," *Medical World News* (March 23, 1987).

4. Mona Shangold, M.D., and Gabe Mirkin, M.D., *The Complete Sports Medicine Book for Women* (New York: Simon and Schuster, Inc., 1985), pp. 111–124.

5. Elizabeth Kaufmann, "Working Out Your Period," *American Health* (November 1987), p. 30.

6. Joan Ullyot, M.D., "Birth Control and Performance," *Runner's World* (November 1986), pp. 78–79.

7. Keith Haglund, "Cancer Down in Women on the Run," *Medical Tribune* (April 2, 1986), p. 23.

8. "Inactivity the Key to Breast, Colon Cancer?" *Medical World News* (August 10, 1987), p. 24.

9. Felicia Halpert, "Wasting Away," *The Runner* (October 1986), pp. 8–9.

10. *Facts About Anorexia Nervosa* (Washington, DC: National Institute of Child Health and Human Development, undated).

11. *Osteoporosis* (Washington, DC: National Institute of Arthritis and Musculoskeletal and Skin Diseases, May 1986).

12. "Exercise and Bone Status," *Complementary Medicine* (May/June 1986), p. 31.

13. "Skeletal Benefit of Exercise Clearer," *Medical World News* (March 23, 1987), p. 24.

14. Dick Patrick, "Benoit Out of the Running for Seoul," *USA Today* (April 28, 1988), p. C1.

15. Patricia Long, *The Nutritional Ages of Women* (New York: Macmillan Publishing Company, 1986), pp. 153–167.

16. Frank Murray, "Why Good Nutrition Improves an Athlete's Performance," *Better Nutrition* (February 1984), pp. 22–25, 48.

17. Doug Henderson, *FDA Consumer* (May 1987).

18. "Athletes Risk Iron Deficiency," *Food & Nutrition News* (May/June 1986).

19. Carlson Wade, "Nutrient Guidelines for Female Athletes," *Today's Living* (June 1988), pp. 8–11; 25–26.

20. Evelyn P. Whitlock, M.D., *The Calcium Plus Workbook* (New Canaan, Conn.: Keats Publishing, Inc., 1988), pp. 12–17.

21. Joe Nicholson, "Women Smokers Risking Strokes," *New York Post* (April 14, 1988), p. 26.

22. Henley Gibble and Ellen Wessel, *Running Women—The First Steps* (Alexandria, Va.: The Road Runners Club of America, 1987).

23. Jane E. Brody, "Exercise in Pregnancy Found Unharmful to Fetus," *The New York Times* (May 28, 1988), p. 8.

24. "Maternal Instincts," *Runner's World* (February 1988), p. 19.

25. Marc Bloom, "You've Come a Long Way, Baby," *The Runner* (December 1986), pp. 26–36.

26. *Women in Long-Distance Running* (Indianapolis: American College of Sports Medicine, undated).

27. Nancy Enright, "Women Who Exercise Need More B-Vitamin," American Chemical Society News Service, April 10, 1984.

28. Richard A. Schwartz, *Walking and Weight Loss: Walking Is the Best Diet to Permanent Weight Loss* (Marlboro, Mass.: The Rockport Walking Institute, 1987).

29. Gayle Olinekova, *Go for It!* (New York, NY: Simon and Schuster, 1982), p. 123.

30. Kurt Butler, M.S., and Lynn Rayner, M.D., *The Best Medicine* (San Francisco: Harper & Row, 1985), p. 25.

31. Deana Lorentzen and LaJean Lawson, "Sports Bras: Which Ones Give the Best Support?" *Physician & Sportsmedicine* (May 1987), p. 128.

32. Christine E. Haycock, M.D., "Breast Problems in Athletics for Women," *Physician & Sportsmedicine* (March 1987), p. 89.

33. Cynthia Cummins, "The Complete Guide to Sports Bras," *Women's Sports & Fitness* (September 1987), pp. 52–58.

34. "Best Health/Support Bets for Active Breasts: Researchers Rate 8 Sports Bras," *Self* (December 1987).

35. Terry Monahan, "Sports Bras: Musts for Busts?" *The Walking Magazine* (June/July, 1987), p. 26.

Chapter 13

Socks

Before an Englishman first invented a machine to knit stockings in 1589, human beings had devised a variety of foot and leg coverings to protect themselves against the weather and obstructions in their path. Although the Roman soldiers who followed Julius Caesar during the conquest of Gaul wore various types of sandals, their short military tunics exposed their legs and thighs to the cold and thorns and briars of the forest. By contrast, the Gauls discovered that they could better withstand the cold, as well as hunt and fight better, if they wrapped rolls of cloth or leather around the loose breeches that they favored, says Milton N. Grass in *History of Hosiery*.[1] The Roman soldiers called these wrappings *tibialae,* which is plural for a kind of stocking or legging.

After the Gauls had been subdued by the Romans and had adopted many of their customs, continues Grass, the Gauls introduced the element of style to the *tibialae* that they wore. Their *tibialae* consisted of two or more colored strips, which looked like checked and striped stockings. Returning Roman soldiers brought this fashion idea back to Rome, and the striped *tibialae* became the familiar striped and colored trunk-hose of medieval Europe.

Although *tibialae* and *fasciae,* another type of legging, were simply wrapped around the foot or leg, *udones* (plural of *udo*) were inner-foot coverings that resemble the modern-day sock, in that they fit the contours of the feet. *Udones* were made of felt, goatskin or goat hair.

In 303 A.D., Emperor Diocletian dictated what was *de rigueur* for the Roman citizen to wear, and he outlined the articles of wearing apparel that the *bracarius* or tailor should design, including mantles, cloaks, breeches and *udones.*

Within 100 to 150 years, continues Grass, the sock-like *udo,* which covered the foot and shinbone, became the full-length, cut and sewed stocking commonly worn by the laity of the Roman Empire. Between the fourth and fifth century A.D., the Catholic Church adopted what we would call stockings as part of the dress and liturgical vestment of the Christian clergy.

"The mosaics in the Church of San Satino, near Milan, Italy, which date back to the fifth century A.D., help us to establish a date, within limits, when full-length, cut and sewn stockings were first worn. These mosiacs, as well as those in other churches, distinctly show bishops wearing *udones* as a part of their liturgical vestures," adds Grass.[1]

He adds that *The Catholic Encyclopedia* reports that, at the beginning of the fifth century, the priestly wardrobe was not too much different from secular dress, in either form or ornament. Therefore, it can be concluded that full-length, cut and sewn stockings, made form linen or silk, were worn by Romans between 325 A.D., the date of Diocletian's edict, and before 400 to 500 A.D., when the mosaics were laid in the Church of San Satino. And, continues Grass, over 1,200 years would pass, from the day that the poet Hesiod wrote about the *piloy*, the first sock-like covering worn by a Greek farmer, before the *fasciae*, *tibialae* and *udones* of the Romans would become the cut and sewn stockings that are familiar today.

The word "stocking" is Anglo-Saxon in origin; "hosiery" can be traced to the Anglo-Saxon, Scotch and Teutonic languages; while "sock" is derived from the Greek word *sykhos*. The Romans changed the word to *soccus,* which turned up as *socc* in Anglo-Saxon, and finally *sock*.[1]

"In ancient Greek," says Grass, "the word *sykhos* originally meant a low, soft shoe. It was a part of the feminine dress and it would have been considered shameful for a man to have worn it. To further accentuate the *kothornos* as a mark of tragic characterization, the *sykhos* was adapted to the theater as a mark of the comic character. . . . As the *sykhos* was the mark of a comedy in the Greek theater, the *soccus* became the mark of a comedy in the Roman theater, and came into common usage."[1]

Factors to Consider

Aside from those who go barefoot, most joggers, racewalkers, runners and walkers prefer socks. But, of course, this is a matter of personal preference. Dr. John L. Marshall—whose patients included Billie Jean King, Rosie Cassals, Arthur Ashe, Julius Irving and other athletes while he was at the Hospital for Special Surgery in New York—says that it is not a good idea to exercise without socks, mainly because there is friction between the bare foot and the shoe.[2]

If shoes were molded to perfectly fit the contours of your feet, socks would be required only to collect dead cells and dirt rubbed off from the feet, keeping shoes free from such debris and the odor resulting from the bacteria, according to Dr. Mona Shangold, who is assistant professor of obstetrics and gynecology at Georgetown University School of Medicine, and Dr. Gabe Mirkin, who is associate clinical professor of pediatrics at the same university.[3] But, since shoes do not fit precisely, socks are useful in filling the empty spaces to make the shoes fit better. Socks are also helpful in preventing friction caused by any rough spots inside the shoes. The most obvious injury is a painful blister, which can make exercise very uncomfortable.

The softest materials make the best socks. Since cotton is both soft and absorbs moisture it has two things going for it. Wool is also soft, it absorbs moisture and it retains heat even when wet. Wet cotton socks are probably too uncomfortable in cold weather, but wet woolen socks might even keep your feet warm, they explain.

If your sport requires high shoes or boots, the authors continue, select socks that will extend above the shoe tops. Actually, in most instances your socks should extend above your shoe tops. Women often prefer the low golf socks, which extend only a bit higher than the top of a standard shoe and which have a pom-pom at the back of the top, keeping the sock from slipping into the shoe. These are usually made of terry cloth, which is soft, comfortable and absorbent, even though it eventually stiffens from wear, perspiration and washing.

"As with all underwear," say Drs. Shangold and Mirkin, "you should find a pair of comfortable socks and replace them with the same product when they wear out. Stick with any product you like."[3]

Improperly fitted shoes are obviously the main cause of blisters and chafing, and the blisters become apparent where the rubbing is the greatest. Therefore, if your socks are too bulky, say the researchers, and permit the feet to move around a lot inside your shoes, you might try thinner socks or no socks at all.

"If you get a blister," they continue, "be careful to keep the top layer of the skin in place. The blister will heal much faster and with much less pain. Removing the fluid will also help healing and relieve pain. Make a small hole at the edge of the blister with a sterilized needle. Press gently with your fingers to force out the fluid. Then apply an antiseptic ointment to prevent infection, and cover this with tape. If redness or pus develops around the blister, check with your doctor to see if you have an infection. If you do, you'll need an antibiotic to treat it."[3]

Writing in *Walking*, Dr. John Pleas, assistant professor of psychology at Middle Tennessee State University, Murfreesboro, suggests that socks should fit as snugly as shoes, with sufficient room to move your toes.[4] He recommends seamless socks, especially in areas that are prone to chafing, such as the heels and balls of your feet. Obviously, they should fit the contours of your feet.

"Heavy wool socks or two pairs of lighter socks are often worn by hikers and long-distance walkers, but they are not needed for daily brisk walking," explains Dr. Pleas. "Socks made from natural products (light wool and cotton) that breathe, absorb perspiration, provide a good fit, and do not move around on the foot are recommended. Socks that are too small or too large can be as much of a problem as shoes that are too small or too large. Tight socks constrict the blood vessels in the feet, and loose socks that slide around on your feet as you are walking can contribute to the formation of blisters."[4]

Dr. Pleas recommends that you press the sock firmly against your foot and smooth out any folds before putting on your shoes. He points out that a folded sock during a long walk can be as irritating as a rock in your shoe and can be almost as damaging.

While on a day-long walk, change your socks and shoes at least once, usually after lunch, advises Gary Yanker.[5] This not only insures fresh, dry feet, but also enables the other shoes and socks to dry and air out.

During the switchover, he recommends that you change to your lighter pair of shoes, as outlined elsewhere in this book. Moving from heavier to lighter shoes is somewhat like a foot massage, he insists. And the light-weight shoes reduce the pressure on the top of your feet, thus giving your foot muscles time to relax.

Design construction and thickness are probably more important than fabric when selecting socks, he continues. Walking socks should preferably have extra padding under the forefoot, about the heels and across the top of the feet about where your toes end. But, he says, socks should not be so thick that they promote sweating.

Yanker adds that, although wool has been the traditional favorite for hiking because of warmth and moisture absorption, combinations of wool, cotton and synthetic materials provide a lightweight, thinner sock that permits the foot to breathe as well as providing cushioning. Since both approaches are valid, the choice will probably boil down to individual preference.

"If you want your socks to cushion your feet, wear two pairs, a regular pair outside of a thin pair," he adds. "To keep your feet drier, the thin pair can be replaced as it gets wet. I find that layering two pairs of socks feels more comfortable than one thick pair. Pack extra pairs for training and event participation. Fresh socks will not only help you keep your feet drier and blister-free, they will also give you a psychological boost. The feel of fresh, dry socks on your feet goes to your head. You feel less tired."[5]

Athletic socks can be characterized as tube, anklet or regular, and personal preference usually dictates which style to buy. Since tube socks are shapeless at the ankle and toe, they have a tendency to move around as you run. For that reason, Bob Glover and Jack Shepherd, in *The Runner's Handbook,* do not recommend this style.[6] Ankle socks cover the feet to the ankle and are preferred by some runners in summer and by others because they are lighter than other socks. Regular socks, of course, are cushioned and tapered to fit around toes and ankles, and they go up to mid-calf. The authors prefer ankle socks for racing and when it is raining.

"Always wear clean socks; dirty socks may also cause blisters, and they wear out sooner," the authors continue. "Also, when buying socks look carefully for deformities or rough spots that might irritate your feet."[6]

In the cotton-wool vs synthetic fiber controversy, Glover and Shepherd say that Orlon in a cotton sock helps wick away moisture and it doesn't get as wet or abrasive.

"Acrylic or Orlon also increase the bulk of the sock and its sponginess," they continue. "Nylon added to cotton makes it more elastic; the sock stays up better. I (Glover) use cotton socks year-round except when running in cold rain, snow or slush. Then I switch to wool. Wool is warmer than cotton, and doesn't lose its insulating properties when wet."[6]

They go on to say that polypropylene sock liners with a wool sock on the outside will offer protection on cold and wet days. And this synthetic fabric, or a polypropylene-wool blend sock, keeps feet dry and warm. If you purchase socks with extra cushioning at the heel, toe and ball of your foot, make sure that this extra bulk does not interfere with the fit of your running shoes.

It goes without saying, adds Raymond Bridge, that you should run in a combination of shoes and socks that are comfortable for long distances, rather than a brand-new pair of racing shoes.[7]

On the other hand, Hal Higden reports in *Beginner's Running Guide* that he normally does not wear socks while running, especially in warm weather.[8] He admits that, although the idea of not wearing socks tricks him into thinking that he is saving weight and running faster, the benefits are negligible and are probably psychological. "It feels better to be 'one' with your running shoes," is the way he puts it.[8]

One reason for going sockless, especially in races where you may be running faster and longer than while training, he says, is that this removes one more obstacle that might cause problems. For example, socks can bunch up and cause a blister. Except in freezing weather, he feels that you can go without socks, especially if your running shoes fit properly.

"A few runners I know use half-socks as sort of a compromise between regular socks and none; women, more often than men, go this route, because they sometimes wear such items with their regular street shoes," he says.[8]

Aside from comfort and warmth, socks do soak up sweat and provide some protection for your shoes against "runner's stink," he adds. Although you can dump a lot of foot powder on your running shoes to absorb the moisture and make them smell better, clean socks every day are probably a more practical solution. And, of course, perspiration-soaked shoes shorten the life of the shoe. Although he prefers nylon socks, he says that cotton is probably better.

As a runner, he advises, you probably should shy away from tube socks. Since there is no great necessity to keep your calves warm, socks that are too tight above the calves might impair circulation, or, if they become loose, they might move down around your ankles.

Panty hose for men are another matter, he continues. "I recall Frank Shorter appearing in the National AAU cross-country championship on a cold November day in Chicago one year wearing panty hose for warmth. This was long before Joe Namath appeared in the famous panty hose TV commercials. Shorter at least had a practical reason for donning panty hose; Namath did it only for the money."[8]

The height of the sock, whether below the ankle or over the calf, is simply a matter of preference, according to Terry Moffatt in *The Walking Magazine*.[9] However, Moffatt adds, support hose and socks that provide some compression against the ankle and calf may appreciably reduce fatigue in the feet and lower legs. Compression, which is provided by spandex or elastomer fibers, is said to increase blood flow and enhance the action of the valves in the veins.

"Do not wear over-the-calf socks with elastic bands at the top to hold them, though," Moffatt adds. "The band can act as a tourniquet and restrict blood flow through the leg. Padding or cushioning, which is usually built into the stock by adding a terry or pile surface to one side of the fabric, is a key feature of most sports-specific socks. Manufacturers claim that the placement and density of the pads are what differentiate each type of sport sock."[9]

Adds Dr. Douglas Ritchie, a podiatrist and clinical instructor at Los Angeles County USC Medical Center, "an overpadded sock could compromise the fit of the shoe. The purpose of padding is to protect the foot. It shouldn't make you feel as if you're walking on a pillow."[10]

Shopping for Socks

Walking socks are available at most department stores, sporting goods shops and athletic footwear outlets, as well as at mass merchandisers, drug stores and in mail-order catalogs. Moffatt reports that the leading labels of walking socks are Burlington, Fox River, Ridgeview, Russell National, Thor-Lo and Wigwam. Prices range from $4 to $7 per pair, generally.

Athletic socks are also available in the fast-growing, all-sock stores that are springing up around the country, such as the Sox Appeal chain based in Minneapolis. Founder Gibson Carothers had received permission to operate franchises in all 50 states, reports *The Walking Magazine*.[10]

Prices for the various types of socks range from $2.50 for a basic sock to a lace bodystocking from Switzerland that retails for $109. The sports sock is the fastest growing line in his stores, says Carothers, with designer labels from Calvin Klein, Perry Ellis and others.

"Active, outdoor people have become a very important market," Carothers continues. "We already have some beautifully made socks for hiking and walking, and we're really going out of our way to improve our sports department. Socks are no longer something you just put on before your shoes."[10]

Sock Construction

All you ever wanted to know about socks, including fashion and style; construction and finishing; yarn and fibers; and measurements is included in an informative 28-page booklet from E. I. DuPont de Nemours & Company, Inc., Hosiery Marketing, 1251 6th Ave., New York, NY 10020, or 6310 Fairview Rd., Charlotte, NC 28210. It is titled *All About Socks*.

Although socks seemingly come in many lengths, there are actually only four categories as established by the National Association of Hosiery Manufacturers. The four categories are:

Knee-highs, which is hosiery with a top extending above the calf but not over the knee.

Mid-calf/Crew refers to hosiery that has a top above the ankle but not beyond the largest part of the calf.

Anklets, as you might surmise, are hosiery with a top designed to cover the ankle bone, extending less than one-third of the way up the largest part of the calf.

Footsocks are hosiery that does not go beyond the ankle bone.

Socks are knitted in a variety of designs, depending on the type and style of hosiery. These designs include cable, fair isle, argyle, basketweave, flame stitch, clock patterning, diagonal rib and plaid.

"Construction is the way the sock is made and is therefore an important element of style as well," says the booklet. "The one common denominator in all socks is that they are produced on circular knitting machines. In knitting, fabric is constructed by the interlooping of yarn loops by the use of knitting needles mounted in either single cylinders (for flat knots) or double cylinders (for ribs). Cylinders create stitches at a rate of between 50 and 500 revolutions per minute, depending on the type of equipment and the style of sock being made.''

Vertical rows of stitches are known as "wales," while horizontal rows are called "courses." The number of wales in an inch will depend on the size of the yarn and the number of needles mounted on the circumference of the machine's cylinder or cylinders. This is referred to as "needle count."

If a manufacturer is making a fine, lightweight men's sock, the needle count may be 176, contrasted with a coarse hunting sock with a needle count of 60. Athletic socks generally have a count of 108, while typical men's casual socks and women's knee-highs are usually made with a count of about 84. Manufacturers also refer to "knit gauge," which is the number of needles per 1½-inch on the cylinder.

Major construction methods are generally characterized as:

1. Ribbed.
2. Flat knit.
3. Cushioned.
4. Jacquard.
5. Mesh.

Obviously, each sock may require more than one construction method. For example, athletic socks can be both ribbed and cushioned.

Sock Fibers

Sock manufacturers basically use nine varieties of yarn and fiber, depending on the purpose of the sock and the aesthetics desired. The familiar fiber families are:

1. *Acrylic*. This is a man-made fiber, such as Orlon, which is spun into yarn. It is highly regarded for its shapekeeping properties and resilience, softness, easy care, low-shrinkage, rich colorations and the fact that it does not itch. A member of this family is hi-bulk Orlon, which has the above properties, as well as a lightweight, low-density bulk with a cushiony, very soft feel. A special advantage for sports socks is that acrylic moves sweat away from the feet and through the sock to the top, where the moisture is evaporated.

2. *Cotton*. This soft and heat-resistant vegetable fiber, from the cotton plant, has been used in garments since 3,000 B.C. It absorbs and retains moisture but is easily washed. Unlike synthetic fibers, whose characteristics are relatively stable, cotton is available in a variety of grades, qualities and performance levels. The various family members include Sea Island, Egyptian, "upland," Pima and Mercerized cotton.

3. *Nylon*. Made from coal, air and water, this fiber can be dyed to a variety of colors; it has exceptional strength and abrasian resistance. It is easily washed and dryed and, in men's socks, it is often combined with other fabrics.

4. *Polyester*. Another man-made fiber, polyester is available in a variety of tradenames, such as Dacron. It is abrasion resistant, washes easily, is readily heat-settable and dyeable and is fast-drying. It is used especially in mens' and

boy's dress socks, notably in decorative applications such as cross-dyeing and jacquards, as well as in reinforcements.

5. *Rayon*. Generally made from regenerated cellulose, rayon washes and dyes well and it has a soft hand, high moisture absorbency and retention.

6. *Silk*. Produced by silkworms, this luxurious natural filament features a high luster, soft hand, high tensile strength and thermal properties.

7. *Spandex*. A man-made fiber, it can stretch over five times its relaxed strength and then return to its original position. It is often used in sock tops for its stretch-recovery properties and for keeping the socks up. It is especially noted for insuring a proper fit and comfort. Lycra is the DuPont tradename.

8. *Wool*. This is the soft, curly hair of sheep that is spun into yarn. Wool for clothing is categorized as Shetland (Scottish) and Merine (Spanish), but woolen yarn for socks generally comes from the United States, Australia and other wool-producing countries. Alpaca and cashmere are hairs from other animals and are not called wool. Known for centuries for being warm, sturdy and durable, wool has a crisp, resilient hand and exceptional insulating properties. After all, it keeps the sheep warm.

Although the terms "yarn" and "fiber" are often used interchangeably, "fiber" actually refers to the basic filament or hair-like structure which is spun into a yarn. The term also refers to filament yarns, which are the nylon yarns used in toe and heel reinforcement. Specialists use the term "fiber" to refer to the raw material—such as acrylic, cotton or wool—from which the yarn for a sock is made. "Yarn" is the grouping of fibers or filaments that are twisted together to make a continuous strand.

"The diameter of the nylon determines the thickness of the sock and is measured in terms of 'yarn count,' " adds the DuPont booklet. "The higher the yarn count, the sheerer the sock. Lycra and the filament yarns referred to above, however, are measured in 'deniers.' Deniers are a weight-per-unit length measurement in which the low numbers represent the finer sizes. In this case, the lower the denier the thinner the sock."[11]

Although this booklet does not go into great detail, yarn manufacturers are combining a variety of natural and synthetic fibers to produce yarns with an almost endless list of applications. Polypropylene, as an example, is gaining acceptance for making socks, often combined with other fibers.

As for blends, the DuPont publication refers to "covered" Lycra, which is Lycra yarn that is wrapped with one or two nylon filaments and is plaited into the sock. Uncovered Lycra is often plaited into the sock to maintain its shape, better fit and stay-up properties. This fiber is often laid-in instead of knitted-in, especially in tops.

A relatively new stabilized corespun yarn results when acrylic or other fibers are spun around the core of Lycra. This results in socks appreciated for their stretch and recovery properties, found in Lycra, and the softness, warmth and durability of spun yarns.

Since there are no industry-wide standards for determining the sock size in relation to your shoe size, various manufacturers publish their own charts. These sizes may vary from one manufacturer to the next, but typical sizes are shown in Table 7.

Table 7

SOCK SIZES

MEN'S

Shoe size	Sock size
6½–7	10
7½–8	10½
8½–9	11
9½–10	11½
10½–11	12
11½–12	13
12½–13	14

INFANTS, GIRLS' & WOMEN'S

Wearer's Foot Length (Inches)	Shoe Size	Sock Size
3¼–3¾	0–1	4
3¾–4¼	1½–2½	4½
4¼–4¾	3–4	5
4¾–5¼	4½–5½	5½
5¼–5¾	6–7	6
5¾–6¼	7½–8½	6½
6¼–6¾	9–10	7
6¾–7¼	10½–11½	7½
7¼–7¾	12–1	8
7¾–8¼	1½–2½	8½
8¼–8¾	4–5	9
8¾–9¼	5½–6½	9½
9¼–9⅝	6½–7½	10
9⅝–10	8–9	10½
10–10⅜	9½–10½	11

Charts courtesy "All About Socks," from DuPont.

References

1. Milton N. Grass, *History of Hosiery* (New York: Fairchild Publications, Inc., 1955), pp. 4–9; 68–71; 80–84.

2. John L. Marshall, M.D., with Heather Barbash, *The Sports Doctor's Fitness Book for Women* (New York: Delacorte Press, 1981), p. 345.

3. Mona Shangold, M.D. and Gabe Mirkin, M.D., *The Complete Sports Medicine Book for Women* (New York: Simon & Schuster, Inc., 1985), pp. 173–174.

4. John Pleas, Ph.D., *Walking* (New York: W. W. Norton & Co., 1981), pp. 66–67.

5. Gary Yanker, *Gary Yanker's Sportwalking* (Chicago: Contemporary Books, Inc., 1987), pp. 221–223.

6. Bob Glover and Jack Shepherd, *The Runner's Handbook* (New York: Penguin Books, 1985), pp. 176–177.

7. Raymond Bridge, *The Runner's Book* (New York: Charles Scribner's Sons, 1978), p. 195.

8. Hal Higden, *Beginner's Running Guide* (Mountain View, Cal., 1978), pp. 114–115.

9. Terry Moffatt, "Which Is the Real Walking Sock?" *The Walking Magazine* (June/July, 1987), pp. 34–37.

10. "Strictly Socks," *The Walking Magazine* (December/January 1988), p. 17.

11. *All About Socks* (New York: E. I. DuPont de Nemours & Co., Inc., undated).

Appendix 1:

Buyer's Guide

Air Fresheners

Unique Sports Products, Inc., 840 McFarland Rd., Alpharetta, GA 30201; 800-554-3707; in GA, 404-442-1977.
  Air freshener for bags, lockers, closets, cars.

Ankle Aids

Ankle braces

Dr. Leonard's Health Care, 74 20th St., Brooklyn, NY 11232. 718-768-0010.
  Ankle supports.

Pro Orthopedic Devices, Box 27525, Tucson, AZ 85726. 602-790-9330.
  Rubberized sleeves.

Unique Sports Products, 840 McFarland Rd., Alpharetta, GA 30201. 800-554-3707; in GA, 404-442-1977.
  Ankle wraps.

Apparel

Bras, sport

Eddie Bauer, 15010 N. E. 36th St., Redmond, WA 98052. 206-882-6100.

The Finals, 21 Minisink Ave., Port Jervis, NY 12771. 800-431-9111.

Jembra, 2215 N. Beachwood Dr., Hollywood, CA 90068. 213-851-4444.

Jogbra, Inc., 1 Mill St., Burlington, VT 05401. 802-863-3548.

Lily of France, 136 Madison Ave., New York, NY 10016. 212-696-1110.

Olga, 7915 Haskell Ave., Van Nuys, CA 91409. 818-782-7568.

Royal Textile Mills, Box 250, Yancyville, NC 27379. 800-334-9361. In NC, 919-694-4121.

Sport Europa, 7871 N.W. 15th St., Miami, FL 33126. 305-477-9341.

Unique Sports Products, 840 McFarland Rd., Alpharetta, GA 30201. 800-554-3707; in GA, 404-442-1977.

Fleecewear

Adidas, 15 Independence Blvd., Warren, NJ 07060. 201-580-0700.

Asics, 10540 Talbert Ave., West Bldg., Fountain Valley, CA 92708. 800-854-6133.

Bassett Walker, Box 5423, Martinsville, VA 24115. 703-632-5601.

Eddie Bauer, 15010 N.E. 36th St., Redmond, WA 98052. 206-882-6100.

L. L. Bean, Freeport, ME 04033. 800-221-4221.

Champion Products, 3141 Monroe Ave., Rochester, NY 14618. 716-385-3200.

Eastern Mountain Sports, 1 Vose Farm Rd., Peterborough, NH 03458. 603-924-9571.

The Finals, 21 Minisink Ave., Port Jervis, NY 12771. 800-431-9111.

Le Coq Sportif, 28 Englehard Dr., Cranbury, NJ 08512. 800-524-2377. In NJ, 609-655-1515.

Nike, 9000 S.W. Nimbus Dr., Beaverton, OR 97005. 503-641-6453.

Pannill Knitting, 202 Cleveland Ave., Martinsville, VA 24115. 703-638-8841.

Patagonia, Box 86, Ventura, CA 93002. 800-523-9597. In CA, 800-432-0241.

Pony Sports and Leisure, 201 Rte. 17 N., Rutherford, NJ 07070. 201-896-0101.

Puma, 492 Old Connecticut Pathway, Framingham, MA 01701. 508-875-4803.

Recreational Equipment, Inc., Box 88125, Seattle, WA 98138. 206-323-8333.

Reebox International, 100 Technology Dr., Stoughton, MA 02072. 617-341-5000.

Russell Athletic, Box 272, Alexander City, AL 35010. 800-526-5256.

Sierra Designs, 2039 Fourth St., Berkeley, CA 94710. 415-843-2010.

Swingster, Box 2987, Shawnee Mission, KS 66201. 816-943-5002.

Norm Thompson, Box 3999, Portland, OR 97208. 800-547-1160.

Tultex, 22 E. Church St., Martinsville, VA 24112. 703-632-2961.

Woolrich, Woolrich, PA 17779. 717-769-6464.

Gloves

Eddie Bauer, 15010 N.E. 36th St., Redmond, WA 98052. 206-882-6100.

Gates-Mills, Harrisen St., Johnstown, NY 12095. 518-762-4526.

Nike, 9000 S.W. Nimbus Dr., Beaverton, OR 97005. 503-641-6453.

Orvis, Box 12000, Roanoke, VA 24022. 703-345-6789.

Patagonia, Box 86, Ventura, CA 93002. 800-523-9597. In CA, 800-432-0241.

Rainbow Racing System, Box 18510, Spokane, WA 99208. 800-962-1011. In WA, 509-326-5470.

Recreational Equipment, Inc., Box 88125, Seattle, WA 98138. 206-323-8333.

Hats, caps, hoods

Adidas, 15 Independence Blvd., Warren, NJ 07060. 201-580-0700.

Eddie Bauer, 15010 N.E. 36th St., Redmond, WA 98052. 206-882-6100.

L. L. Bean, Freeport, ME 04033. 800-221-4221.

Body Glove, Inc., 530 Sixth St., Hermosa Beach, CA 90254. 213-374-4074.

Columbia Sportswear Co., Box 83239, Portland, OR 97283. 800-547-8066.
  Orange, waterproof hats.

Decent Exposure, Box 591, Columbus, GA 31902. 404-322-4145.

Hart Hat, Box 6300, Tamarack, MN 55787. 218-357-2635.
  One-piece hood for head, face, etc.

Mature Wisdom, Bldg. 28, Hanover, PA 17333. 800-621-5800.

Nike, 9000 S.W. Nimbus Dr., Beaverton, OR 97005. 503-641-6453.

Orvis, Box 12000, Roanoke, VA 24022. 703-345-3600.

Outdoor Research, 1000 First Ave. S, Seattle, WA 98134. 206-467-8197.

Pony Sports and Leisure, 201 Rte. 17 N., Rutherford, NJ 07070. 201-896-0101.

Puma, 492 Old Connecticut Pathway, Framingham, MA 01701. 508-875-4803.

Recreational Equipment, Inc., Box 88125, Seattle, WA 98138. 206-323-8333.

Reebox International, 100 Technology Dr., Stoughton, MA 02072. 617-341-5000.

Unique Sports Products, 840 McFarland Rd., Alpharetta, GA 30201. 800-554-3707. In GA, 404-442-1977.
  Suncaps.

Vermont Country Store, Box 3000, Manchester Center, VT 05225. 802-362-4667.

Outerwear, rainwear

Adidas, 15 Independence Blvd., Warren, NJ 07060. 201-580-0700.

Alitta, 75 Spring St., New York, NY 10012. 212-334-1390.

Asics, 10540 Talbert Ave., West Bldg., Fountain Valley, CA 92708. 800-854-6133.

Eddie Bauer, 15010 N.E. 36th St., Redmond, WA 98052. 206-882-6100.

L. L. Bean, Freeport, ME 04033. 800-221-4221.

Blair, 220 Hickory St., Warren, PA 16366. 800-458-6057.

CB Sports, 210 South St., Bennington, VT 05201. 802-447-7651.

Champion Products, 3141 Monroe Ave., Rochester, NY 14618. 716-385-3200.

Columbia Sportswear, 6600 N. Baltimore, Portland, OR 97203. 503-286-3676.

Eastern Mountain Sports, 1 Vose Farm Rd., Peterborough, NH 03458. 603-924-7231.

The Finals, 21 Minisink Ave., Port Jervis, NY 12771. 800-431-9111.

Forrester's, 1734 N.E. Broadway, Portland, OR. 800-556-4653.

Gander Mountain, Box 248, Wilmet, WI 53192. 800-558-9410.

Head Sportswear, 9198 Red Branch Rd., Columbia, MD 21045. 301-730-8300.

Hind Performance Sportswear, Box 12609, San Luis Obispo, CA 93406. 805-544-8555.

JanSport, 2425 W. Packard St., Appleton, WI 54913. 414-734-5708.

Lands' End, Lands' End Lane, Dodgeville, WI 53595. 800-356-4444.

Le Coq Sportif, 28 Englehard Dr., Cranbury, NJ 08512. 800-524-2377. In NJ, 609-655-1515.

Marmot Mountain Works, 545 31st Rd., Grand Junction, CO 81504. 303-434-6688.

Nautica, 10 W. 33rd St., New York, NY 10001. 212-947-4041.

New Balance, 38 Everett St., Boston, MA 02134. 617-783-4000.

Nike, 9000 S.W. Nimbus Dr., Beaverton, OR 97005. 503-641-6453.

The North Face, 999 Harriston St., Berkeley, CA 94710. 800-446-5522.

Orvis, Box 12000, Roanoke, VA 24022. 703-345-3600.

Outdoor Products, 533 S. Los Angeles St., Los Angeles, CA 90013. 800-438-3353. In CA, 800-626-6678.

Patagonia, Box 86, Ventura, CA 93002. 800-523-9597. In CA, 800-432-0241.

Pony Sports and Leisure, 201 Rte. 17 N., Rutherford, NJ 07070. 201-896-0101.

Puma, 492 Old Connecticut Pathway, Framingham, MA 01701. 508-875-4803.

Recreational Equipment, Inc., Box 88125, Seattle, WA 98138. 206-323-8333.

Reebox International, 100 Technology Dr., Stoughton, MA 02072. 617-341-5000.

Russell Athletic, Box 272, Alexander City, AL 35010. 800-526-5256.

Sierra Designs, 2039 Fourth St., Berkeley, CA 94710. 415-843-2010.

Swingster, Box 2987, Shawnee Mission, KS 66201. 816-943-5052.

Tultex, 22 E. Church St., Martinsville, VA 24112. 703-632-2961.

Vital Concepts, 925 Delaware St., S.E., Minneapolis, MN 55459. 800-642-8482.

Woolrich, Woolrich, PA 17779. 717-769-6464.

Pants

Eastern Mountain Sports, 1 Vose Farm Rd., Peterborough, NH 03458. 603-924-7231.

Hind, no address. 800-426-4463; 805-544-8555.

Lands' End, Lands' End Lane, Dodgeville, WI 53595. 800-356-4444.

Le Coq Sportif, 28 Englehard Dr., Cranbury, NJ 08512. 800-524-2377. In NJ, 609-655-1515.

New Balance, 38 Everett St., Boston, MA 02134. 617-783-4000.

Nike, 9000 S.W. Nimbus Dr., Beaverton, OR 97005. 503-641-6453.

Patagonia, Box 86, Ventura, CA 93002. 800-523-9597. In CA, 800-432-0241.

Recreational Equipment, Inc., Box 88125, Seattle, WA 98138. 206-323-8333.

Reebox International, 100 Technology Dr., Stoughton, MA 02072. 617-341-5000.

SportHill, 1035 Conger, Eugene, OR 97402. 503-345-9623.

Woolrich, Woolrich, PA 17779. 717-769-6464.

Shorts

Adidas, 15 Independence Blvd., Warren, NJ 07060. 201-580-0700.

Alitta, 75 Spring St., New York, NY 10012. 212-334-1390.

Asics, 10540 Talbert Ave., West Bldg., Fountain Valley, CA 92708. 800-854-6133.

L. L. Bean, Freeport, ME 04033. 800-221-4221.

Champion Products, 3141 Monroe Ave., Rochester, NY 14618. 716-385-3200.

Eastern Mountain Sports, 1 Vose Farm Rd., Peterborough, NH 03458. 603-924-7231.

The Finals, 21 Minisink Ave., Port Jervis, NY 12771. 800-431-9111.

In-Sport, no address. 800-652-5200.

Lands' End, Lands' End Lane, Dodgeville, WI 53595. 800-356-4444.

Le Coq Sportif, 28 Englehard Dr., Cranbury, NJ 08512. 800-524-2377.
In NJ, 609-655-1515.

New Balance, 38 Everett St., Boston, MA 02134. 617-783-4000.

Nike, 9000 S.W. Nimbus Dr., Beaverton, OR 97005. 503-641-6453.

The North Face, 999 Harrison St., Berkeley, CA 94710. 800-446-5522. In CA, 415-527-9700.

Patagonia, Box 86, Ventura, CA 93002. 800-523-9597. In CA, 800-432-0241.

Pony Sports and Leisure, 201 Rte. 17 N., Rutherford, NJ 07070. 201-896-0101.

Recreational Equipment, Inc., Box 88125, Seattle, WA 98138. 206-323-8333.

Reebox International, 100 Technology Dr., Stoughton, MA 02072. 617-341-5000.

Sport Europa, 7871 N.W. 15th St., Miami, FL 33126. 305-477-9341.

Norm Thompson, Box 3999, Portland, OR 97208. 800-547-1160.

Woolrich, Woolrich, PA 17779. 717-769-6464.

Socks

Adidas, 15 Independence Blvd., Warren, NJ 07060. 201-580-0700.

Asics, 10540 Talbert Ave., West Bldg., Fountain Valley, CA 92708. 800-854-6133.

Eddie Bauer, 15010 N.E. 36th St., Redmond, WA 98052. 206-882-6100.

L. L. Bean, Freeport, ME 04033. 800-221-4221.

Beta Socks/Singer Hosiery, 710 Jacob St., Thomasville, NC 27360. 919-475-2161.

Burlington Socks, 2303 W. Meadowview Rd., Greensboro, NC 27284. 919-379-2000.

Champion Products, 3141 Monroe Ave., Rochester, NY 14618. 716-385-3200.

Eastern Mountain Sports, 1 Vose Farm Rd., Peterborough, NH 03458. 603-924-7231.

The Finals, 21 Minisink Ave., Port Jervis, NY 12771. 800-431-9111.

Foot-Joy, 144 Field St., Brockton, MA 02403. 508-586-2233.

Fox River Mills, Box 298, Osage, IA 50461. 800-247-1815.

Gates-Mills, Harrison St., Johnstown, NY 12095. 518-762-4526.

Le Coq Sportif, 28 Englehard Dr., Cranbury, NJ 08512. 800-524-2377.
In NJ, 609-655-1515.

Mephisto, 520 E. Hyman, Aspen, CO 81611. 800-443-3661. In CO, 303-925-8220.

New Balance, 38 Everett St., Boston, MA 02134. 617-783-4000.

Nike, 9000 S.W. Nimbus Dr., Beaverton, OR 97005. 503-641-6453.

Patagonia, Box 86, Ventura, CA 93002. 800-523-9597. In CA, 800-432-0241.

Pony Sports and Leisure, 201 Rte. 17 N., Rutherford, NJ 07070. 201-896-0101.

Puma, 492 Old Connecticut Pathway, Framingham, MA 01701. 508-875-8333.

Recreational Equipment, Inc., Box 88125, Seattle, WA 98138. 206-323-8333.

Reebox International, 100 Technology Dr., Stoughton, MA 02072. 617-341-5000.

Rockport, 72 Howe St., Marlboro, MA 01752. 800-343-9255. In MA, 617-485-2090.

Norm Thompson, Box 3999, Portland, OR 97208. 800-547-1160.

Thor-Lo, Box 5440, Statesville, NC 28677. 800-438-0209. In NC, 704-872-6522.

Unique Sports Products, Inc., 840 McFarland Rd., Alpharetta, GA 30201. 800-554-3707. In Ga. 404-442-1977.

Vermont Country Store, Box 3000, Manchester Center, VT 05225. 802-362-4667.

Wigwam Mills, Box 818, Sheboygan, WI 53082. 414-457-5551.

Winter Silks, Box 130, Middleton, WI 53562. 800-648-7455.

T-Shirts

Vantage Communications, Inc., Box 546, Nyack, NY 10960. 800-872-0068.

Tights

Alitta, 75 Spring St., New York, NY 10012. 212-334-1390.

Asics, 10540 Talbert Ave., West Bldg., Fountain Valley, CA 92708. 800-854-6133.

L. L. Bean, Freeport, ME 04033. 800-221-4221.

Champion Products, 3131 Monroe Ave., Rochester, NY 14618. 716-385-3200.

The Finals, 21 Minisink Ave., Port Jervis, NY 12771. 800-431-9111.

Pony Sports and Leisure, 201 Rte. 17 N., Rutherford, NJ 07070. 201-896-0101.

Puma, 492 Old Connecticut Pathway, Framingham, MA 01701. 508-875-4803.

Wags, 280 Bridge St., Dedham, MA 02026. 617-329-9030.

Underwear, thermal

Eddie Bauer, 15010 N.E. 36th St., Redmond, WA 98052. 206-882-6100.

L. L. Bean, Freeport, ME 04033. 800-221-4221.

Duofold, 350 Fifth Ave., New York, NY 10118, 212-736-4228.

Eastern Mountain Sports, 1 Vose Farm Rd., Peterborough, NH 03458. 603-924-7231.

The Finals, 21 Minisink Ave., Port Jervis, NY 12771. 800-431-9111.

Orvis, Box 12000, Roanoke, VA 24022. 703-345-3600.

Patagonia, Box 86, Ventura, CA 93002. 800-523-9597. In CA, 800-432-0241.

Puma, 492 Old Connecticut Pathway, Framingham, MA 01701. 508-875-4803.

Recreational Equipment, Inc., Box 88125, Seattle, WA 98138. 206-323-8333.

Norm Thompson, Box 3999, Portland, OR 97208. 800-547-1160.

Winter Silks, Box 130, Middleton, WI 53562. 800-648-7455.

Back Aids

Dricast Orthopedics, 2709 Via Orange Way, Spring Valley, CA 92078. 800-331-9421.
Back supports.

Pro Orthopedic Devices, Box 27525, Tucson, AZ 85726. 602-790-9330.
Rubberized sleeve.

Canteens

Mark Pack Works, 230 Madison, Oakland, CA. 415-452-0243.
Canteens.

Rainbow Racing System, Box 18510, Spokane, WA 99208. 800-962-1011. In WA, 509-326-5470.
Water bottles.

Dog Deterrents

Advanced Security Products, 5 Chestnut, Tenafly, NJ 07024. 201-567-8363.
Security device.

Unique Sports Products, 840 McFarland Rd., Alpharetta, GA 30201. 800-554-3707. In GA, 404-442-1977.
Dog repellent.

Elbow Aids

Pro Orthopedic Devices, Box 27525, Tucson, AZ 85726. 602-790-9330.
Rubberized sleeves.

Eyeglass Holders

Unique Sports Products, 840 McFarland Rd., Alpharetta, GA 30201. 800-554-3707. In GA, 404-442-1977.

First-Aid Kits

Coghlan's, 121 Irene St., Winnipeg, Man., Canada R3T 4C7. 204-284-9550.
Foot care kits, insect relievers, snake bite kits.

Outdoor Research, 1000 First Ave., S., Seattle, WA 98134. 206-467-8197.
First-aid kits.

Foot Aids

Allor Project, 1 Maple St., Concord, NH 03301. 603-228-0121.
Foot care, hygiene products.

Brookstone, 5 Vose Farm Rd., Peterborough, NH 03458. 603-924-7181.
Foot heaters, toenail cutters, massagers.

Cadillac Shoe Products, 4444 Second Blvd., Detroit, MI 48201. 313-832-4334.
Deodorants.

Clairol Research, 345 Park Ave., New York, NY 10154. 212-644-2990.
Foot baths, massagers.

Dr. Leonard's Health Care, 74 20th St., Brooklyn, NY 11232. 718-768-0010.
Foot care products.

Foot Care Connection, 419 N. Larchmont Blvd. Los Angeles, CA 90004. 213-467-3668.
Foot baths, gels, lotions.

Gander Mountain, Box 248, Wilmot, WI 53192. 800-558-9410.
Foot warmers.

Hammacher Schlemmer, 147 E. 57th St., New York, NY 10022. 212-421-9000.
Heated foot massager.

Mature Wisdom, Bldg. 28, Hanover, PA 17333. 800-621-5800.
Pedicure scissors.

Micro Balanced Products, 25 Aladdin Ave. Dumont, NJ 07628. 201-387-0200.
Lavilin deodorants for the feet and underarms.

Norm Thompson, Box 3999, Portland, OR 97208. 800-547-1160.
Foot massagers, warmers.

Orvis, Blue Hills Dr., Roanoke, VA 24022. 703-345-3600.
Foot and hand warmers.

Professional Foot Care Products, 74 20th St., Brooklyn, NY 11232. 718-768-7383.
All types of foot care products.

Scholl, 3030 Jackson Ave., Memphis, TN 38151. 901-320-2011.
Foot care products.

Solutions, Box 6878, Portland, OR 97228. 800-342-9988.
Foot massagers

Spenco Medical, 6301 Imperial Dr., Waco, TX 76710. 800-433-3334.
Foot paddings, blister kits, dressings.

Vermont Country Store, Box 3000, Manchester Center, VT 05225. 802-362-4667.
Toenail clippers, foot creams.

Warner Lambert Co., Box 597, Morris Plains, NJ 07950. 800-223-0182. In NJ, 201-540-2000.
Foot lotion.

Headbands, Sweatbands

RaceAid, Box 1470, Pinellas Park, FL 34290. 800-237-5656. In FL, 813-546-9002.

Unique Sports Products, 840 McFarland Rd., Alpharetta, GA 30201. 800-554-3707. In GA, 404-442-1977.

Insoles, Heel Cushions, Orthotics

Brookstone, 5 Vose Farm Rd., Peterborough, NH 03458. 603-924-7181.
Innersoles.

Calderon Products, Box 5387, Akron, OH 44313. 216-864-8100.
Heel pillows.

Chattanooga Corp. Box 4287, Chattanooga, TN 37405. 615-870-2281.
Insoles.

Combo, 1101 Westchester Ave., White Plains, NY 10604. 800-431-2610. In NY, 914-694-5454.
Insoles.

Comfort Connection, 1931 Lakeview Dr., Ft. Wayne, IN 46808. 800-533-3416. In IN, 219-436-1686.
Insoles.

Dr. Leonard's Health Care, 74 20th St., Brooklyn, NY 11232. 718-768-0010.
Insoles.

Energy Impact, 4905 Pine Cone Dr., Durham, NC 27707. 800-333-7680.
Insoles.

Frelonic, Box 169, Salem, MA 01970. 508-744-0300.
Insoles.

Mature Wisdom, Bldg. 28, Hanover, PA 17333. 800-621-5800.
Insoles.

Scholl, 3030 Jackson Ave., Memphis, TN 38151. 901-320-2011.
Insoles, heels.

Spenco Medical, Box 2501, Waco, TX 76702. 800-433-3334. In TX, 817-772-6000.
Insoles.

Sure Foot Corp, Box 40, Grand Forks, ND 58206. 800-722-FOOT.
Insulator for cold weather.

Key Holders

Unique Sports Products, 840 McFarland Rd., Alpharetta, GA 30201. 800-554-3707. In GA, 404-442-1977.

Knee Aids

Cho-Pat, Inc., Box 293, Hainesport, NJ 08036. 609-261-1336.
Knee strap.

Dricast Orthopedics, 2709 Via Orange Way, Spring Valley, CA 92078. 800-331-9421.
Knee supports.

Dr. Leonard's Health Care, 74 20th St., Brooklyn, NY 11232. 718-768-0010.
Knee supports.

Mature Wisdom, Bldg. 28, Hanover, PA 17333. 800-621-5800.
Knee supports.

Pro Orthopedic Devices, Box 27525, Tucson, AZ 85726. 602-790-9330.
Rubberized sleeves.

Natural Foods, Beverages, Supplements, Etc.

Beverages

Corr's Natural Beverages, Box 1240, Gary, IN 46407. 219-886-1025.

Crystal Geyser Water, 501 Washington St., Calistoga, CA 94515. 707-942-0500.

Knudsen & Sons, Inc., Box 369, Chico, CA 95927. 916-891-1517.

Mountain Sun, 18390 Hwy. 145, Dolores, CO 81323. 303-882-2283.

Old Chicago, 9744 Alburtis Ave., Santa Fe Springs, CA 90607. 619-232-6136.

Perrier, 777 West Putnam Ave., Greenwich, CT 06836. 203-531-4100.

Food Supplements

Alacer Corp., 7425 Orangethorpe, Buena Park, CA 90621. 800-854-0249.

Alta Health Products, 1979 E. Locust St., Pasadena, CA 91107. 818-796-1047.

American Health Plus Corp., P.O. Box 119, Pearl River, NY 10965. 914-735-0640.

Auro Trading, 18A Hangar Way, Watsonville, CA 95076. 800-225-6111.

Bio-Botanica, Inc., 75 Commerce Dr., Hauppauge, NY 11788. 516-231-5522.

Bioforce of America, Kinderbrook, NY 12106. 518-758-6060.

J. R. Carlson Laboratories, Inc., 15 College Dr., Arlington Heights, IL 60004. 708-255-1600.

Dynamic Power Labs, Box 224, Wheeler, IN 46393. 219-759-4422.

Earthrise Co., Box 1196, San Rafael, CA 94915. 415-485-0521.

Enzymatic Therapy, Inc., Box 1508, Green Bay, WI 54305. 414-437-1061.

Excel, 3280 W. Hacienda, Las Vegas, NV 89118. 702-795-7464.

Global Marketing Associates, 435 Brannan St., San Francisco, CA 94107. 415-495-8524.

Gold's Gym Products, 358 Hampton Dr., Venice, CA 90291. 800-3-GOLDS-3; in CA, 800-346-5373. 213-392-3005.

Green Foods Corp., 620 Maple Ave., Torrance, CA 90503. 213-618-0678.

Hoffman's, Box 1707, York, PA 17405. 717-764-0044.

Inter-Cal Corp., 421 Miller Valley Rd., Prescott, AZ 86301. 602-445-8063.

Kyolic/Wakunaga, 23501 Madero, Mission Viejo, CA 92601. 714-855-2776.

L&S Research Corp., 33 Beaverton Blvd., Brick, NJ 08723. 201-477-4880.

Lewis Laboratories, 49 Richmondville Ave., Westport, CT 06880. 203-226-7343.

Makers of KAL, Box 4023, Woodland Hills, CA 91365. 818-340-3035.

Modern Products, Inc., 3015 W. Vera Ave., Milwaukee, WI 53209; 414-352-3333.

Montana Naturals, Inc., 19994 Hwy. 93, Arlee, MT 59821. 406-726-3214.

Natren, 10935 Camarillo St., North Hollywood, CA 91602. 818-766-9300.

Natrol, Box 5000, Chatsworth, CA 91311. 818-701-9966.

Naturade Products, Inc., 7110 E. Jackson St., Paramount, CA 90723. 213-531-8120.

Naturally Vitamin Supplements, Inc., 14851 N. Scottsdale Rd., Scottsdale, AZ 85254. 602-991-0200.

Nature's Bounty, Inc., 105 Orville Dr., Bohemia, NY 11716. 516-567-9500.

Nature's Herbs, Box 336, Orem, UT 84057. 801-225-4443.

Nature's Plus, 10 Daniel St., Farmingdale, NY 11735. 516-293-0030.

Nature's Way Products, 10 Mountain Springs Parkway, Springville, UT 84663. 801-489-3631.

Now Foods, 2000 Bloomingdale Rd., Glendale Heights, IL 60139. 312-893-1330.

Nutrition 21, 1010 Turquoise St., San Diego, CA 92109. 619-488-1021.

Nu Life, 3300 Hyland Ave., Costa Mesa, CA 92626. 714-556-8400.

Pep Products, Inc. Box 715, Castle Rock, CO 80104. 800-624-4260.

Plus Products, 3300 Hyland Ave., Costa Mesa, CA 92626. 800-438-8216.

Pure-Gar, Inc., Box 98813, Tacoma, WA 98498. 206-582-6421.

Radiance Products Co., 15 Dexter Plaza, Pearl River, NY 10965. 914-735-0640.

Rainbow Light, 207 McPherson, Santa Cruz, CA 95060. 800-635-1233.

Richlife, Inc., 3300 Hyland Ave., Costa Mesa, CA 92626. 714-556-8400.

Schiff BioFoods, Inc., Moonachie, NJ 07074. 201-933-2282.

Solgar, Box 330, Lynbrook, NY 11563. 516-599-2442.

Source Naturals, Box 2118, Santa Cruz, CA 95063. 408-438-1144.

Sun Chlorella, 4025 Spencer St., Torrance, CA 90503. 800-537-0077; in CA, 800-537-0088.

Thompson, 23529 S. Figueroa St., Carson, CA 90745. 213-830-5550.

TwinLabs, 2120 Smithtown Ave., Ronkonkoma, NY 11779. 516-467-3140.

UniPro, Inc., 47823 Westinghouse Dr., Fremont, CA 94539. 415-490-9000.

Vegetarian Products, 465 Production St., San Marcos, CA 92069. 619-744-7040.

Viobin Corp., Waunakee, WI 53597. 608-849-5944.

Weider Health & Fitness, 21100 Erwin St., Woodland Hills, CA 91367. 818-884-6800.

Yerba Prima Botanicals, Box 2569, Oakland, CA 94614. 415-632-7477.

Herbal/homeopathic remedies

Ellon Bach USA, 644 Merrick Rd., Lynbrook, NY 11563. 516-593-2206.

Bio-Botanica, Inc., 75 Commerce Dr., Hauppauge, NY 11788. 516-231-5522.

Bioforce of America, Kinderhook, NY 12106. 518-758-6060.

Boiron/Borneman, Box 54, Norwood, PA 19074. 215-532-2035.

Longevity Pure Medicine, 9595 Wilshire Blvd., St. 706, Beverly Hills, CA 90212. 213-273-7423.

Nature's Herbs, Box 336, Orem, UT 84059. 800-HERBALS.

Nature's Way Products, 10 Mountain Springs Parkway, Springville, UT 84663. 801-489-3631.

NatureWorks, Inc. 5341 Derry Ave., Agoura, CA 91301. 818-889-1602.

NuAge Labs, 4200 Laclede Ave., St. Louis, MO 63108. 314-533-9600.

Similasan Corp., 23224 - 94th Ave., S., Kent, WA 98031. 206-859-9072.

Standard Homeopathic Co., Box 61067, Los Angeles, CA 90061. 213-321-4284.

Tiger Balm, 3450 3rd St., San Francisco, CA 94124. 415-826-6006.

Suntan Products

Aubrey Organics, 4419 N. Manhattan Ave., Tampa, FL 33614. 813-877-4186.

Borland of Germany, Box 1487, New London, NH 03257. 603-526-2076.

Carme, Inc., 84 Galli Dr., Novato, CA 94949. 415-382-4000.

4-D Hobe Marketing Corp., 201 S. McKemy, Chandler, AZ 85226. 602-257-1950.

Ivo of California, 8533 Seranata, Whittier, CA 90603. 213-947-4100.

Jason Natural Products, 8468 Warner Dr., Culver City, CA 90232. 213-838-7543.

Michael's Health Products, 7040 Alamo Downs Pkway, San Antonio, TX 78238. 512-647-4700.

Naturade Products, Inc., 7110 Jackson St., Paramount, CA 90723. 213-531-8120.

Orjene Natural Cosmetics, 5-43 48th Ave., Long Island City, NY 11101. 718-937-2666.

Rachel Perry, 9111 Mason Ave., Chatsworth, CA 91311. 818-888-5881.

Stearns, Inc., 21601 Devonshire St., Chatsworth, CA 91211. 818-718-1420.

Twin Laboratories, Inc., 2120 Smithtown Ave., Ronkonkoma, NY 11779. 516-467-3140.

Ointment, Herbal

Penn Herb Co., 605 N. 2nd St., Philadelphia, PA 19123. 215-925-3336.

Pedometers, Pulse Monitors, Etc.

Accusplit, 2290 Ringwood Ave., San Jose, CA 95131. 800-538-9753. In CA, 408-432-8228.
Pedometers.

Aristo Import, 15 Hunt Rd., Orangeburg, NY 10962. 914-359-0720.
Pedometers.

Eddie Bauer, 15010 N.E. 36th St., Redmond, WA 98052. 206-882-6100.
Pertable thermometers.

L. L. Bean, Freeport, ME 04033. 800-221-4221.
Pedometers.

Brookstone, 5 Vose Farm Rd., Peterborough, NH 03458. 603-924-7181.
Pedometers, map meters.

Casio/Sports Time/Hanhart, 300 Valley View Dr., Franklin Lakes, NJ 07417. 800-272-0272.
Chronographs, stop watches.

Creative Health Products, 575 Saddle Ridge Rd., Plymouth, MI 48170. 800-742-4478. In MI, 313-453-5309.
Pedometers, pulse monitor, fat calipers.

The Finals, 21 Minisink Ave., Port Jervis, NY 12771. 800-431-9111.
Stop watches.

Free Style, 21025 Osborn St., Canoga Park, CA 91304. 818-709-0795.
Watches.

Hammacher Schlemmer, 147 E. 57th St., New York, NY 10022. 212-421-9000.
Pedometers.

Heart Rate, 3186 Airway Ave., Costa Mesa, CA 92626. 714-850-9716.
Pulse meters.

Innovative Time, 6054 Corte Del Cedro, Carlsbad, CA 92008. 800-854-3831. In CA, 800-432-7451.
Pedometer, chronographs.

Leichtung Workshops, 4944 Commerce Parkway, Cleveland, OH 44128. 216-831-6191.
Distance converter for maps.

Nike, 9000 Nimbus Dr., Beaverton, OR 97005. 503-641-6453.
Speed, distance, pace, stride, pulse rate meters.

Precise International, 3 Chestnut St., Suffern, NY 10901. 800-431-2996.
Pedometers.

Push Pedal Pull, 3100 W. 12th St., Sioux Falls, SD 57104. 800-237-9973. In SD, 800-654-8865.
Pedometers, pulse monitors.

Recreational Equipment, Inc., Box 88125, Seattle, WA 98138. 206-323-8333.
Chronographs, thermostats, pulse monitors, etc.

Solutions, Box 6878, Portland, OR 97228. 800-342-9988.
Pedometers.

Sun, 11413 W. 48th Ave., Wheat Ridge, CO 80033. 303-424-4651.
Thermometers.

Norm Thompson, Box 3999, Portland, OR 97208. 800-547-1160.
Pedometers.

Transource Corp., 4725 N. 43rd St., Phoenix, AZ 85031. 602-997-8101.
Pedometers.

Tunturi, 1776 136th Pl., N.E. Bellevue, WA 98009. 800-426-0858.
Pulse monitors.

Vanguard, 1865 Miner St., Des Plaines, IL 60016. 800-634-5463. In IL, 800-542-7981.
Pedometer/odometer, calories burned, etc.

Radios, Stereos, Cassettes, Etc.

Medical and Sports Music, 1200 Executive Parkway, Eugene, OR 97401. 503-344-5323.
Cadence cassette.

Tune Belt, 2601 Arbor Place, Cincinnati, OH 45209. 513-531-1712.
Radio, cassette carrier.

Reflective Wear, Gear

Jog-a-Lite International, Box 125, Silver Lake, NH 03875. 603-367-4741.
Reflective bands, belts, vests, etc.

Kenyon Consumer Products, 200 Main St., Kenyon, RI 02836. 401-792-3704.
Reflective tape.

Nathan & Co., 920 Broadway, New York, NY 10010. 800-835-0800. In NY, 212-473-8408.
Reflective gear.

Unique Sports Products, 840 McFarland Rd., Alpharetta, GA 30201. 800-554-3707. In GA, 404-442-1977.
Reflective vests, wrist band, armband, headband, sash, shoe spots.

Scales

Health O Meter, 7400 W. 100th Place, Bridgeview, IL 60455. 708-598-9100.
Digital cordless scale.

Shoe Cleaners, Repair Aids

Cadillac Shoe Products, 4444 Second Blvd., Detroit, MI 48201. 313-832-4334.
Shoe cleaners, refinishers.

Secondwind, Box 2300, Paso Robles, CA 93447. 805-239-2555.
Shoe cleaners, protectors.

Unique Sports Products, 840 McFarland Rd., Alpharetta, GA 30201. 800-554-3707. In GA, 404-442-1977.
Shoe repair cement, sealers, cleaners, etc.

Shoe Dryers

Gander Mountain, Box 248, Hwy. W., Wilmot, WI 53192. 414-862-2331.

Shoelaces

Mature Wisdom, Bldg. 28, Hanover, PA 17333. 800-621-5800.

Shoestring, Inc., Box 2311, Ketchum, ID 83340. 208-726-7533.

Shoe Pockets

Unique Sports Products, 840 McFarland Rd., Alpharetta, GA 30201. 800-554-3707. In GA, 404-442-1977.

Shoes

Adidas, 15 Independence Blvd., Warren, NJ 07060. 201-580-0700.

Asics, 10540 Talbert Ave., West Bldg., Fountain Valley, CA 92708. 800-854-6133.

Autry, 11420 Reeder Rd., Dallas, TX 75229. 800-872-8879. In TX, 800-892-8878.

Avia, 16160 S. W. Upper Boones Ferry Rd., Portland, OR 97223. 800-652-2223. In OR, 503-684-0490.

G. H. Bass, 360 U.S. Rte. 1, Falmouth, ME 04105. 800-535-5004. In ME, 207-781-3180.

Brooks, 9341 Courtland Dr., Rockford, MI 49351. 800-233-7531.

Brown, 8300 Maryland Ave., St. Louis, MO 63166. 314-854-4000.

California Footwear, 3100 Rolisen Rd., Redwood City, CA 94063. 415-364-9928.

Converse, 1 Fordham Rd., North Reading, MA 01864. 508-664-1100.

Danner, 5188 S. E. International Way, Portland, OR 97222. 800-345-0430. In OR, 503-251-1100.

Dexter, 1230 Washington St., West Newton, MA 02165. 617-332-4300.

Dunham, Cotton Mill Hill, Brattleboro, VT 05301. 802-257-0324.

Ellesse USA, 1430 Broadway, New York, NY 10018. 212-840-6111.

Etonic, 147 Centre St., Brockton, MA 02403. 508-583-9100.

Fabiano, 850 Summer St., Boston, MA 02127. 617-268-5625.

Fila Athletic Footwear, 200 International Circle, Hunt Valley, MD 21301. 301-785-7530.

Foot-Joy, 144 Field St., Brockton, MA 02403. 508-586-2233.

Hersey Custom Shoes, RFD 3, Box 7390, Farmington, ME 04938. 207-778-3103.

Hi-Tec Sports, 4400 North Star Way, Modesto, CA 95356. 800-521-1698. In CA, 800-558-8580.

Kaepa, 5410 Kaepa Court, San Antonio, TX 78218. 512-661-7463.

KangaRoos, 1809 Clarkson Rd., Chesterfield, MO 63017. 314-532-5104.

Kinney, 233 Broadway, New York, NY 10279. 212-720-3700.

L. A. Gear, 4221 Redwood Ave., Los Angeles, CA 90066. 213-822-1995.

Le Coq Sportif, 28 Englehard Dr., Cranbury, NJ 08512. 800-524-2377. In NJ, 609-655-1515.

Lowell Shoe, 8 Hampshire Dr., Hudson, NH 03051. 603-880-8900.

Lydico, 6680 Beta Dr., Mayfield Village, OH 44143. 216-446-1000.

Mason, 1251 First Ave., Chippewa Falls, WI 54729. 715-723-1871.

Mephisto, 520 E. Hyman, Aspen, CO 81611. 800-443-3661. In CO, 303-925-8220.

Milo 1933, 18 Railroad St., Andover, MA 01810. 508-683-9090.

Musebeck, 803 Westover St., Oconomowoc, WI 53066. 800-558-0182. In WI, 414-567-5564.

New Balance, 38 Everett St., Boston, MA 02134. 617-783-4000.

Nike, 9000 Nimbus Dr., Beaverton, OR 97005. 503-641-6453.

Pony, 201 Rte. 17 N., Rutherford, NJ 07070. 800-654-7669.

Propet, 20206 87th St., S., Kent, WA 98032. 206-872-7944.

Puma, 492 Old Connecticut Pathway, Framingham, MA 01701. 508-875-4803.

Reebok International, 100 Technology Dr., Stoughton, MA 02072. 617-341-5000.

Revelations, 16 E. 34th St., New York, NY 10016. 212-683-2600.

Rockport, 72 Howe St., Marlboro, MA 01752. 800-343-9255. In MA, 508-485-2090.

Ryka, 3 Industrial Park, 36 Finnell Dr., Weymouth, MA 02188. 617-331-8800.

Saucony, Box 6046, Peabody, MA 01960. 508-532-9000.

Sporto, 65 Sprague St., Boston, MA 02137. 617-426-2121.

Technica, Box 551, West Lebanon, NH 03784. 800-258-8032. In NH, 603-298-8032.

Thom McAn, 67 Millbrook St., Worcester, MA 01606. 508-791-3811.

Timberland, Box 5050, Hampton, NH 03842. 603-926-1600.

Turntec, 16542 Milliken Ave., Irvine, CA 92714.

U. S. Shoe, 1 Eastwood Dr., Cincinnati, OH 45227. 513-527-7000.

Walk Over Shoes, 31 Perkins St., Bridgewater, MA 02324. 508-697-6104.

Shoes, Resoling

Athletic Shoe Service, 2901 S. Main St., Santa Ana, CA 92707. 714-751-0272.

Mercury Shoe Outlet, Inc., 350 Green St., North Andover, MA 01845. 508-682-8768.
  Resoling: Adidas, Saucony, New Balance, Tiger.

The Sole Source, 8400 Hilltop Road, Fairfax, VA 22031. 703-876-4800 (D.C. and environs); elsewhere, 800-876-SHOE.

Stroller, Baby

Racing Strollers, 516 N. 20th Ave., #8, Yakima, WA 98902. 800-548-7230.

Uni-USA, 8025 S.W. 185th, Aloha, OR 97007. 800-832-2376.

Sunglasses

Barracuda Sports Products, 0224 S. W. Hamilton, Portland, OR 97201. 503-241-0528.

Eddie Bauer, 15010 N.E. 36th St., Redmond, WA 98052. 206-882-6100.

Bausch & Lomb, 42 East Ave., Rochester, NY 14603. 716-338-6000.

L. L. Bean, Freeport, ME 04033. 800-221-4221.

Bolle America, 3890 Elm St., Denver, CO 80207. 303-321-4300.

Bucci, Inc., Box 66888, Scotts Valley, CA 95066. 800-222-8224. In CA, 800-332-8224.

Carrera, 135 Maple St., Norwood, NJ 07648. 800-631-1580.

Gander Mountain, Box 248, Wilmot, WI 53192. 414-862-2331.

Jones Optical Co., Box 3096, Boulder, CO 80307. 800-321-8300. In CO, 303-447-8727.

Recreational Equipment, Inc., Box 88125, Seattle, WA 98138. 206-395-3780.

Style Eyes of California, 839 Hinckley Rd., Burlingame, CA 94001. 415-692-2594.

Tasco, Box 520080, Miami, FL 33152. 305-591-3670.

Norm Thompson, Box 3999, Portland, OR 97208. 800-547-1160.

Tura, 130 Cuttermill Rd., Great Neck, NY 11022. 800-645-9235. In NY, 516-487-8200.

Uvex Winter Optical, 10 Thurber Blvd., Smithfield, RI 02917. 401-232-1200.

Vuarnet-France, Box 823, El Segundo, CA 90245. 800-421-2344.

Training Belts

York Barbell Co., Inc., Box 1707, York, PA 17405. 717-767-6481.

Walking Canes, Sticks, Rods

L. L. Bean, Freeport, ME 04033. 800-221-4221.
  Walking sticks.

Genuine Montana, 9387 Miller Creek Rd., Missoula, MT 59803, 800-533-4684.
  Walking sticks.

House of Canes and Walking Sticks, 5628 Vineland Ave., N. Hollywood, CA 91601. 818-769-4007.

L. I. Engineering, 125 Jeranios Court, Thousand Oaks, CA 91362. 805-492-1784.

Stan Novak, 115 W. 30th St., New York, NY 10001. 800-443-7310. In N.Y., 212-947-8466.
  Walking sticks.

Power Pole, 3023 W. Northwide Dr., Jackson, MS 39213. 800-453-6500.
  Walking sticks.

Wallets

Unique Sports Products, 840 McFarland Rd., Alpharetta, GA 30201. 404-442-1977.
Clip-on wallet, wrist wallet.

Weights

Ajay/Vitamaster, 1501 E. Wisconsin St., Delavan, WI 53115. 414-728-5521.
Ankle and wrist weights.

American Athlete, 200 American Ave., Jefferson, IA 50129. 800-247-3978.
Hand weights.

Bodyshrinkers, Inc., 18755 Century Park East, Los Angeles, CA 90067. 213-837-7675.
Bandoliers.

Bollinger Industries, 222 W. Airport Freeway, Irving, TX 75062. 800-527-1166; in TX, 214-445-0386.
Ankle/wrist, belt, leg, hand and vest weights.

Excel, 9935 Beverly Blvd., Pico Rivera, CA 90660. 213-699-0311.
Ankle and wrist weights.

Heavyhands, 1000 Nabor, Pittsburgh, PA 15205. 800-922-3827.
Hand weights.

Ivanko Barbell, Box 1470, San Pedro, CA 90733. 213-514-1155.
Handweights, barbells.

Mr. America, Box 587, Ooltewah, TN 37363. 800-251-6040; In TN, 615-238-5388.
Ankle and wrist weights.

Push Pedal Pull, 3100 W. 12th St., Sioux Falls, SD 57104. 800-237-9973; in SD, 800-654-8865.
Ankle, hand, wrist weights.

Spenco Medical, Box 2501, Waco, TX 76702. 800-433-3334.
Hand, wrist, belt weights.

Weider Health and Fitness, 21100 Erwin St., Woodland Hills, CA 91367. 818-884-6800.
Ankle, hand, wrist weights.

Weight Room, 245 N. Bridge St., Anthony, ID 83445. 208-624-3115.
Weighted vests.

York Barbell Co., Inc., York, PA 17405. 717-767-6481.
Barbells, dumbells and other weight-training equipment.

Whistles

L. L. Bean, Freeport, ME 04033. 800-221-4221.
Whistle, compass and match holder.

Unique Sports Products, 840 McFarland Rd., Alpharetta, GA 30201. 800-554-3707; in GA, 404-442-1977.
Whistles.

Wristbands

Unique Sports Products, 840 McFarland Rd., Alpharetta, GA 30201. 800-554-3707; in GA, 404-442-1977.

Appendix 2:

Addresses to Remember

Organizations

Aerobics and Fitness Foundation, 15250 Ventura, Ste. 310, Sherman Oaks, CA 91403. 818-905-0040.

American Athletic Union, Box 68207, Indianapolis, IN 46268. 317-872-2900.

American College of Sports Medicine, Box 1440, Indianapolis, IN 46206. 317-637-9200.

American Podiatric Medical Association, 9312 Old Georgetown Rd., Bethesda, MD 20814. 301-571-9200.

American Running and Fitness Association, 9310 Old Georgetown Rd., Bethesda, MD 20814. 301-897-0197.

Coors Light Biathlon Series, Box 236, Lake Oswego, OR 97034. 503-655-4721.

New York Road Runners Club, 9 E. 89th St., New York, NY 10128. 212-860-4455.

President's Council on Physical Fitness and Sports, Washington, DC 20001. 202-272-3421.

Road Runners Club of America, 8208 E. Boulevard Dr., Alexandria, VA 22308. 703-836-0558.

The Rockport Walking Institute, Box 480, Marlboro, MA 01752. 508-485-2090.

Women's Sports Foundation, 342 Madison Ave., Ste. 728, New York, NY 10173. 800-227-3988.

Periodicals

Health

Alive, 4728 Byrne Rd., Burnaby BC, Canada V5J 3H7. 604-438-1919.

American Health, 80 Fifth Ave., New York, NY 10011. 212-242-2460.

Better Nutrition for Today's Living, 390 Fifth Ave., New York, NY 10018. 212-613-9700.

Delicious, 81301 Spruce St., Boulder, CO 80302. 303-939-8440.

East West, 17 Station St., Brookline, MA 02147. 617-232-1000.

Health News & Review, 27 Pine St., New Canaan, CT 06840. 203-966-8721.

Healthworld, 1477 Rollins Rd., Burlingame, CA 94010. 415-343-1637.

Let's Live, 444 N. Larchmont Blvd., Los Angeles, CA 90004. 213-469-8379.

New Age Journal, 342 Western Ave., Brighton, MA 02135. 617-787-2005.

Prevention, 33 E. Minor St., Emmaus, PA 17405. 215-967-5171.

Vegetarian Times, Box 570, Oak Park, IL 60303. 708-848-8100.

Sports

Runner's World, 33 E. Minor St., Emmaus, PA 18098. 215-967-5171.

The Walking Magazine, 711 Boylston St., Boston, MA 02116. 617-236-1885.

Some Popular Races

Boston Marathon, Box 1990, Hopkinton, MA 01748. 508-435-6905.

Chicago Marathon. 312-951-0660.

Coors Light Biathlon Series, Box 236, Oswego, OR 97034. 503-655-4721.

Dallas White Rock Marathon, Box 743335, Dallas, TX 75374.

Kansas City Marathon, 2018 W. 48th St., Westwood, KS 66205. 913-362-7223.

L'Eggs Running Program, 9 E. 89th St., New York, NY 10128.

Los Angeles Marathon, 11110 West Ohio Ave., Ste. 100, Los Angeles, CA 90025. 213-444-5544.

Montreal Marathon, Box 1570, Sta. B., Montreal, PQ, Canada H3B 3L2. 514-879-1027.

New York City Marathon, 9 E. 89th St., New York, NY 10128. 212-860-4455.

Philadelphia Distance Run, Box 43111, Philadelphia, PA 19129.

Pittsburgh Marathon, 638 USX Bldg., Pittsburgh, PA 15230. 412-391-2800.

Portland Marathon, Box D, Beaverton, OR 97075. 503-226-1111.

The Revco/Cleveland Marathon, Box 550, Twinsburg, OH 44087.

San Francisco Marathon. 415-896-1530.

Stamford Marathon, 880 Canal St., Stamford, CT 16902. 203-359-1248.

Toronto/Wang Marathon, 1220 Sheppard Ave., E. Willowdale, Ont., Canada M2K 2X1.

Twin Cities Marathon, 6th and Marquette, Minneapolis, MN 55480.

Utica Boilermaker Road Race, Box 4729, Utica, NY 13504.

For the dates and locations of other marathons, running camps, etc., throughout the United States, Canada and abroad, contact *Runner's World,* 33 E. Minor St., Emmaus, PA 18098. Always confirm dates and places before going to the city.

Index